# Risk Measurement and Monitoring

## THE FERMA-RIMAP® SERIES

*The FERMA-rimap® Series* serves as a proactive, continuous and dynamic learning and research platform to respond to risk managers' present and future educational and professional needs. The volumes set a flexible and dynamic measurable standard taxonomy for European Risk Managers and essential reading for students gaining their qualification. The scope of *The FERMA-rimap® Series* is to reach out to experienced or junior risk professionals, whatever their background is, and wherever their career is heading. All risk professionals have a duty to stay in contact with the evolution of the risk landscape.

# Risk Measurement and Monitoring

EDITED BY

**SIMON GRIMA**
*University of Malta, Malta*

**MARÍA ISABEL MARTÍNEZ TORRE-ENCISO**
*Universidad Autónoma de Madrid, Spain*

AND

**MAURIZIO CASTELLI**
*Augustas Risk Services SpA, Italy*

emerald PUBLISHING

United Kingdom – North America – Japan – India – Malaysia – China

Emerald Publishing Limited
Emerald Publishing, Floor 5, Northspring, 21-23 Wellington Street, Leeds LS1 4DL.

First edition 2025



**British Library Cataloguing in Publication Data**
A catalogue record for this book is available from the British Library

ISBN: 978-1-83662-311-3 (Print)
ISBN: 978-1-83662-310-6 (Online)
ISBN: 978-1-83662-312-0 (Epub)

# Contents

# Preface

Risk measurement and monitoring are fundamental to modern risk management practices, enabling organisations to assess, quantify, and respond to uncertainties effectively. In today's complex and rapidly evolving risk landscape, financial institutions, corporations, and policymakers require sophisticated measurement techniques to make informed decisions and ensure resilience against unforeseen disruptions.

This volume, *Risk Measurement and Monitoring*, is a vital resource designed to equip risk professionals with the necessary knowledge, tools, and methodologies to measure, monitor, and mitigate risk effectively. It serves as a bridge between academic research and practical application, ensuring that risk managers can make informed decisions based on data-driven analysis and strategic foresight.

The book delves into both quantitative and qualitative risk assessment techniques, offering a multidimensional perspective on risk measurement. Covering essential topics such as uncertainty modelling, portfolio risk management, operational risk, corporate governance, supply chain risk, and cybersecurity, this volume provides a holistic view of the risk landscape. It also addresses contemporary challenges such as emerging risks, geopolitical threats, environmental risks, and the impact of artificial intelligence on risk management.

By integrating theoretical models with practical examples, the book offers valuable insights into modern risk management frameworks, emphasising regulatory compliance, decision-making under uncertainty, and enterprise risk management (ERM). Furthermore, the book highlights best practices in risk communication, reporting, and stakeholder engagement, reinforcing the importance of transparency and accountability in risk management.

As a part of the *FERMA-rimap® Series*, this book aligns with the European certification standards for risk professionals, ensuring that both experienced practitioners and newcomers in the field can benefit from its structured and forward-looking approach. Whether used as an educational tool or a professional reference, this book is an indispensable guide for navigating the complexities of risk measurement and monitoring in today's dynamic environment.

The book *Risk Measurement and Monitoring* specialises in enterprise risk management (ERM) and risk measurement methodologies, with a strong emphasis on quantitative techniques, strategic risk integration, and regulatory frameworks. It serves as a key educational and professional development resource for risk managers, financial analysts, auditors, and executives responsible for risk oversight.

The book is structured around core risk measurement topics, including:

- Uncertainty Modelling – Exploring historical data methods, expert-based analysis, and hybrid approaches for predicting and mitigating risk.
- Portfolio Risk and Efficient Frontier – Applying financial principles to optimise risk-taking in investment and corporate decision-making.
- Corporate Social Responsibility (CSR) and ESG Risk – Integrating environmental, social, and governance risks into enterprise risk management.
- Risk Communication and Governance – Understanding the role of corporate governance and effective communication in risk mitigation.
- Operational and Supply Chain Risk Management – Addressing systemic risks, compliance challenges, and third-party risk mitigation.
- Cybersecurity and Emerging Threats – Managing risks associated with cyber threats, data privacy, and artificial intelligence-driven vulnerabilities.
- Mergers, Acquisitions, and Financial Risk – Evaluating the risks involved in corporate restructuring, financial modelling, and regulatory compliance.
- Terrorism and Geopolitical Risks – Assessing the impact of terrorism, political instability, and macroeconomic disruptions on risk exposure.
- Reputational Risk and Crisis Management – Strategies to manage and recover from reputational crises and stakeholder challenges.

This book serves as an essential guide for professionals in risk management, finance, insurance, and corporate governance, offering both foundational knowledge and advanced methodologies to enhance risk resilience and decision-making.

We extend our sincere gratitude to the contributing authors, industry experts, and academic professionals who have shared their insights and expertise in shaping this publication. Their dedication ensures that this book remains a valuable resource for risk managers, corporate leaders, policymakers, and students alike. This book series is a testament of FERMA's (Federation of European Risk Management Associations) unwavering commitment to promoting excellence in risk management through education, research, and professional development.[1]

[1]To know more FERMA's commitment to risk management, please visit www.ferma.eu

# Acknowledgements

**Industry experts (FERMA materials)**
The structure of the following document is based on the FERMA rimap® Body of Knowledge developed in 2015 by a team of European risk managers representing their national risk management associations, members of FERMA, to serve as a basis for a European Risk Management certification. The FERMA rimap® Body of Knowledge was designed under the supervision of Prof. María Isabel Martínez Torre-Enciso, Doctor in Business and Economics by UCM, Professor of Corporate Finance in UAM, MBA, RIMAP, vice-president of ACdP-Fundación Universitaria San Pablo CEU.

Prof. Jean-Paul Louisot, Docteurès Sciences de Gestion de la Sorbonne, MBA, ARM, FIRM, acted as FERMA's subject matter expert to ensure greater consistency between the numerous topics of the Body of Knowledge, the ANZIIF existing learning materials and the new content developed to enrich the document. Amar Rahman, Principal Risk Engineer/Global Practice Leader Natural Hazards Resilience at Zurich Insurance Company Ltd.

**Instructional design and copy editing (FERMA materials)**

Stephanie Heriot AE, ANZIIF (Allied), Grad Dip Editing & Publishing, Cert. IV TAE

- ANZIIF expressly disclaims any and all liability to any person in respect of the consequences of anything done or not done by any person in reliance upon the contents of this subject material.

- **www.anziif.com and www.ferma.eu**

- **Industry experts (ANZIIF source modules)**

Simon R. Doherty
*BAppSc (TourMgt), Grad Cert Bus (Dpl & Trade) and Grad Cert Emerg Hth*

Deanne Keetelaar
*CPRM*

Kevin W Knight AM
*CPRM, Hon FRMIA, FIRM (UK), LMRMIA, ANZIIF (Mem)*

Kimberley Turner
*CPRM*

Mark Wheatley
*CPRM*

Lynda Fay
*ANZIFF Admin*

Mikaela Reynoldson
*MBA, LLB, BComm, GAICM*

Bob Anderson
*ANZIFF Admin*

Gordon Taylor
*ANZIIF Fellow, CIP, Adv. Dip FS, Hon Life Member*

Peter Moloney
*ANZIFF Admin*

Shaun Wilkinson
*ANZIIF (Fellow), FCII, Dip Bus Studs (Ins Mgt), FIRM*

Stuart Bassett
*LLB, BComm, FICSM, ASA, AAII, AIRM*

Gordon Young
*BA, MSc, ARM, AFRMIA, CPRM*

Harry Rosenthal
*BA, MBA, ARM, CPCU*

Ian Deayton
*Dip RM, AII (Assoc), RMIA (Mem)*

Vanessa Dallan
*ANZIIF (Fellow) CIP, MRM*

Tom Beer
*DSc, PhD, FEIA*

Gordon Young
*BA, MSc, ARM, CPRM, AFRMIA*

J. Peter Clarke
*FCA, MBA*

Roger Clarke
*BCom, MCom, PhD, FACS*

Chapter 1

# Uncertainty Modelling

## Introduction

The Volkswagen emissions testing scandal that sent shock waves throughout the industry in Europe is a vivid reminder of how events that are hard to foresee can still disturb profitability and threaten an organisation's survival. Producers are not only subject to these kinds of random events but also to shocks due to shifting consumers' tastes, volatile exchange rates, business cycles and technological developments; these are just some of the factors that can alter an organisation's fortunes. Executives must make forward-looking decisions in the face of all these uncertainties – but how?

It requires a new expanded definition of risk. Therefore, the 'new' risk manager must think and look beyond the organisation's frontiers, more specifically to include all economic partners, indeed all stakeholders of the organisation. Special attention will have to be devoted to the procurement chain and the interdependences of all parties and this includes a solid understanding of modelling uncertainty.

As a matter of fact, risk management is maturing into a fully-fledged branch of managerial sciences dealing with the handling of uncertainty, both threats and opportunities, to which all organisations are confronted due to more or less predictable changes in the internal and external context in which they operate as well as evolutions in their ownership and stakeholders' expectations and their impacts on objectives.

Enterprise-wide risk management is involved both in the design and implementation of strategies that must include provisions for adaptations and/or anticipations of these changing conditions and put in place sentinel events to warn of possible ruptures as early as possible. This will deliver value by facilitating prompt reaction and pre-emptive actions to allow managers to reach their optimal objectives, goals, and missions under any circumstances while coping with surprises, even of cataclysmic proportions.

**Risk Measurement and Monitoring, 1–14**

**doi:10.1108/978-1-83662-310-620251002**

However, this organisational resilience can be achieved only through the implementation of a continuous process of risk management at all levels in the organisation stemming from a clearly defined risk management strategy approved by the board in which the risk appetite is defined and communicated. This process loops through the review and audit process of the risk management programme to ensure that the key objectives are the centre of all decision-making and are achieved through a proper implementation of the plans.

Judgement can be applied to decision-making in risk-related issues, but rational and transparent processes called for by good governance practices require that risks be quantified to all extents possible. When data are insufficient, unavailable or irrelevant, expertise must be called upon to quantify impacts as well as likelihoods. Therefore, the risk manager must understand and be able to guide the implementation of the appropriate quantification tools at all three steps of the risk management process: risk assessment (identification, analysis and evaluation), risk treatment (reduction and financing), and monitor and review to validate the results and improve the future direction of the major models and provide illustrations on how they could apply.

This chapter will provide a description of the major models and provide illustrations on how they could be applied.

## Learning Outcomes

By the end of this chapter, you should be able to:

- define different approaches to modelling uncertainty;
- describe the major methods based on historical data;
- distinguish between simple, complex and matrix organisational structures;
- define data-based approaches to modelling uncertainty.

## Modelling Methods

Forecasting models based on probabilities and trend analysis are part of the risk manager's fundamental tool kit, and the question of analytics should be at the top of any new risk manager's agenda.

The mass of data that flows through the organisation and that is relevant to risk management is such that computer-based systems are early in the game.

There are analytical tools available to risk management professionals to measure the degree of uncertainty and to predict how an organisation will fare depending on various influencing factors and strategies.

Organisations assess the impact of uncertainty – that is, risk – through the development and use of empirical models. These models assist decision-makers in simulating, testing, and predicting outcomes and learning from the information produced.

The information derived from models helps in making decisions at all levels: strategic, tactic, and operational.

The methods for modelling uncertainty are traditionally split into three broad categories:

- methods based on historical data
- methods based primarily on expert input
- hybrid methods based on a combination of historical data and expert input.

Beyond these three categories, the methods could be viewed as a continuum and they should be each analysed for their benefits and limitations depending on the context and needs of the organisation.

When it comes to using the different methods, it is unlikely that each organisation would use all of them.

*Modelling Continuum*

| **Historical Data Analysis** | **Hybrid Models** | **Expert Input** |
|---|---|---|
| Empirical distribution | | Bayesian networks |
| Fit parameters of theoretical probability density functions | | |
| Stochastic differential equations | | |
| Extreme value theory | | |

## Methods Based on Historical Data

Traditionally, insurers approach uncertainty and predictive issues based on historical data and past patterns and this has been carried over to the risk management community.

The following are the major methods based on historical data:

- empirical distribution
- fit parameters of theoretical probability density functions
- stochastic differential equations (SDE)
- extreme value theory (EVT)
- regression analysis.

*Empirical Distribution*

An empirical distribution develops the theoretical probability distribution function of a set of many observations of a random variable (X1, X2, ... XN) forming a sample of observations. The most straightforward approach to constructing an empirical distribution is to form the hypothesis that the future is a reflection of the past and that the sample is a precise extraction of the population. In such a situation, the analyst can infer a discrete probability distribution.

Therefore, an empirical distribution is often represented by a series of steps representing the cumulative distribution from which the sample is drawn. As an illustration, organisations can use such an approach to predict the future return of a portfolio provided the portfolio has generated enough data to offer complete, reliable and consistent data, i.e. credible inputs.

This requirement is the limitation of this approach; it assumes that the organisation has been able to gather complete, consistent and reliable data in a stable context, including extreme events.

### *Fit Parameters of Theoretical Probability Density Functions*

One way to manage the limitations of empirical distribution is to assume that the uncertainty – the risk – lends itself to a continuous probability density function. In such a situation, the analyst will compute the parameters of the distribution that best fit the sample available. However, this implies that the analyst has reasons to select a form of distribution, not always the normal distribution already defined in a previous rimap Block. For instance, in the case of property-casualty losses, their frequency is often assumed to follow a Poisson or negative binomial distribution, both non-symmetrical and presenting a thick tail (risk of catastrophic frequency). When it comes to the severity, experience has proved that assuming a lognormal distribution or a Pareto distribution (or conditional, or tail) is a better fit.

### *Stochastic Differential Equations*

SDE represent the change between the value of a variable (for instance an interest rate or the quote of a share in the portfolio of an investor) between instant $t$ and $t+1$, one period later. The change is expressed as the combination of a predictable (certain) change and a random change during the time span considered. The random change is represented by a random variable following a specified probability distribution (typically, the normal distribution is chosen as it is simply defined by two factors: mean and standard deviation). Using an initial value, an SDE helps to roughly develop a scenario in which value changes over time can be produced this way. Thus, scenarios can be represented as probability distributions for each point in time over the forecast timeline and can be used by management to develop forecasts to assist in strategic decision-making.

### *Extreme Value Theory*

EVT is a subset of the discipline of statistics. Rather than creating a model based on the assumption that values or returns are normally distributed, risk managers can use EVT to include extreme or rare deviations from the median of probability distributions. As an analytical and a statistical tool, it aims to analyse probability distributions generated by processes. In the realm of risk, these processes may be natural forces such as erratic weather, one-hundred-year floods or earthquakes. More recently, EVT events have included finance and banking organisations' significant or 'extreme' exposure to poorly performing collateralised debt obligations. For this reason, EVT has utility in assessing risk from infrequently-occurring but high-severity types of losses.

### *Statistics and Trend Analysis*

Establishing forecasts on the basis of past data, i.e. using probability or trend analysis, is founded on the hypothesis that the future will reflect the past. Starting on this hypothesis, forecasts can be developed:

- On probability analysis: the world is stable and the future is a strict reproduction of the past.
- On trend analysis: the evolution of the world is stable and the evolution schemes of the past will continue in the future.

Whatever the circumstances, one of the basic objectives of risk forecasting is to evaluate the costs of future claims of a given organisation (from the viewpoint of the insurer and the reinsurer), or the future cash flows associated with uncertain future outcomes (from the viewpoint of the risk manager).

However, forecasts for the future are not used only in risk management, and using what the past teaches us of the future is a key to any rational management decision for a future that is intrinsically uncertain.

Just as a reminder, forecasts in the economic world are always based on past data. Only empirical probabilities can be used, by opposition to mathematical probabilities that can be computed without any sample or past experience (throwing dice, playing cards, etc.). The economic phenomena or situations are far too complex to lend themselves to a priori mathematical modelling as opposed to experience-based modelling. Therefore, they rely heavily on the accuracy of past data and the appropriate hypotheses on the foreseeable evolution of the mathematical relationship between key variables.

The major difference between 'management' and 'risk management' is in the word risk, meaning the degree of uncertainty. When the law of large numbers applies and reasonably accurate forecasts can be developed, there is no risk and it is just efficient management of a cost or profit centre (see Frequency risks). The problem is that when a real uncertainty (a serious risk) is involved, the data available may be too short to constitute a reliable sample to develop a probability distribution or a credible trend analysis.

This knowledge of the past must be translated in numbers to be used in all these forecast models. Therefore, collecting data, or learning from past experience, is a key to any rational approach to managing risks. (Any reader interested in furthering their knowledge of the field will find easily a number of books on forecast for beginners.)

Any useful data must be:

- exhaustive
- coherent (and stable)

- pertinent
- in order.

*Exhaustivity*

The risk manager relies on all the department heads to gather data, and all other information necessary to establish reserves and forecast future losses. Incident reports and quasi-accident information must be reported, otherwise the risk management process will be based on truncated information and therefore may lead to ill-informed decisions.

*Consistency (and Stability)*

In probability, consistency refers to the fact that the data in the sample are drawn from the same probability distribution. In practice, data must be collected and evaluated on the same basis.

To fix this idea, let us illustrate with an automobile fleet. If we want to use a five-year claim history, all claims must be expressed with the same monetary unit (adjusted for inflation). Also, the evolution of the park (model types and numbers) and drivers (retirement, resignations, new recruitments, etc.) will have to be accounted for as well as the modification of the environment (competition, laws, etc.).

*Relevance*

This is particularly difficult, as one makes sure that the data are related directly to the phenomena to be explained.

Let us illustrate by the same example. The climatic conditions at the site of a car accident can provide insights into the behaviour of drivers or cars under given conditions. On the other hand, the temperature in Tokyo on the day of an accident in Europe may be totally irrelevant.

*Order*

Data must be ordered in a way that makes sense with regard to the independent variables that will be the basis for the analysis. One of the most frequent is time, but it can be also turnover for product liability claims and salaries for workers compensation.

***Statistics***

Probability analysis can be used only provided the world is stable. This supposes that the world of the future is identical to the world of the past. Then, and only then, can a probability distribution be drawn from past data, the sample, to forecast the future.

What do we mean by probability? It is the relative frequency of an outcome; that is, the ratio of the number of occurrences of one of the outcomes to the totality of possible cases. It is represented by a number between 0 and 1, usually given as a per cent.

Let us summarise here the characteristics of a probability distribution.

### *Central Tendency*

The most common measure is the mean. Most probability distributions are more or less clustered around the most probable value, called the mode. Finally, a value leaves the same probability for the outcome to be higher or lower, it is the median. The mean is estimated by the arithmetic average of the sample.

### *Dispersion*

Most readers are likely to be familiar with the 'bell-shaped' curve, or normal distribution, also known as Gauss Law. Intuitively, one may understand that the bell may be wide open, spreading over a large interval, or narrowly pointed around its mean. It is easy to figure that a narrow curve will provide a more precise evaluation of the future than the broader one.

The measure of this dispersion is called the standard deviation. As a reminder, the standard deviation is the square root of the variance. The variance is the sum of the square of the distance of every possible outcome to the mean multiplied by its probability. The shape of the curve is really given by the dispersion index equal to the standard deviation divided by the mean.

### *Symmetry*

Some probability distributions are symmetrical, others are asymmetrical (Poisson, or binomial, distribution). This means they have a tail on one side. A distribution that is not symmetrical is skewed to the right or to the left. Most distributions found in the risk management world tend to be skewed to the right. In the case of a severity distribution, this means that there is a non-negligible probability that a catastrophic loss may be suffered.

The law of large numbers states that the larger the sample drawn from a population, the more trustworthy are the conclusions drawn.

Going back to the simplified risk mapping in four quadrants, it is clear that only risks with high frequency and low frequency will lend themselves easily to probability analysis. It is where the impact of prevention instruments can be assessed with some degree of accuracy.

However, the severe restriction due to the 'world stability' hypothesis reduces the domain where probability analysis can be applied as most elements of any organisation and its environment are always changing. This hypothesis can be partially lifted through trend analysis.

## ***Trend or Regression Analysis***

Trend or regression analysis consists in acknowledging the evolution of the environment and the system. However, it poses the hypothesis that the evolution follows mathematical relations between better-known dimensions (independent variables) and other variables (dependent variables). It is always essential to make a judicious choice of parameters, the evolution of which must be better known to forecast how the dependent variable may move in the future.

If linear regression is easier to use, it is not the only mathematical relation that may be used in modelling for forecasting the future. Furthermore, one dependent variable may require several independent variables to explain its future behaviour. The formidable advances in computing capacity have made possible multiple regression analysis and the processing of a large number of data, which was impossible by hand in the past.

Here are some illustrations of regression that might prove fruitful for the risk manager:

- number of vehicles in a fleet explaining the variation in yearly total losses from the fleet;
- annual turnover and total amount of product liability claims (with a possible lag time between the two);
- number of employees and frequency of workers compensation claims.

But also consider product liability claims related to 'quality budget'.

Let us remember if that dealing with uncertainty is at the heart of any rational management process, it is even more essential than the management of risks, intended to handle situations of extreme uncertainty. Probability, trend analysis, and modelling (Monte-Carlo, etc.) all rely heavily on the quality of data collected first through the past history of the organisation but also on the experience of similar organisations or industry wide data.

However, the rapidly changing and somewhat erratic world that we have experienced over the last 10 or 20 years has made modelling based on probability and trend analysis at best unreliable, if not totally obsolete. It remains to evaluate the new breach in forecasting future states of systems that will bring new developments in the mathematical world like chaos theory and the transposition of existing concept physics like entropy and other laws of thermo-dynamics into the economic sphere.

**Note:** When using regression analysis, it is essential to validate the quality of the regression thanks to the determination of efficient R2. R2 is between 0 and 1; the closer to 1, the better (more reliable) the regression. c is the most probable (see graph below).

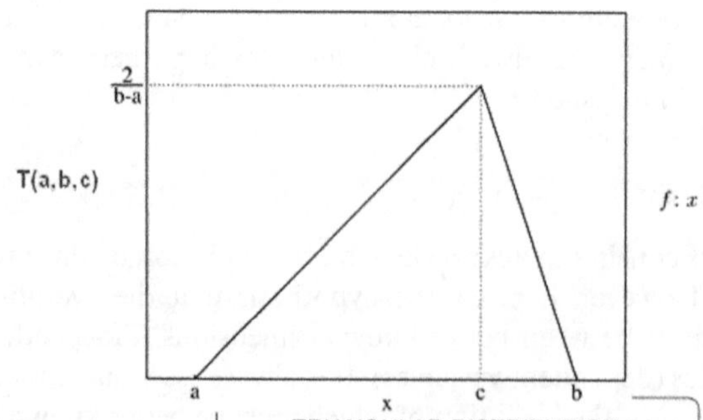


TRIANGULAR DISTRIBUTION

$$f : x \mapsto \begin{cases} \dfrac{2(x-a)}{(b-a)(c-a)} & \text{si } a \leq x \leq c \\ \dfrac{2(b-x)}{(b-a)(b-c)} & \text{si } c \leq x \leq b \\ 0 & \text{sinon} \end{cases}$$

### *Most Common Probability Distributions*

These distributions are either created from real life models – such as Weibull distribution, used to represent lifetime of objects in reliability theory – or from mathematical inference. For instance, the square value of a normally distributed variable follows a so-called Chi-squared distribution.

All distributions can be useful in some risk analysis applications. The most useful distributions for a risk manager are likely to be:

- normal or Gaussian distribution, used to represent the impact of common events;
- Poisson distribution, used generally to represent the frequency of events;
- Gumbel or extreme value distribution, used to represent the impact of uncommon events;
- general histogram distribution;
- triangular distribution.

#### *Normal or Gaussian Distribution*

The normal distribution is typically used to model a variety of natural or behavioural phenomena. The wide use of this distribution is a consequence of the central limit theorem (below). In all situations where many small effects are added together into an observable variable, the use of the normal distribution can be theoretically justified.

The Gaussian distribution parameters are:

- $\mu$: the mean of the observed phenomenon;
- $\sigma$: the standard deviation of the observed phenomenon.

#### *Example of Normal/Gaussian Distribution*

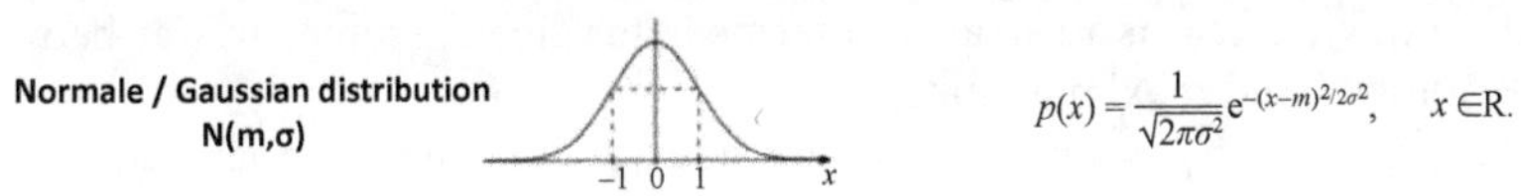


$$f(x)=\frac{1}{\sqrt{2\pi\sigma}}e^{\frac{1}{2}\left(\frac{x-\mu}{\sigma}\right)^2}$$

#### *Poisson Distribution*

The Poisson distribution is a discrete probability distribution. It expresses the probability of a number of events occurring in a fixed time if these events occur with a known average rate and are independent of the time since the last event. In the field of risk management, it is often used to model the frequency of a given event.

This distribution has only one parameter:

- $\lambda$ is the expected number of events during the considered period.

*Example of Poisson Distribution*

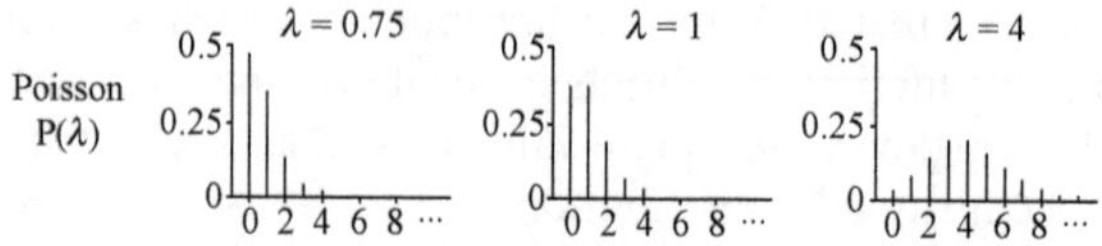


$$\mu = \sum_{n \geq 0} e^{-\lambda} \frac{\lambda^n}{n!} \delta_{(n)}$$

$$f(x) = \frac{\lambda^x - e^{-\lambda}}{x!}$$

*Gumbel or Extreme Value Distribution*

In the 1950s, the German mathematician Gumbel proposed a statistical theory of extreme events (EVT or extreme value theory). This theory has now abundant applications, for instance when modelling large insurance losses, financial intra-day risk, and extreme floods or waves.

Gumbel distribution is a special case of the Fisher–Tippett distribution. Gumbel distribution is obtained when $\mu = 0$ and $\beta = 1$.

*Example of Gumbel/Extreme Value Distribution*

$$f(x) = \frac{z.e^{-z}}{\beta}$$

$$\text{where } z = e^{\left(-\frac{x-\mu}{\beta}\right)}$$

*General Histogram Distribution*

Histograms are used to represent the distribution of empirical data.

The parameters of this distribution are:

- the minimal and maximal value of the available data;
- $\{x\} = \{x_1, x_2, \ldots, x_N\}$ is an array of intermediate values, assumed to stay between the minimal and maximal limits;
- $\{p\} = \{p_1, p_2, \ldots, p_N\}$ is an array of each interval cumulated probability.

*Example of General Histogram Distribution*

**Gumel distribution (μ,β)**

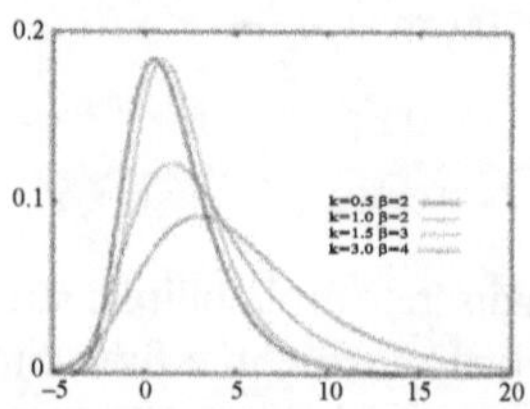


$$P(z) = \frac{\exp(-z)\, z}{\beta}$$

$$\text{avec } z = \exp\left[-\frac{x-\mu}{\beta}\right]$$

$$f(x) = p_i + \left[\frac{x - x_i}{x_{i+1} - x_i}\right](p_{i+1} - p_i)$$

*Triangular Distribution*

This distribution is generally used to represent an expert's view of a random variable.

One important point must be mentioned: Most of the usual mathematical distributions are unbounded, which means that they can take infinite values, because they were usually designed as limits or generalisations of discrete distributions. Using unbounded distributions, and hence potentially infinite outcomes, may be nonsensical in risk management applications.

Most of the literature on quantitative risk management is about mathematics. For a non-mathematician reader, this literature is often dense and incomprehensible. However, it must be always kept in mind that mathematical tools are used only to combine or derive beliefs in a rational way. In other words, all mathematical developments on probabilities build on top of a simple initial belief or theory. This initial belief is then unfolded as much as possible using mathematical inference *within the framework of probability theory* and yields quantitative results that may seem difficult to assimilate.

Probability theory is a mathematical framework to rationally combine beliefs. It will not provide any information on what deciders should or should not believe when making decisions. This is an incredibly powerful tool: from the specification of very simple beliefs or assumptions, probability distributions can be rationally inferred. One of the most usual and powerful tools of probability theory is the central limit theorem, which guarantees that the sum of a large number of identically distributed random variables will converge to a normal law.

In the field of risk management, only finance and insurance can really benefit from mathematical developments of probability theory because these two fields deal with frequent random events. Indeed, at a cumulated level, most random phenomena exhibit organised features. When dealing with discrete and specific uncertain events, every professional has to build their own beliefs. To do so, they may rely on experts, specifically on causal models designed by experts, or simulate too-scarce events.

Triangular distribution can prove useful when no law seems to apply to the data available. If an expert suggests that the variable should be between $a$ and $b$ then it is possible to construct a distribution that can be used, for example to use a Monte-Carlo approach.

## Methods Based on Expert Input

### *Bayesian Networks*

A Bayesian network is a probabilistic causal graph.

The graph represents the structure of knowledge about a given domain: concepts or variables are connected by oriented links. A link is the expression of a causal dependency.

*Nodes and Variables*

In a Bayesian network, each node represents a discrete random variable, i.e. a variable with at least two possible outcomes.

Bayesian networks can in principle deal with continuous variables, but discrete nodes are more usual. Furthermore, using continuous variables in Bayesian networks imposes restrictions for architecture and usable algorithms. In practice, as far as prospective risk analysis is concerned, the use of discrete or discretised variables would be generally appropriate and even recommended for a better communication of the models.

*Probabilities*

Since each variable is considered random, its distribution must be defined. This means that the probabilities of the different outcomes must be defined.

*Dependencies*

A link in a Bayesian network is interpreted as a causal relationship, i.e. A→B means that A is one of the causes of B. In other words, if A and B are uncertain variables, and the causal relation A→B holds, then the distribution on B will be different for different outcomes of A.

*Inference*

The main use of Bayesian networks is inference. A Bayesian network represents the dependency structure of a knowledge domain. Once the graph has been created and the probability tables defined, a Bayesian network software will calculate the overall distribution of the set of variables.

*Learning*

A Bayesian network contains knowledge in two different forms:

- the causal structure of the graph
- the probability tables.

Knowledge can be generally obtained from two sources: either empirically (i.e. from data) or from domain experts. This holds also for Bayesian network, at least in theory. In practice, experts will help build the causal structure of the model, and the quantitative part of the model (probability tables) will be inferred from statistical data.

In theory, it could be possible to derive the causal structure directly from data. Specific learning algorithms can be used for that purpose. However, building the model structure directly from data is usually not feasible because no statistical database would be available where all useful variables are simultaneously present.

*Extension to Influence Diagrams*

Bayesian networks represent specific domain knowledge in a probabilistic graph. In all their applications, and especially for risk management, this knowledge will be used to support some sort of decision.

Influence diagrams are extended Bayesian networks that can be helpful for decision under uncertainty. In influence diagram, special nodes called decision nodes are used to represent various alternatives.

### *Monte Carlo Simulation*

Sometimes it may prove impossible to effectively combine beliefs (or local probability distributions). This may be impossible analytically, or there may be no mathematician at hand, or simply one may be too lazy. In any of these situations, using Monte Carlo simulation may prove the next best solution.

Monte Carlo simulation is a very powerful mathematical tool when dealing with uncertainty. It is widely applied in many application domains, such meteorology, finance, epidemiology, drug design and quantum physics. The complete mathematical developments of Monte Carlo simulation are far beyond the scope of this chapter. The purpose here is to introduce the basics of this technique for application in risk management.

A simple way to understand why risk managers need to understand Monte Carlo simulation is to realise that if they do not, their organisation may lose money when dealing with people who do master this method. It is clear for most people knowing the basics of probabilities that a casino owner is almost certainly rich. Thanks to Monte Carlo simulation, it is possible to understand why some fund managers are so efficient.

#### *Sampling Random Numbers*

Sampling random numbers is about to create a well-balanced set of possible results of a random experiment. When an experiment cannot be repeated, for which some conditions are considered random, an alternative is to simulate it, that is, run the experiment on paper or, more realistically, on a computer. In other words, simulated experiments are considered representative of actual ones; however, it remains necessary that at least that the random part of the real and simulated experiments is similar (has the same distribution). If for instance the experiment involves some binary random event of probability – 50% – then it would be realistic to flip a coin to simulate this. If the distributions involved are more complex, then computerised tools will be called for – there are no coins that you can flip to simulate a normal distribution.

The basic tool needed is a uniform sampler, which is a computerised function capable of drawing a number uniformly distributed between 0 and 1. Although this is not a simple function to create, this discussion will not be entered here, and it can be assumed for instance that the RAND () function available within Excel is actually such a function.

The principle of Monte Carlo simulation has been introduced here to show how to evaluate the distribution of some random variable, assuming it depends of other random variables, through a calculation or decision process. In some circumstances, it would be possible to calculate analytically the distribution of the random variable to be studied but this would not always be the case.

## Summary

Please keep in mind the following points:

- The core mission of risk management is to inform top management on uncertainties and be able to narrow down as best possible the outcome of the future.
- Forecasting models based on probabilities and trend analysis are part of the risk manager's fundamental tool kit.
- The mass of data that flows through the organisation and that is relevant to risk management is such that computer-based systems are early in the game.
- There are analytical tools available to risk management professionals to measure the degree of uncertainty and to predict how an organisation will fare depending on various influencing factors and strategies.
- Organisations assess the impact of uncertainty, i.e. risk, through the development and use of empirical models. These models assist decision-makers in simulating, testing and predicting outcomes and learning from the information produced.
- The information derived from models helps in making decisions at all levels: strategic, tactic, and operational.
- The methods for modelling uncertainty are traditionally split into three broad categories:

  - Methods based on historical data
  - Methods based primarily on expert input
  - Hybrid methods based on a combination of historical data and expert input.

Beyond these three categories, the methods could be viewed as a continuum and they should be each analysed for their benefits and limitations depending on the context and needs of the organisation. When it comes to using the different methods, it is unlikely that each organisation would use all of them.

- Typically, an organisation will tailor a model to best suit its needs and may require a very detailed approach.

Chapter 2

# Present Value, Portfolio Approach and Efficient Frontier

## Introduction

The sustainability of an organisation relies on its financial efficiency and the two key objectives of finance are optimising return while avoiding bankruptcy. This is the reason why the modern approach to selecting investments and sources of funds relies on the present value of cashflows. In most organisations, financial decisions are based on the present values of cashflows generated by a proposed investment. This is why risk managers must be aware of this approach and the criteria attached to it, especially the net present value (NPV).

However, there are underlying assumptions that must be considered; primarily the link between risk and return where risk is traditionally measured by uncertainty or the volatility of the cashflows.

Analysing individual investments in an organisation is not enough and the risk management professional must understand how risks interact with each other and the meaning of correlation and covariance so that they can assess the integrated of a risk/assets portfolio.

Theories have been developed to help model the integration of risk in an organisation's portfolio so as to reach its efficient frontier based on its tolerance/appetite for risk.

The present chapter aims at equipping risk management professionals with the tools to understand the approach to making financial decisions and providing top management with the information they need to make informed decision.

**Risk Measurement and Monitoring, 15–34**

**Published under exclusive licence by Emerald Publishing Limited**
**doi:10.1108/978-1-83662-310-620251005**

**Learning Outcomes**

By the end of this chapter, you should be able to:

- define the present value approach to selecting investments;
- apply different criteria to make risk management decisions;
- define the relationship between risk and return;
- distinguish between Value at Risk (VaR) and Cash Flow at Risk (CFaR).

## Present Value and Criteria to Select Investments

The below case study is based on the facts of the Indigo Company case. To successfully complete this case study, you should understand five capital budgeting concepts:

- discount rate
- present value
- net present value
- internal rate of return
- time-adjusted period of return.

### *Discount Rate*

The discount rate is the rate used to calculate, or discount, the value of a dollar that will be received in the future into current dollars. The term 'discount' is used because a dollar received in the future is worth less than a dollar received today, after accounting for the future dollar's opportunity cost, which is the interest that the dollar would have accumulated between today and the time it is actually received.

Although the terms 'discount rate' and 'interest rate' are often used interchangeably, a discount rate is used to calculate a dollar's present value, while an interest rate is used to calculate a dollar's future value.

### *Present Value of Cash Flows*

Present value is the current value of money that will be received in the future, calculated using a discount rate, or the equivalent today of the sum to be received in the future, reduced by the cumulated interest that will not be earned over the period due to delayed inflow; alternatively, it is the sum that invested today at the relevant rate would accumulate to the expected cashflows.

### *NPV of an Investment*

NPV is the present value of cash inflows, minus the present value of cash outflows, resulting from a proposed expenditure for a given rate of return on an investment. Knowing how to calculate the NPV of an investment proposal is vital to understanding this approach to selecting investment and/or financing mechanisms. This calculation incorporates several elements:

- the amount of the investment at time zero;
- the estimated additional cash outflows, if any, that the project will require;
- the number of years of the project's useful life;
- the organisation's required rate of return;
- the cash inflows that the project is expected to generate;
- the organisation's depreciation method (for example, straight-line or accelerated) for capital projects;
- the organisation's effective tax rate on inflows from the die project.

### *Internal Rate of Return*

Internal rate of return (IRR) is the discount rate at which the present value of a proposal's net cashflow is zero. It is another method, in addition to the die NPV method, for evaluating investment proposals.

### *Time-Adjusted Period of Return*

The time-adjusted period of return is a calculation of the time required for the present value of the net cash flows generated from a project, when discounted at the required rate of return, to equal the initial investment. That is, the time-adjusted period of return is the length of time required for the organisation to recover its initial investment.

#### ***Case study – The Emerald Company***

The Emerald Company is contemplating investing in new equipment to boost its production capacity for a total cost of 360 M€. The new equipment would increase net annual revenues by 106.5 M€ during its estimated useful life of 12 years. However, the annual maintenance costs will be 7.3 M€. The equipment will have no residual value at the end of its useful life and the company uses linear depreciation for its assets. Emerald management has set its return target at 16%. Emerald tax rate is 38%.

The present value of an annual flow of € 1 for 12 years may be calculated using various interest rates:

- € 5.197 at 16% interest
- € 5.421 at 15% interest
- € 5.660 at 14% interest.

Furthermore, at 14% interest, an annual flow of € 1 for 10 years is € 5.216 and, for 11 years, € 5.453.

**Step 1: Deciding on a Given Investment Based on Present Values**

To determine whether to accept or reject the investment the Emerald Company is contemplating, it should calculate first the investment's NPV. This incorporates the following factors:

| | |
|---|---|
| • *2360 M€* | is the amount of the investment at time zero. |
| • *n* | is the number of years of the project's useful life. |
| • $NOCF_{BT}$ | is the net discounted cashflow (before taxes). |
| • $NDCF_{AT}$ | is the net discounted cashflow (after taxes). |
| • *PVs* | is the present value of cash flows generated by the investment. |

*Given the facts, should Emerald Company choose to invest in the purchase of the equipment?*

**Data summary in € million:**

$I° = €\ 360$

$n = 12$ years

--› Annual depreciation = $I°/n = €\ 30$

Required rate of return = 16%

Inflow 106.5

Outflow (maintenance) – 7.3

$NDCF_{ar} = €\ 99.2$

NDCF $_{Br}$ 99.20

– Annual depreciation 30.0

= Taxable income € 69.2 × 38% —▶— Taxes 26.30

= $NDCF_{AT}$ € 72.90

NPV = $PV(NDCF) - I° = NDCF_{Ar} - I°$

NPV = 72.90 × 5.197 – 360= 378.86 – 360 = +18.86

NPV = +€ 18,860

The NPV is positive; therefore, the investment should be approved.

**Note:** Using the IRR method would have resulted in the same decision.

**Step 2: Including the Cost of Risk in the Decision Process**

The preceding assessment did not consider uncertainty, i.e. risk. Should the equipment representing the investment be damaged by fire, for example, the expected cash inflows to be generated would be reduced. Based on Emerald's previous loss history with similar machinery, the risk management professional devises a probability distribution of expected losses in any given year.

| Probability loss (in € million) | |
|---|---|
| 0.740 | 0 |
| 0.110 | 10 |
| 0.080 | 50 |
| 0.065 | 100 |
| 0.004 | 400 |
| 0.001 | 1,000 |

*If the Emerald Company chose to finance its risk through retention, would the investment still be justified?*

Assuming that the 'annual cost of risk' incurred is equal to the expected value of the losses (average losses over time), then the cost of risk is:

$$E(\text{losses}) = (0.740 \times 0) + (0.11 \times 10) + (0.08 \times 50) + (0.065 \times 100) + (0.004 \times 400) + (0.001 \times 1{,}000) = €14.20$$

**Data summary in € million:**

$I° = €\ 360$

$n = 12$ years

Annual depreciation $I°/n = €\ 30$

Required rate of return = 16%

| | |
|---|---|
| Inflow | 106.5 |
| Outflow (maintenance) | –7.3 |
| Expected annual loss/Cost of risk | –14.20 |

$NDCF_{Br} = €\ 85.00$

| | |
|---|---|
| $NDCF_{Br}$ | 85.00 |
| – Annual Depreciation | 30.00 |

= Taxable income € 55.00 × 38% —▶ — Taxes 20.90

= *NDCF* € 64.10

NPV = $PV(NDCF) - I° = NDCF_{Ar} - I°$ = 64.10 × 5.197 – 360 = 333.13 – 360 = –€ 26.87

Because the NPV is negative when the cost of risk has entered the picture, Emerald Company should not purchase the equipment if it maintains the goal of reaching its target of a minimum rate of return of 16%.

**Step 3: Considering Risk Control/Reduction Measures**

The Emerald Company risk management team has developed a loss control programme that would reduce the expected value of fire losses to € 2.30 but would require implementing control procedures that would cost € 3.00 annually. The implementation of this loss reduction programme would modify the return of the proposed Emerald company's investment.

*If the Emerald Company implements the proposed risk reduction measure, would the investment be justified?*

In this context, the cost of risk (in € million) consists of two elements: the cost of implementing the loss reduction measure and the reduced expected annual loss. Thus, it is equal to € 2.30 + € 3.00 = € 5.30 and this is the only change in the data.

**Data summary in € million:**

$I°$ = € 360

$n$ = 12 years

– Annual depreciation = $I°/n$ = € 30

Required rate of return = 16% Inflow 106.5

| | |
|---|---|
| Inflow | 106.5 |
| Outflow (maintenance) | –7.3 |
| Cost of risk | –5.3 |
| NDCF*8r* = | € 93.90 |

$NDCF_{ar}$ 93.90

– Annual Depreciation 30.00

= Taxable income € 63.90 × 38% —▶ — Taxes 24.28

= NDCFAT € 69.62

NPV – PV(NDCF) – I °= $NDCF_{Ar}$ – I° = 69.62 × 5.197 – 360 = 361.18 – 360 = +1.18

If the loss reduction (loss control) measures were to be implemented, the NPV would be positive. Hence, the company could invest in this new equipment and obtain the desired rate of return of 16%.

**Step 4: Buying Insurance Cover to Transfer the Financial Consequences**

The Emerald Company could choose to transfer the financial burden of the fire losses due to the proposed new equipment to an insurer. It has obtained a quote for fire insurance coverage at € 4.80.

*If in view of view its risk appetite, the Emerald Company decides that it must purchase insurance covers; in this case, would the investment still be justified?*

If an insurer is ready to offer coverage at € 4.80, it is not in a situation where it would be buying 'the € 14.2 expected value of losses', but rather the value obtained at step 3, thanks to the implementation the proposed loss reduction program. Therefore, the cost of risk is equal at the sum of two factors, the cost of the reduction measure and the cost of the insurance; hence to € 3.0 plus € 4.8, which is € 7.8.

**Data summary in € million:**

$I°$ = € 360

$n$ = 12 years

Annual depreciation = $I°/n$ = € 30

Required rate of return = 16%

| | |
|---|---|
| Cash inflow | 106.5 |
| Outflow (maintenance) | –7.3 |
| Expected annual loss | –7.8 |
| $NDCF_{8r}$ = | € 91.40 |

| | | |
|---|---|---|
| $NDCF_{8r}$ = | € 91.40 | |
| – Annual Depreciation | 30.00 | |
| = Taxable income | €61.40 × 38% – | – Taxes 23.33 |
| | | = $ADCF_{AT}$ € 68.07 |

NPV = $PV(NDCF) - I° = NDCF_{Ar} - I°$ = 68.07 × 5.197 – 360 = 353.75 – 360 = – 6.26 = (€6.260)

When insurance covers are purchased, the investment's NPV is negative; therefore, Emerald Company should not purchase the equipment if it maintains 16% as its desired rate of return.

**Step 5: The Impact of Tax Policy on the Choice of Investment**

Assuming that the proposed investment is desirable for society at large, the government might consider a reduction in Emerald's tax bracket to allow it to make the investment while obtaining its desired rate of return of 16%.

*By how much would the tax rate have to be reduced to make it worthwhile for Emerald to make the investment?*

If Emerald is to obtain the desired 16% return on its investment, the $NDCF_{Ar}$ must be at least equal to $I°$ divided by the present value factor (360/5.197 = 69.27).

The income tax must be reduced so that the $NDCF_{Ar}$ is raised to be at least equal to the desired minimum. The needed amount is the difference between the current value and the desired minimum (68.22 – 69.27, or –1.05), which represents less than 2% of the taxable income. The government would have to reduce the tax rate from 38% to 36% for Emerald to achieve its goal.

At a tax rate of 36%, taxes become 61.40 × 0.36 = 22.10, and the $NDCF_{Ar}$ is € 69,300 (€ 69,270).

In the event of such a tax reduction (2%), the NPV would be positive, so the company could invest in the new equipment and obtain the desired 16% rate of return.

When the economy is weak or public policy focus is on 'green' solutions to risk control challenges, the potential implications of tax policy should not be ignored.

**Step 6: Volatility or the Level or Uncertainty Must Be Considered**

Having reviewed the available options described above, Emerald's top management is ready to sacrifice on return in order to avoid unpleasant surprises (such as an uninsured major fire loss). Management would be willing to accept a 15% or 14% rate of return on its investment provided the equipment is fully insured. *In view of these considerations, what would be Emerald's optimal decision?*

If management is ready to accept a 15% rate of return on its investment, it must compute the NPV for this rate when insurance coverage is purchased:

NPV = $PV(NDCF) - I° = NDCF_{AF} - I°$ = 68.22 × 5.421 – 360 = 369.82 – 360 = + 9.82 = € 9,820

Because the NPV is positive, the investment is acceptable. At 14%, the NPV would be even greater but the computation would be without merit.

From the calculations of the previous steps, the recommendation to Emerald Company leadership would be to invest in the equipment, implement the risk reduction programme and purchase the insurance cover as this would entail accepting a limited reduction in the rate of return (the risk premium to be insured would be less than 1%).

Therefore, here is Emerald's risk management professional's final recommendation to Emerald's board of directors:

- Purchase the equipment
- Implement the loss control (risk reduction) measures
- Purchase the proposed fire insurance.

**Step 7: Time-Adjusted Payback Period**

When evaluating a potential investment, many companies also consider the period needed to recover cash invested in equipment, or the payback period. If the funds are generated quickly, they will be available for other purposes, which is an important factor when considering dynamic modelling. Therefore, the payback period is one factor in prioritising investments. However, when cash inflows occur over several years, the traditional cash 'payback period' fails to include the loss of income in the meantime. Therefore, the evaluation of an investment should incorporate the time value of money (an actualised period of return).

As an illustration, in Emerald Company's case, for evaluation purposes, it must determine how long it will take for the present value of the cash inflow to equal the initial investment, assuming a 14% return rate. The present value factor of the investment is the initial investment divided by the net discounted cashflow, which in this case is 360 divided by 68.22, or 5.277.

The present value factor at 14% of an annual flow of € 1 is 5.216 for 10 years and 5.453 for 11 years. The present value factor for this investment at 14% is 5.277, which is between the present value factors for 10 and 11 years. Thus, the time-adjusted period of return is a little over 10 years.

This approach also provides an insight into what information and data should be verified, as they are crucial for regaining the initial investment.

### *Limits of Using Present Value Criteria to Make Risk Management Decisions*

While using the present value approach to select risk management options has the advantage of putting them in the same framework as all other corporate decisions, there are limits that must be considered.

- In a business environment, it is often necessary to evaluate investment opportunities as a portfolio, rather than individually, as present value analysis as presented here does.
- Budgetary constraints may force an organisation to forgo or postpone some desirable opportunities. And the interactions between proposals are not readily considered.

- Only purely financial issues are considered, and such considerations as ethics and values issues, are not integrated in the decision process.
- Cash flows evaluated at the 'expected value' do not reflect the reality especially when the uncertainty involved is extremely volatile. Therefore, special attention must be paid to 'tails of distributions' (black swans, etc.) such as catastrophic developments.
- The further into the future inflows are expected to occur, the less accurate those projected inflows are likely to be. It is possible for good maths to be crushed by bad estimates of future occurrences.
- The portfolio approach will lead planners to consider the synergies and probabilistic relationships among the many assets involved, which are not considered in the present value approach.
- The finance supply side (such as access to additional long-term funds and short-term cash facilities from external providers) is not directly given due consideration.

## Optimising Risk Taking

When confronted with a given investment project, in competition with other opportunities for a limited budget, any organisation should engage in a global approach including the expected return and the risk associated with the project. In accordance with the modern theory initiated in 1951 by Harry Markowitz, the return must include a 'risk premium' commensurate with the risk accepted.

Therefore, managers, including risk managers, responsible for strategic planning must understand the risk–return relationship associated with investments in projects and initiatives; they also should understand the importance of weighing risks against potential financial gains or losses. At the end of the day, they have to understand their organisation's risk tolerance and/or appetite level.

### *Risk and Return Are Related*

When risk and return are mentioned in a financial context, 'risk' refers to the degree of uncertainty about possible outcomes. An organisation must assess whether the return for a given investment is likely to meet projected expectations, exceed those expectations, or fall short of them. The organisation will have to establish target returns on investments in various organisational projects based on a number of assessment methods like those explored in the previous block.

Usually, decisions concerning high risk, hence high return, projects, strategic in nature, are made by senior managers or even at the executive/board level. Day-to-day decisions and tactical or operational investment/expenses involving lower levels of risk are generally delegated to operational or business-level managers.

### *The Portfolio Approach*

Rather than assessing a single exposure, risk management professionals are generally confronted with the analysis of the range of risks – the portfolio – the organisation faces. Therefore, it is crucial that they can assess how adding risk to an organisation affects its overall risk portfolio. This is key when making risk management decisions to create value for the organisation.

Therefore, when evaluating the risks an organisation faces, a risk management professional should use a portfolio approach. This means evaluating each risk not only on its own impact but also on how it interacts with all other risks in the portfolio. This approach involves evaluating several factors:

- expected return of each risk in the portfolio
- volatility of the return of each risk in the portfolio
- overall return of the portfolio
- overall risk of the portfolio
- impact to overall portfolio performance of adding individual risks.

The portfolio approach, which helps organisations determine which risks to integrate or eliminate from their overall risk profiles, can be applied to both financial and non-financial assets. Correlation and covariance are statistical measures used in the portfolio approach. Optimising risk taking also involves identifying and quantifying risk metrics.

#### *Modern Portfolio Theory (MPT) and Financial Assets*

When finance professionals make decisions regarding investments or potential investments, they evaluate not only the risk and return associated with a given investment, but also how the proposed investment would influence other investments in the existing portfolio. This approach is commonly referred to as MPT or simply the 'portfolio approach'. MPT states that investors, through diversification, optimise their portfolios by maximising return or minimising risk by considering both the risk inherent to the proposed investment and the overall portfolio risk due to the way all investments interact.

To assess the effect of adding a new investment to a portfolio and of overall portfolio performance it is usual to plot the portfolio's investments in a graph that shows the investments' relationship to an 'efficient frontier'. The efficient frontier is a graphical representation of a financial portfolio's rate of return and volatility. An optimal portfolio generates the highest return for a given volatility or the lowest volatility for a given return.

*The Efficient Frontier on the Return/Risk Plan*

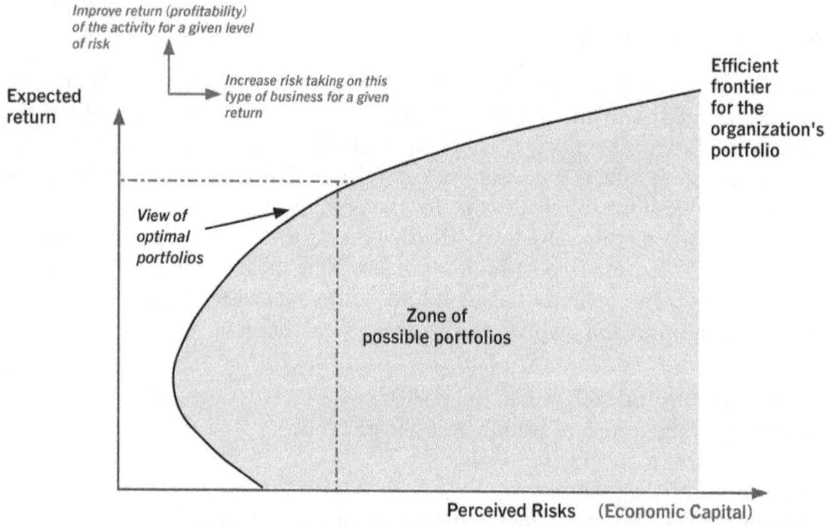


Moving left along a horizontal axis or up along a vertical axis towards the frontier represents an improvement in the risk/return frontier of a portfolio. If adding an investment to the portfolio moves a portfolio closer to the efficient frontier (the desired direction), then adding that investment is a good decision. Once the efficient frontier is reached, no new investments, or real-locations of existing investments, can improve the portfolio (or make it more efficient). A higher return may be generated by taking on more volatility, i.e. more risk. However, at this point, movement cannot occur horizontally or vertically, but only along the efficient frontier trading off risk (volatility) and return. Stated differently, portfolios that reach the efficient frontier are optimised because they provide a maximal expected rate of return for a given level of risk tolerance and minimal risk for a given level of expected return.

## *MPT and Non-Financial Assets*

MPT can also be applied to decision-making regarding non-financial (or physical) assets such as real estate or personal property. When risk management professionals, using a holistic approach, consider the global portfolio of risks their organisations face, including risks to both financial and non-financial assets, the overall portfolio must be assessed while considering the interrelationships among those assets.

Risk managers can assess the threats and opportunities (i.e. the risks and rewards) associated with each risk and how those risks (portfolio elements) affect the organisation's overall risk profile. Through this approach, the organisation is led to select only those investment risks that move it closer to its targeted position on the efficient frontier.

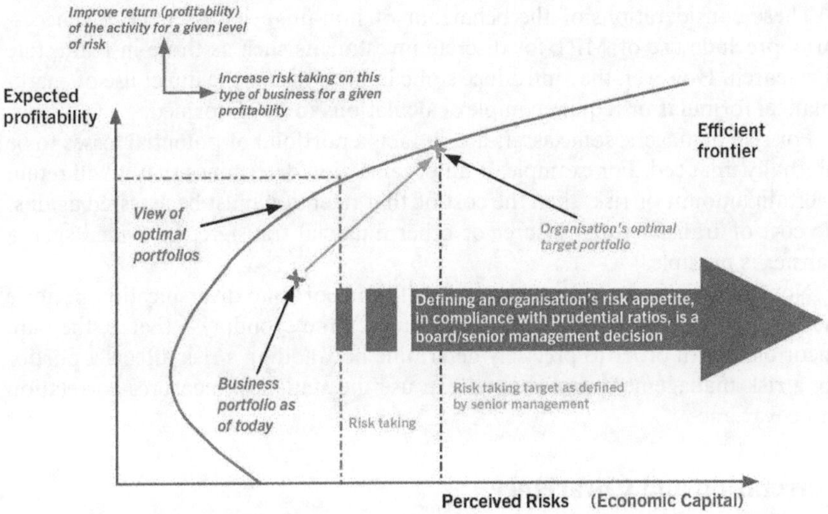


However, when the MPT is used to optimise portfolios that consist totally or partially of non-financial assets, the behaviour of those assets differs from the behaviour of financial assets. Therefore, the following considerations should be addressed:

- Financial assets are divisible into small units that facilitate optimisation. For example, a stock portfolio (large unit) can be optimised on a per-share basis. For example, for a portfolio constituted by three types of shares, the optimal position for the three shares, in term of units, might be 50%, 40%, and 10%. Non-financial assets are not as divisible. For example, single investments in new real estate, software development or product development usually cannot be divided into components or split into instalments. For these non-financial assets their specific nature might limit the capability of attaining in real life the theoretical optimal solution.
- Financial assets can be easily purchased or sold in active markets in which the assets are continually valued (they are fungible). For example, shares and bonds are traded daily. Non-financial assets are typically less liquid than financial assets. For example, it might take months or even longer for an organisation to find a buyer for facilities it wishes to dispose of. Or, if a new product development project is interrupted, the 'sunk funds' already spent for that project might be totally lost – there is no resale value.
- Financial assets typically produce returns that follow a normal distribution (represented by a rounded, shorter peak and a thin tail). Put another way, financial assets tend not to produce fat tail distributions. Non-financial assets

are typically more likely than financial assets to be subject to wide-ranging variations in return. For example, a biotech firm's investment in development of a new molecule can produce a very successful drug or end up in a dead end (total loss).

These considerations of the behaviour of non-financial assets do not necessarily preclude use of MPT for discrete investments such as those in real estate or research. However, they introduce some limitations for the direct use of mathematical formulas or require complex calculations to be performed.

For risk managers, some assets are, in fact, a portfolio of potential losses to be internally financed. For example, if an organisation determines that it will retain a certain amount of risk, then the cost of that retention must be assessed against the cost of transfer to an insurer or other financial transferee, provided such a transfer is possible.

Non-financial risks offer an opportunity for portfolio diversification because they are largely disconnected from the state of the economy – that is, they are uncorrelated. In order to precisely determine how adding a risk affects a portfolio, a risk management professional can use the statistical measures correlation and covariance.

## Correlation and Covariance

Correlation and covariance are key concepts within the studies of probability and statistics that are necessary for understanding portfolio selection:

- Correlation is usually represented by a single number – the correlation coefficient – that is a scaled version of the covariance.
- Covariance is a statistic used to convey the direction of and strength of association between two variables (risks). Covariance indicates the extent to which two variables change together.

Risk management professionals use correlation and covariance measurements for several purposes:

- identify and quantify relationships among risks (the portfolio approach);
- communicate risks to management;
- prioritise investments in risk control;
- optimise financing mechanisms that cover multiple risks;
- evaluate risk management programme effectiveness.

Both correlation and covariance provide quantification of the relationship between two or more elements (risks) in the portfolio. For a risk management professional, correlation and covariance measurements provide a common, precise language for the description of the relationship among risks. The interaction among risks can have a significant impact on risk management decision making and an organisation's view of risk appetite.

A common misconception about correlation is that it is the same as causality.

- Correlation is purely a statistical relationship between two random variables and is not a measure or even implication of causality. Correlation only measures a statistical relationship, not causality.
- Causality indicates a practical, replicable cause and effect; stated differently, it explains how a chain of events may be triggered. In some cases, causality is clear, in others it may require in-depth analysis to reveal causality (root-cause analysis) and sometimes, in complex situations, causality may not be identified.

Common, underlying factors are a frequent cause of positive or negative correlations between two variables. Underlying factors can be obvious or, on occasion, difficult to identify. Risk management professionals must confirm underlying variables when analysing correlations, because many risk control and financing applications are only effective when tied to an underlying variable.

As with any statistical measure, the interpretation of the results of correlation analysis must be cautious. Correlation, like any single statistical measure, is subject to inaccuracy and may be skewed by abnormal observations in the data used to obtain them, inaccuracy in data collection, or an insufficient number of observations. Accordingly, a risk management professional should review the two variables' relationship across the entire set of data, rather than relying on a singular statistical calculation.

### *Correlation/Covariance Matrices*

When a risk management professional is considering how one risk interacts with a group of other risks (rather than just one other risk variable), correlation and covariance are still used and are typically reported in the form of a correlation or covariance matrix.

The matrix reports either the correlation or covariance for each pair of risks in the portfolio. A covariance matrix is usually represented as a triangle with the variance of each risk along the diagonal. A correlation matrix is reported the same way, only with a correlation of '1' shown along the diagonal.

When considering a correlation matrix, note that risks that have low positive correlations, no correlations, or negative correlations are generally good risks to add to the portfolio (all factors that could influence the correlations being equal), because they will tend to move the organisation closer to the efficient frontier. Risks that have high positive correlations with other risks in the portfolio, all else being equal, generally will not move the organisation closer to the efficient frontier, because the additional risk does not significantly alter the risk/return profile of the organisation.

#### *Extreme Events and Copulas*

While correlation coefficient and covariance are important and commonly used statistical measurements, both have significant limitations. Under a number of scenarios, neither is capable of fully describing the relationship and dependence between two variables. Two instances when a covariance matrix may incompletely explain a relationship between variables are extreme events and copulas. Extreme events are referred to as 'outliers' in statistics. The difference between traditional distributions and fat tail distributions is that the latter include extreme events. Copulas, which provide links between two statistical observations, express the correlations among fat tails.

Outlier events, particularly those for which there is no historical data, may not be fully represented in a covariance matrix.

## At-Risk Metrics

At-risk metrics, which are obtained from risk measures, are used to characterise the level of risk present in a portfolio. Risk metric actual results are compared to the organisation's acceptable standards or thresholds to identify any variance.

Most at-risk metrics share a simple key idea: that potential loss is the likelihood that some asset will fall below some threshold level. A probabilistic model is used to illustrate this concept; more precisely, by fractals on a loss distribution. In statistical terms, this means the probability the asset will fall into the tail. The essential idea that unites many of these 'at-risk' concepts is a cumulative (loss) distribution.

Two types of risk measures are VaR and CFaR:

- VaR is used primarily by financial firms, which depend on asset values.
- CFaR is used primarily by non-financial firms, which depend on cash flows.

However, the current trend is to overlook the distinction between these two main categories.

The major drawback of at-risk metrics is that they take into account only the quantifiable consequences of uncertainty (or at least those that can be assessed) in financial terms and do not contemplate the influence of non-financial consequences, such as social, environmental and human, that should be considered in the decision-making process. This is one reason why decision makers must exercise post-optimal analysis and judgement.

### *Value at Risk*

VaR is the measure of loss at a given probability. VaR, which was developed by the financial industry, is defined as the maximum loss (ML) expected to be incurred over a certain time horizon, traditionally a short terra, at a given probability, or VaR one day at 99% of confidence. The cumulative (loss) distribution generally used is a standard normal distribution.

VaR provides decision makers with three key benefits:

- The potential loss associated with a decision can be quantified.
- Complex positions are expressed as a single figure.
- Loss is expressed in monetary terms that are easily understood.

However, VaR also has two major limitations:

- It does not indicate how much worse a loss might be compared to the VaR.
- It is not a coherent risk measure. A coherent risk measure, one that reduces dependence on a single source of income by spreading losses over several comparable sources, does not increase risk.

The second VaR limitation can be addressed with the conditional value at risk (CVaR) metric. CVaR provides the same benefits as VaR but is a coherent measure of risk that considers the extremely large losses that may occur, even with very low probabilities, in the tau of a value distribution. CVaR is defined as the expected loss given that the loss is greater than or equal to the VaR value.

Initially developed for the banking and finance industries, VaR and CVaR have been used as risk measures by other industries such as the agricultural industry, which has used it for decisions regarding crop selection. It has also been used by utilities in deregulated markets to determine plant capacities. The VaR concept can also be applied in the context of economic capital (capital at risk, which differs on distribution [non-normal], time horizon [longer] and confidence level [lower]).

### *Application of the VAR to Determine Economic Capital (EC) and Regulatory Capital (RC)*

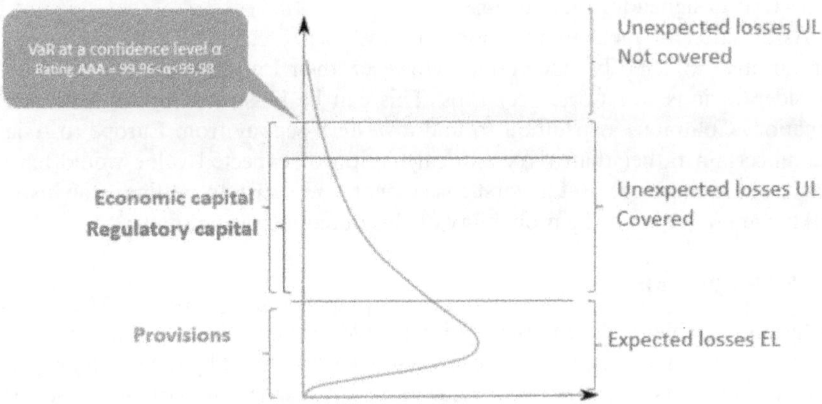


| Rating | Regulatory | BBB | A | AA | AAA |
|---|---|---|---|---|---|
| α | 99% | 99.75% | 99.9% | 99.95% | 99.97% |
| Return time 1/(1-α) | 100 days | 400 days | 4 years | 8 years | 13 years |

### *Cash Flow at Risk*

CFaR is analogous to VaR but it uses as metrics the cash flows extracted from the profit and loss statement (income statement) instead of the asset value extracted from the balance sheet. CFaR assumes that cash flows are a random variable based on a normal probability distribution and assumes that the cash flows will remain above a given threshold defined by the organisation's leadership. It is therefore primarily concerned with liquidity risks and how organisations can manage them.

The benefits and limitations noted for VaR also apply to CFaR, with the exception that it reflects the metrics or cash flows that dictate directly whether a business can survive as a going concern, because an organisation cannot always readily transform asset values into cash to protect itself from bankruptcy.

## Extreme Events and Stress Scenarios

As previously noted, most probabilistic models are based on normal distributions and therefore do not integrate the extreme loss scenarios that are by nature present only in distribution tails. Therefore, they are valid only under 'normal' circumstances and do not reflect extreme environments. Thus, probabilistic models could lead decision-makers to feel dangerously comfortable even when vital security issues are at stake. This is why it is essential to complement these models with stress scenarios that will reflect those extreme events. Capturing the risk of extreme events is precisely why Basel II and Basel III for banks and Solvency 2 for insurance companies (in the European Union) assess compliance using specific stress tests designed for that purpose.

As a matter of fact, organisations are not able to calculate expected values for variables affected by uncertainty. However, their leaders must be willing to consider various worst-case scenarios. This can be illustrated by an historical situation: Columbus' expedition to find a western seaway from Europe to Asia was uncertain rather than risky and calculation of expected value would have been quite a challenge. But a worst-case scenario was easy to outline – the boats sinking at sea – even if the probability of this outcome was unknown.

## Risk Integration

Determining which risks an organisation should or could accept requires careful analysis. The risk manager, or the decision-maker informed by the risk manager, must not only assess the risk and return associated with any particular risk (or portfolio element) being considered, but also how the addition of this risk to the existing portfolio of risks will affect the organisation's overall risk profile. With this approach, organisations should only consider risks that move them towards their targeted risk/reward profile, being careful to add only those risks that have the right combination of volatility, return and correlation with their existing risks.

Risk integration analysis and the portfolio approach will result in some organisations accepting risks that other organisations might avoid. Because different

Portfolio Optimising Return for the Defined Risk Appetite

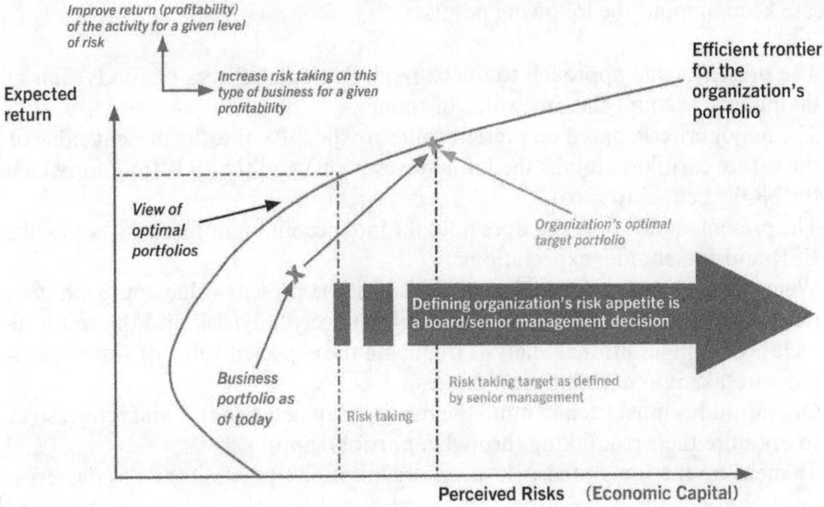


organisations have different risk profiles, certain risks will move some organisations towards the efficient frontier and others away from it. Understanding an organisation's current risk profile is vital to understanding which risks are acceptable and which are not.

### *Built-in Flexibility*

In a time of highly volatile environment coupled with increasing interdependencies and complexity, organisations may benefit from flexible strategies that clearly recognise that risk factors can take on different values. Flexible strategies design operations and processes that enable the organisation to respond quickly and optimise its operations whatever conditions it is confronted with.

In academic terms, the organisation strives to make profits into a convex function of the risk factor; this means that profitability for a flexible organisation increases as the environment becomes more volatile.

Flexibility in operations would be designed so that costs increase only minimally when there is a volume surge, or that contracts with suppliers and sub-contractors allow for rapid change in volume orders, also using temporary workforce and leasing capacity rather than owning it.

In marketing, it would entail segmenting the markets so as to adapt and anticipate changes in demand levels. In control, it would entail organising lines of control in the firm to be more flexible.

## Summary

Please keep in mind the following points:

- The present value approach to selecting investments/sources of funds aims at taking into account the time value of money.
- The major criteria based on present value are the NPV (i.e. the present value of the future cashflows minus the initial investment) and the IRR (rate for which the NOV is equal to zero).
- The present value approach does not take into account non-financial issues like CSR and stakeholder expectations.
- When applied to risk management decisions, the present value approach does not take into account the level of volatility/uncertainty/risk and that must be included in an additional analysis (reducing the expected value of future cash-flows to take into account the riskiness).
- Organisations must keep in mind the relationship between risk and return so as to optimise their risk taking through a portfolio approach.
- To measure the integrated risk of an organisation's portfolio of risks/assets it must consider the correlations, covariances and covariance matrices that link its various financial and non-financial assets.
- One way to take into account risk is to understand two essential concepts: VaR mostly used for financial institutions and CFaR for non-financial organisations.
- When extreme events are to be considered, the normal distribution may prove misleading and stress tests are key to making informed decisions.
- In all situations, risk integration is key to evaluating how the proposed investments would impact the overall organisation's risk profile.

# Chapter 3

# Corporate Social Responsibility

## Introduction

This chapter looks at what defines corporate social responsibility (CSR) and the guidance on social responsibility. It also describes the European Commission's strategy and other standards globally.

## Learning Outcomes

By the end of this chapter, you should be able to:

- define CSR;
- identify the key elements that compose social responsibility;
- describe the standards and principles in Europe and globally;
- understand the impacts to organisations regarding positive social responsibility.

## Corporate Social Responsibility (CSR)

CSR is defined by the European Commission as 'the responsibility of enterprises for their impact on society'. It can be seen as one of the more controversial areas in relation to corporate disclosures because it goes to the heart of the debate on whether companies exist purely for generating shareholders' profits or whether society is entitled to expect organisations to act in the general public interest, especially on issues such as the environment and social change.

**Risk Measurement and Monitoring, 35–40**

**Published under exclusive licence by Emerald Publishing Limited**
**doi:10.1108/978-1-83662-310-620251008**

***Case Study – James Hardie***

The Australian Securities and Investment Commission's (ASIC) proceedings against James Hardie arise from ASIC's investigation of matters identified by the Special Commission of Inquiry into the Medical Research and Compensation Foundation. ASIC filed civil penalty proceedings in the Supreme Court of New South Wales relating to disclosures by James Hardie Industries Limited (JHIL) in respect to the adequacy of the funding of the Medical Research and Compensation Foundation. One of the allegations raised related to the assertion that the company failed to disclose certain important information to the Australian Securities Exchange (ASX) regarding the cancellation of the partly paid shares in JHIL; these were held by James Hardie Industries NAV (JOIN) and represented as having been issued for the purpose of JHIL meeting any future liabilities.

> ASIC alleged that JOIN failed to act with the requisite care and diligence in requesting JHIL to cancel those shares. ASIC also sought orders that JOIN execute a deed of indemnity up to a maximum of A$1.9 billion, or such amount as JHIL or its directors considered necessary to ensure that JHIL remained solvent.

## Applying Enterprise Risk Management (ERM) to Environmental, Social and Governance (ESG) Related Risks

In October 2018, COSO and the World Business Council for Sustainable Development (WBCSD) released a Guidance for Applying ERM to ESG related risks.

The guidance for applying ERM to ESG-related risks appeared in the context of an evolving landscape of ESG-related risks, which can impact the profitability, success and even survival of a variety of entities.

COSO and WBCSD have partnered to develop this guidance to help organisations better understand the full spectrum of these risks and to manage and disclose them effectively.

There is no universal or agreed definition of ESG-related risks, which may also be referred to as sustainability, non-financial or extra-financial risks, the guidance explains.

However, showing that a business understands and manages ESG risks, by integrating them into a true business methodology like ERM, will send a powerful signal to investors and society as a whole that they are resilient and prepared to make better informed decisions to remain sustainable in the next decade.

## Standards

As previously described, the definition of CSR is the 'responsibility of enterprises for their impact on society'. The Standards listed in this section have been developed to help guide organisations in understanding their responsibilities relating to their social and societal impact.

In the COSO report, the term 'sustainability' is used synonymously with CSR, corporate citizenship, stewardship and corporate responsibility. This highlights the numerous issues and nuances that fall under CSR.

The basic concept is that organisations should be aware of the impact their activities can have on society, the economy and the environment. They should seek to manage that impact and enhance positive externalities and curb negative externalities. It is closely related to the growing sense of urgency around the need to act on climate change, pollution and future-proofing our resources.

### *Guidance on Social Responsibility*

The International Organisation for Standardisation released a Standard about CSR in 2010. This Standard, *ISO 26000:2010 Guidance on social responsibility*, was designed to guide organisations in ensuring they are operating in a socially responsible way, meaning, according to the ISO, 'in an ethical and transparent way that contributes to the health and welfare of society'.

One key point to note about ISO 26000 is that organisations cannot be certified against it, as it is providing guidance only (not requirements). The aims of this Standard are to clarify key terms, outline how principles can be translated into action and describe global best practice.

In doing so, the Standard has identified seven key elements that compose social responsibility:

- organisational governance
- human rights
- labour practices
- the environment
- fair operating practices
- consumer issues
- community involvement and development.

To see how these elements interconnect, view the poster at: www.iso.org/publication/PUB100259.html

In 2017, *IWA 26 Using ISO 26000 guidance on social responsibility in management systems* was developed to assist organisations in using the original Standard in relation to the management systems standard (MSS) approach, also developed by ISO.

### *European Commission's Strategy on CSR*

To promote CSR throughout the EU, the European Commission developed its own strategy on CSR. The strategy was based in part on ISO 26000 as well as other principles and guidelines related to human rights and social policy. It aims to emphasise the importance of CSR, to improve regulation, disclosure practices and integration of CSR and to align approaches to CSR around the world.

To read more, visit the European Commission website and search for 'strategy on CSR'.

### *Other Standards*

#### *OECD Guidelines for Multinational Enterprises*

These guidelines are recommendations on how to conduct business responsibly in accordance with applicable laws and standards. They are essentially a code of practice that applies to multinational enterprises operating in OECD-adherent countries.

Like ISO 26000, they're not binding, but governments have committed to promoting and adhering to them. http://mneguidelines.oecd.org/guidelines

#### *Guiding Principles for Business and Human Rights (UN)*

These Principles, subtitled *Implementing the United Nations' 'Protect, respect and remedy' framework*, are designed to provide a global standard to prevent human rights from being abused a result of business activities. They tie in with CSR in that their aim is to make organisations accountable for and aware of their effect on societies and the people within them. www.unglobalcompact.org/library/2

#### *UN Global Compact*

Another UN initiative, the UN Global Compact is the world's largest corporate sustainability initiative that aims to mobilise organisations and stakeholders to create a sustainable and ethical world. The Compact was developed to drive awareness and action towards achieving the UN's Sustainable Development Goals (SDGs) by 2030. The 10 Principles of the Compact have been written with this purpose in mind.

The Compact is a non-legally binding voluntary initiative that cannot enforce the behaviour it promotes, but this is not the intention. Instead, it means to increase awareness and to encourage and promote solutions for change. www.unglobalcompact.org

#### *Global Reporting Initiative (GRI)*

This initiative aims to raise the awareness of organisations and governments regarding the effects of business on sustainability issues. GRI has developed three general Standards and numerous topic-specific standards to support organisations to prepare best practice sustainability reports. www.globalreporting.org

#### *Voluntary Principles on Security and Human Rights*

The Voluntary Principles are guidelines aimed at increasing awareness of and respect for human rights specifically by organisations that extract raw materials from the earth. These organisations are collectively known as the *extractive industry*, which includes mining, dredging and oil extraction. Organisations voluntarily adopt the Principles and use them to ensure that their operations are safe, secure, risk aware and respectful of human rights. www.voluntaryprinciples.org

*Extractive Industries Transparency Initiative (EITI)*

This is another initiative that applies to the extractive industry with the intention of promoting the open and accountable management of oil, gas, and mineral resources. The initiative includes the EITI Standard, which requires the oil, gas, and mining sectors to disclose information about their governance processes, including the amount of tax they pay. The information is published by EITI to enable the public to better understand the industry, and so that accountability and transparency increase. The founding belief is that all citizens should benefit from natural resource wealth. https://eiti.org

*Equator Principles*

The Equator Principles (EPs) are a risk management framework specific to environmental and social project risk and aim to provide a global benchmark for the financial institutions that adopt them (these institutions come to be known as EPFIs). They EPs apply to four financial products and restrict EPFIs' ability to deal with clients that cannot comply with the EPs. www.equator-principles.com

*IFC Sustainability Framework*

The International Finance Corporation (IFC) has developed this Framework to express its commitment to sustainability. The Framework contains the Performance Standards, which are globally recognised as a benchmark for managing environmental and social risks in the private sector. www.ifc.org/sustainabilityframework

*UN Principles for Responsible Investment (PRI)*

The PRI promotes responsible investment that gives due consideration to ESG factors. It is again a voluntary initiative that organisations adopt. There are six Principles that require entities to incorporate ESG issues into processes and policies, to seek disclosure on ESG from entities being invested in and to promote and report on the Principles. PRI's aim is to create a sustainable global financial system. www.unpri.org

**Activity | CSR**

Investigate whether your organisation adheres to any of these Standards.

- If it does, describe how that Standard affects your organisation. Have any practices changed as a result?
- If it doesn't, consider whether any of the Standards would be a good fit for your organisation. Describe what would need to change if a Standard were to be adopted.

## Summary

Please keep in mind the following points:

- CSR is defined by the European Commission as 'the responsibility of enterprises for their impact on society'. It can be seen as one of the more controversial areas in relation to corporate disclosures because it goes to the heart of the debate on whether companies exist purely for generating shareholders' profits or whether society is entitled to expect organisations to act in the general public interest, especially on issues such as the environment and social change.
- The basic concept is that organisations should be aware of the impact their activities can have on society, the economy and the environment. They should seek to manage that impact and enhance positive externalities and curb negative externalities. It is closely related to the growing sense of urgency around the need to act on climate change, pollution and future-proofing our resources.
- The seven key elements that compose social responsibility:

  - organisational governance
  - human rights
  - labour practices
  - the environment
  - fair operating practices
  - consumer issues
  - community involvement and development.

- To promote CSR throughout the EU, the European Commission developed its own strategy on CSR. The strategy was based in part on ISO 2600 as well as other principles and guidelines related to human rights and social policy. It aims to emphasise the importance of CSR, to improve regulation, disclosure practices and integration of CSR and to align approaches to CSR around the world.
- The Voluntary Principles are guidelines aimed at increasing awareness of and respect for human rights specifically by organisations that extract raw materials from the earth. These organisations are collectively known as the extractive industry, which includes mining, dredging and oil extraction. Organisations voluntarily adopt the Principles and use them to ensure that their operations are safe, secure, risk aware and respectful of human rights.
- The IFC has developed this Framework to express its commitment to sustainability. The Framework contains the Performance Standards, which are globally recognised as a benchmark for managing environmental and social risks in the private sector.
- The PRI promotes responsible investment that gives due consideration to ESG factors. It is again a voluntary initiative that organisations adopt. There are six Principles that require entities to incorporate ESG issues into processes and policies, to seek disclosure on ESG from entities being invested in and to promote and report on the Principles. PRI's aim is to create a sustainable global financial system.

Chapter 4

# Communication, Consultation, Corporate Governance and the Role of the Board

### Introduction

This section outlines the risk management process and focuses on the primary step of communication and consultation. This critical step aims to establish communication and consultation channels with internal and, in some cases, external stakeholders.

### Learning Outcomes

When you have completed this section, you should be able to:

- define corporate governance;
- understand the role corporate governance plays in ensuring ethical and sustainable behaviour;
- explain effective communication/consultation processes and how they influence decision making;
- define the relationship between organisational structure and communication;
- understand the benefits of effective risk management communication.

## Definition of Corporate Governance

The term 'corporate governance' is reputed to have been first used in the USA in the mid-1970s because of the Watergate Scandal, which involved an abuse of power by the Nixon administration. During the Watergate investigations, it was discovered that many US companies had made secret political contributions and corrupt payments to the Nixon administration, whose corruption in turn diminished the market value of the companies concerned. In the 1980s, these discoveries, together with the collapse of several high-profile companies, rekindled a

**Risk Measurement and Monitoring, 41–79**

**Published under exclusive licence by Emerald Publishing Limited**
**doi:10.1108/978-1-83662-310-620251010**

debate that had started at the time of the 1929 Wall Street crash over the rights and obligations of the parties that influence the direction, strategy and performance of corporations. The debate also focused on the inter relationships between those who own, manage or have an interest in the performance of organisations.

While corporate governance has been actively discussed for over 70 years, there is still no universally accepted definition. Academics and practitioners of corporate governance tend towards a broad definition that focuses on the processes (formal and informal) by which the company is governed as well as the external environment in which the organisation operates. Investors, policymakers, and lawyers favour a narrower definition where corporate governance is defined in terms of the internal structures and processes that determine the control and direction of the corporation and relationships.

Various definitions are set out below for consideration.

- Corporate governance is the system by which businesses are directed and controlled.
  *(The Committee on the Financial Aspects of Corporate Governance and Gee and Co. Ltd 1992 [The Cadbury report])*
- Procedures and processes according to which an organisation is directed and controlled. The corporate governance structure specifies the distribution of rights and responsibilities among the different participants in the organisation – such as the board, managers, shareholders and other stakeholders – and lays down the rules and procedures for decision-making.
  *(European Central Bank 2004)*
- Corporate Governance is concerned with holding the balance between economic and social goals and between individual and communal goals. The corporate governance framework is there to encourage the efficient use of resources and equally to require accountability for the stewardship of those resources. The aim is to align as nearly as possible the interests of individuals, corporations and society.
  *(Cadbury 2000)*
- Corporate governance is concerned with the resolution of collective action problems among dispersed investors and the reconciliation of conflicts of interest between various corporate claimholders.
  *(Becht, Marco, Bolton, Patrick and Röell 2002)*
- The system by which entities are directed and controlled.
  *(SAI Global AS 8000-2003)*

The definitions may vary but there are common themes:

- Governance is not ad hoc but is based on systems and processes.
- Governance provides a framework for the management of risks.
- Governance requires action and is not a passive process.

Entities operate within an environment of constant change and while each has its own goals and milestones, all entities have a common need to respond to new challenges as they arise. (Note that the term 'entity' is used in this chapter interchangeably with 'organisation' to refer to privately owned entities, companies, not-for-profits and public-sector agencies.) The dynamic nature of organisations requires constant revision of their goals and decisions about a range of matters – some of which concern issues of high risk, ethics or the competing needs of shareholders, the community and others with an interest in the organisation.

A useful analogy to use when discussing corporate governance is that of a car and a journey. In accordance with the powers delegated to it, the board (or committee in the case of some not-for-profit entities) decides the journey to be undertaken while the management undertakes the trip on behalf of the board and organises everything that is required in terms of resources for the journey.

Governance is the process by which the car is driven and keeps it headed in the right direction while simultaneously providing a framework for responding to any risks and opportunities that are encountered along the way. While corporate governance cannot itself prevent unethical or criminal conduct, it limits the power of one group or individual to abuse their power simply by putting in place mechanisms which minimise the risks.

Good corporate governance is somewhat akin to the headlights of a car. If two companies are in a daytime race, nothing goes wrong – then they are evenly matched. If the race goes past dusk, however, the company with good governance has the headlights to deal with the problem. *(Felton et al. 1996)*

Corporate governance describes the framework used to:

- determine the journey in terms of direction, goals and time frame;
- manage risks and opportunities experienced during the journey;
- monitor and check progress made during the journey;
- regulate the flow of information required to make decisions to manage the risks and opportunities encountered during the journey;
- make its decision makers accountable for the decisions made during the journey; and
- keep the owners informed of the journey's progress.

### *Corporate Governance and the Financial Crisis*

Since the global financial crisis (GFC) triggered by the subprime crisis in the USA, organisations have been much more aware of corporate governance and the role it must play in ensuring ethical and sustainable behaviour.

It is important to remember that while the financial crisis was significant because of the monetary consequences of the corporate governance and risk management failures, numerous other non-financial catastrophes have resulted from similar shortcomings. Some examples from the non-financial explored in previous blocks include the BP/Transocean oil spill, the Fukushima nuclear meltdown, the Bhopal gas disaster, and the Toyota and Samsung product recalls.

As such, while the financial crisis received widespread attention and triggered numerous process reviews, the issue of poorly conducted corporate governance practices goes far beyond the financial sector.

One of the reviews conducted in the wake of the crisis, was the OECD's investigation into the cause of the crisis. From this, a set of recommendations was developed with the intention of improving adherence to corporate governance Standards and principles throughout the world in financial and non-financial sectors.

The OECD's conclusions were published in a report entitled, 'Corporate governance lessons from the financial crisis'. The conclusions included:

- Corporate governance arrangements did not prevent excessive risk taking
  - information about risk was not always presented to the board or even upper management
  - strategies were approved but not properly implemented or monitored
  - disclosure was insufficient
  - boards did not take their responsibilities seriously
  - some standards and requirements were insufficient.

- Boards should be qualified and competent for financial and non-financial institutions.
- Remuneration and incentive systems were problematic and often provided strong incentives to take risks.

Because of this report, the OECD released recommendations to help organisations overcome corporate governance weaknesses and to better implement the OECD *Principles on corporate governance*. These recommendations have been published in the paper, 'Conclusions and emerging good practices to enhance implementation of the Principles'. Four major areas were identified and key findings and main messages were determined for each of these areas.

1. Governance of the remuneration process
2. Effective implementation of risk management
3. Board practices
4. The exercise of shareholder rights.

It could be considered that recommendations and self-regulation are insufficient given the history of corporate governance failure, and that regulation should be introduced. However, this report argues that corporate governance is too complex to be covered in standard regulation, and instead strongly recommends that jurisdictions regularly review their context to address issues before they result in disaster.

***Box 2 – Key findings and main messages: effective implementation of risk management***

- Perhaps one of the greatest shocks from the financial crisis has been the widespread failure of efficient risk-management and lack of risk management. In many cases, risk was not managed on an enterprise basis and not adjusted to corporate strategy. Risk managers were often separated from management and not regarded as an essential part of implementing the company's strategy. Most important of all, boards were in several cases ignorant of the risk facing the company.

- It should be fully understood by regulators and other standard setters that effective risk management is not about eliminating risk taking, which is a fundamental driving force in business and entrepreneurship. The aim is to ensure that risks are understood, managed and, when appropriate, communicated.
- Effective implementation of risk management requires an enterprise-wide approach rather than treating each business unit individually. It has become essential, and even legally binding in many jurisdictions, that Boards be involved in both establishing and overseeing the risk management structure.
- The Board should also review and provide guidance about the alignment of corporate strategy with risk appetite and the internal risk management structure.
- To assist the Board in its work, it should be considered good practice that risk management and control functions be independent of profit centres and the 'chief risk officer' or equivalent should report directly to the Board of Directors along the lines already advocated in the OECD Principles for internal control functions reporting to the audit committee or equivalent.
- The process of risk management and the results of risk assessments should be appropriately disclosed. Without revealing any trade secrets, the board should make sure the firm communicates to its major stakeholders, material risk factors in a transparent and understandable fashion. Disclosure of risk factors should be focused on those identified as more relevant and/or should rank material risk factors in order of importance based on a qualitative selection whose criteria should also be disclosed.
- With few exceptions, risk management is typically not covered, or is insufficiently covered, by existing corporate governance standards or codes. Corporate governance standard setters should be encouraged to include or improve references to risk management to raise awareness and improve implementation.

*Source: OECD Key Findings*

Also available from the OECD is a report entitled, 'Risk management and corporate governance', which presents the results of a peer review investigating the corporate governance practices of 28 jurisdictions (22 OECD member countries and six others). The peer review involves sending a questionnaire to participants to assess how they implement the *Principles on corporate governance.* The report also presents case studies of three jurisdictions to highlight best practices.

**Activity | Corporate governance**

Review the sound risk governance practices outlined in Annex A of the OECD report 'Risk management and corporate governance 'and consider the following questions.

- How many of these practices does the organisation you work for implement?
- When were these practices implemented, and has there been any change in outcomes since then?
- Are there any not currently implemented that should be adopted?
- Did your organisation suffer losses in the financial crisis? Were any of these practices not in place then, and do you think having those practices would have changed the effects suffered?

## Communication and Consultation Within Organisations

### *Communication: Definition*

McLaughlin (1994) defines communication as:

> ...the transmission of information and understanding from one person or group to another.

### *Effective Communication/Consultation Processes*

The organisation should aim to achieve a culture in which stakeholder's plan and review changes to operating systems and associated risk information in consultation with those who can influence (or will be affected by) the change. The organisation should also consider how system changes affect the flow of risk information to decision makers.

**Self-Help Question 4.1**

List three of the consultation processes in your organisation (for example, meetings).

Answers to self-help questions are provided at the end of each section.

***Direction of Communication***

As the following diagram summarises, integrated management systems allow for more effective communication of information in many directions.

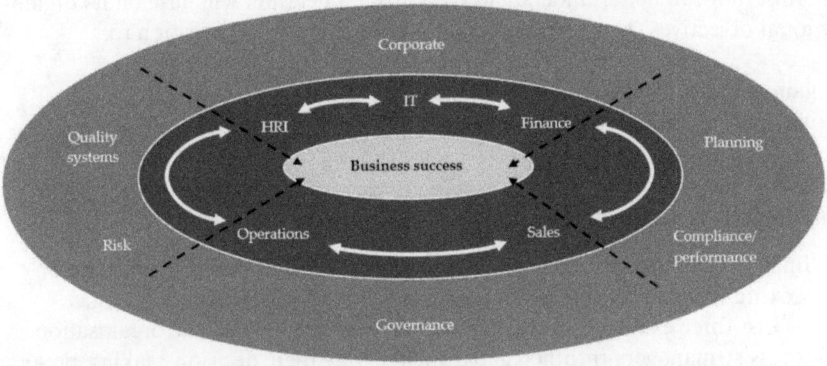


Integrated Management Model

The following table describes these directions.

**The Directions of Effective Communication of Information**

| Direction | Description |
|---|---|
| Horizontally | Across the business lines of the same level |
| Vertically | The organisation can provide senior management with a good understanding of performance issues within a specific area of accountability |
| Holistically | The organisation as a whole |

As previously discussed, organisations need design and structure to facilitate the flow of information. This information is used for decision-making and to monitor progress towards attainment of organisational goals.

***Influencing Strategic and Operational Decision-Making***

One of the major benefits of integrating management systems is the ability to influence both *strategic* and *operational* decision-making processes.

*Sharing Information*

Unless decision-making occurs in conjunction with other areas of the organisation, there is a very real risk of the decisions having a negative impact (or flow-on effect) to other areas. Failing to share information (business and risk) when deciding can also increase the organisation's exposure to negative risk.

Ensuring information management systems are designed to share information across the organisation is critical in avoiding increased negative risk exposures or missed opportunities.

By using the best available and most current business and risk information, the organisation can better understand the impact a decision will have on its organisational objectives. This understanding may enable the organisation to:

- gain a competitive edge in the market
- improve its level of service delivery.

---

**Self-Help Question 4.2**

Imagine you are the manager of the HR department of an organisation seeking to achieve enhanced integration through information sharing.

List three examples of information to be shared across the organisation to assist managers in other departments with their decision-making processes (for example, results of training evaluations).

---

Answers to self-help questions are provided at the end of each section.

---

---

**Self-Help Question 4.3**

A project manager introduces a new IT system without consulting key stakeholders. This lack of consultation results in serious negative consequences for the organisation, including:

- budget blow-outs
- staff resistance to change
- loss of key client data.

Based on your understanding of the benefits of an integrated risk management approach, how do you think the project manager could have improved the outcomes of this project (for example, identifying and engaging key stakeholders from the outset)?

---

Answers to self-help questions are provided at the end of each section.

---

## Organisational Structure and Effective Communication

The effectiveness of the management system relies on the effectiveness of communication. McLaughlin (1994) theorises that:

> [...] the relationship between organisational structure and communication is one of mutual independence.

In summary, the organisational structure can directly influence the effectiveness of communication within an organisation, and vice versa.

### *The Matrix Structure*

Developing a matrix structure facilitates communication between the internal stakeholders 'central to a project, product or client.

In the case of a project, the project manager ensures project managers identify, engage, and share information with key project stakeholders to ensure they can achieve project objectives. Project managers undertake these activities by identifying barriers to communication and either:

- removing them; or
- implementing an intervention that facilitates the improved flow of information.

> **Activity | Communication and consultation barriers**
>
> Can you identify a project in which your organisation broke down communication and consultation barriers to facilitate a more effective flow of information?
>
> Conversely, has failing to remove communication and consultation barriers affected the success of a project?

## The Communication Network

Managers develop a communication network because of the need to communicate information throughout an organisation. This communication network results in a multi-directional flow of communication, which can be categorised into two channels.

### ***Formal Communication***

According to McLaughlin (1994):

> [...] formal channels of communication follow the channels for authority of the organisation.

These formal channels provide managers with the ability to facilitate a flow of information, which enables all staff to complete their jobs with a view to recognising and attaining organisational goals.

Formal channels of communication enable the flow of information throughout the organisation both vertically and horizontally.

*Vertical Communication*

Vertical communication is a bi-directional (top-down and down-up) flow of information.

***Top-Down Communication***

Top-down communication aids the flow of essential information for staff to fulfil their work responsibilities.

Top-down communication is often associated with *directing* and *controlling* performance (Mukhi et al., 1988). It involves the top level of the organisational hierarchy:

- determining the organisation's mission and vision
- communicating these to lower levels of the organisation through setting hierarchical plans.

Establishing a risk management policy, plan and associated guidelines, and taking a 'top-down' approach to implementation, sets a direction for the organisation in terms of managing risk.

Organisations can improve top-down communication by using multiple methods and channels to increase the opportunity for messages to be successfully transmitted (Bartol et al., 2005). Senior managers can also test the success of the information by asking for feedback, or through specific programs such as auditing and review.

**EXAMPLE**

**Risk Tolerance and Authority Levels**

The senior management team defines the requirements for risk tolerance and assigns authority levels for decision-making in association with these requirements.

**Self-Help Question 4.4**

List two reasons why an organisation requires top-down communication.

Answers to self-help questions are provided at the end of each section.

**Self-Help Question 4.5**

List three examples of top-down communication you have experienced in your organisation (for example, policies).

Answers to self-help questions are provided at the end of each section.

**Self-Help Question 4.6**

According to Bartol et al. (2005), top-down communication can often be distorted. List two reasons why a top-down message may not be transmitted as intended (for example, internal mail or email system failure).

Answers to self-help questions are provided at the end of each section.

**Activity | Failing to communicate top-down**

Can you identify an occasion in your organisation in which the top-down communication of information was not successful?

From the previously suggested reasons, can you identify the reason for the failure to transmit the intended message?

Was there an additional or different reason?

### *Down-Up Communication*

Down-up communication occurs when information flows from the lower levels of an organisation to higher levels. Managers often use down-up communication to assist them in making key organisational decisions.

Down-up communication is usually defined by the reporting framework, which facilitates the down-up flow of risk-based information, including the results of:

- risk assessments
- audits
- self-assessments
- performance reviews
- incidents.

The down-up communication reporting framework provides senior managers in an organisation with the information required to effectively make decisions about achieving organisational goals and provides the assurance that risk is managed at all levels.

**EXAMPLE**

**New Risks**

The senior management team defines the requirements for risk tolerance and assigns authority levels for decision-making in association with these requirements.

---

**Self-Help Question 4.7**

List two reasons why an organisation requires down-up communication (for example, understanding opportunities for improvement).

Answers to self-help questions are provided at the end of each section.

---

**Self-Help Question 4.8**

List three examples of the types of down-up communication you have experienced in your organisation (for example, reports, either verbal or written).

Answers to self-help questions are provided at the end of each section.

---

**Self-Help Question 4.9**

Just as top-down communication can often be distorted, so too can down-up communication. List two reasons why a down-up message may not be transmitted as intended (for example, a shoot-the-messenger type culture).

Answers to self-help questions are provided at the end of each section.

### *Horizontal Communication*

Risk management is dependent on the effectiveness of horizontal communication. Although a particular area of the organisation may identify a specific risk, they may depend on interactions with other departments to manage the risk.

Horizontal communication is the flow of information laterally (or diagonally) within the organisation (Bartol et al., 2005; Mukhi et al., 1988). Horizontal communication occurs between:

- departments
- work groups
- project teams
- peers.

Horizontal communication is ultimately important in facilitating the day-to-day operations of an organisation, especially regarding decision-making and work delegation.

Managers use horizontal communication channels to:

- coordinate work requirements
- solve problems (including conflicts)
- share information.

Horizontal communication is an essential factor in facilitating integrated management systems throughout an organisation.

**EXAMPLE**

**An Operational WHS Risk**

The successful management of an WHS risk in an operational area depends on the level of departmental interaction with peer departments experiencing the same risk. The solution may result in an economy of scale, where resources are shared.

**Self-Help Question 4.10**

List three examples of horizontal communication you have experienced in your organisation (for example, telephone calls).

Answers to self-help questions are provided at the end of each section.

**Self-Help Question 4.11**

List two barriers to the effective horizontal transmission of a message.

Answers to self-help questions are provided at the end of each section.

### *Informal Communication*

Formal communication channels are associated with organisational positioning (Bartol et al., 2005) and are by nature planned types of communication. On the other hand, informal communication channels have no association with predetermined requirements.

Informal communication tends to be verbal, in which individuals discuss a central issue and spread the message randomly from person to person. Informal communication may also be referred to as the:

- communication network
- grapevine
- corridor conference.

*Benefits*

The informal channel can be beneficial as it enables managers to discover hidden staff perspectives or identify problems that otherwise would not be apparent through the more formal channels.

Staff members use informal communication channels to make sense of limited or fragmented information (Davidson & Griffin, 2003). They may receive one piece of a message they do not understand and seek further clarification from others. If the source of clarification is reliable (for example, an informed co-worker), the informal channel serves its purpose.

In relation to risk management, a manager may identify areas of risk, or become aware of events that have already occurred, because of listening to the 'grapevine'.

**EXAMPLE**

**Potential Near-Misses**

A manager may be concerned about potential near-misses that are difficult to capture in staff reports.

By spending time in the staff tea-room or listening to the 'corridor conversations', the manager may be able to clarify their concerns.

**Self-Help Question 4.12**

Identify some of the negative influences an informal communication channel may have on staff members.

Answers to self-help questions are provided at the end of each section.

## Remedies for Poor Communication

Managers can mitigate certain negative communication effects by increasing their awareness of the existing organisational communication channels. Managers can also emphasise to staff members that they can and should discuss concerns relating to organisational decision-making (or to their role in the organisation) with a:

- superior
- HR manager
- staff representative.

Managers may also consider providing anonymous question boxes for staff to raise their queries or using a staff survey to capture staff concerns.

***Case Study – Poor Communication***

Jane is a team leader for the design team. Her position requires her to conduct regular audits of her team's work to ensure they are complying with organisational protocols.

### Jane's Quarterly Report

Jane sends her supervisor the completed quarterly report, which needs to be presented to the relevant audit committee. In the following week, Jane speaks with a colleague on the audit committee who informs her there might be a problem with her report.

### The meeting with Jane's supervisor

Approximately four weeks later, the head of the audit committee requests that Jane attend a meeting with her supervisor. During this meeting she discovers the audit committee deemed some of the audit results as unacceptable.

Jane's supervisor informs her that some of the audit parameters (acceptable limits) had changed in a recent policy update and some of the results Jane reported were below acceptable limits.

## The 'missing' memo

Jane has no recollection of the change in audit parameters. Her supervisor indicates that he remembers seeing a memo and forwards it to her for her information.

---

**Self-Help Question 4.13**

1. Identify the channels of communication indicated in the previous case study.

| Communication | Channel |
|---|---|
| | |

2. What are some examples of poor communication described in this case study?

---

Answers to self-help questions are provided at the end of each section.

---

### *Communication and Consultation*

A key action in the risk management process is to establish communication and consultation channels with internal and, in some cases, external stakeholders, two-way communication.

ISO 31000:2018 highlights the importance of communication and consultation by listing it as the first step in the risk management process. This is in recognition of the risk management process as a key component of organisational change and achieving organisational success, of which stakeholder engagement and communication are key principles.

Both communication and consultation are integral to each step in the risk management process, further supporting the need for taking a stakeholder management approach for the management of risk.

Organisations should open and maintain the lines of communication established in this initial phase throughout each subsequent stage of the risk management process to ensure it:

- appropriately and effectively executes each activity
- clearly understands the relevant:
  - responsibilities
  - accountabilities
  - authorities.

Organisations should communicate/consult throughout the risk management process to ensure the risk management programme remains on track and relevant to the organisation's objectives.

***Benefits of Effective Risk Management Communication***

Communication and consultation are important to the success of the risk management process because they:

- make risk management explicit (rather than implicit)
- highlight risk management's relevance to an organisation's operations.

Well-managed communication and consultation ensures the organisation can:

- develop a risk management programme that meets its needs;
- appropriately define the risk management context;
- effectively identify risk exposures;
- bring together different perspectives and expert opinions to analyse and evaluate risk exposures;
- facilitate appropriate change management during risk treatment.

*Collaboration.* A major benefit of good communication and consultation is that they encourage multiple stakeholders to collaborate. This collaboration provides a well-informed understanding of organisational risk exposures and facilitates improved decision making.

Collaboration provides stakeholders with the opportunity to endorse the risk treatment plans, encouraging the ownership of risk exposures. In this sense, communication and consultation are activities closely linked to the broader risk management framework goals of establishing responsibility, accountability and authority.

*Other Benefits.* Extensive communication and consultation in the risk management process:

- identifies barriers and other issues the organisation needs to consider in the risk management framework;
- creates consistency and coherence across business units/departments;

- assists decision making by examining risk management from several perspectives;
- improves an organisation's understanding of:
  - how and why it makes risk management decisions
  - why it takes certain actions
- encourages ownership of risk management activities in the organisation;
- encourages ownership of specific risk exposures;
- facilitates appropriate change management during risk treatment;
- assists in the development of a common view of risk, which is so often lacking in organisations without a risk management programme. For example, stakeholder A may consider a risk as significant, while stakeholder B may assess the risk as immaterial.

### *Maintaining Communication and Consultation Throughout the Risk Management Process*

Organisations need to open and maintain the lines of communication established in this initial phase throughout each subsequent stage of the risk management process.

### *Communication Types*

#### *Communication Out*

Communication out is communication by the risk team and includes:

- the risk policy and framework
- risk tools and templates
- agreed implementation time frames
- resourcing requirements
- reporting requirements.

#### *Communication In*

Communication in is communication to the risk team and includes:

- board and executive requirements (such as reporting)
- the organisation's risk appetite
- line management implementation issues (such as resourcing constraints)
- management views on risk and how it is controlled (through workshops and meetings)
- progress on risk mitigation plans— usually through a risk manager–developed reporting process, which allows management to report their progress using:
  - meetings
  - audits
  - an intranet portal
- the communication of risk events, such as:
  - staff accidents/incidents
  - compliance breaches
  - product failures

- existing risk management processes, such as WHS systems
- new strategies and programmes that could lead to new material risks such as:
  - a new government programme the organisation has to administer
  - the execution of a major project.
- changed external factors which also could impact risk, such as:
  - the introduction of a new industry regulator
  - a deterioration in the economy, which may impact social welfare agencies.

## Communication Plans

Understanding the needs and concerns of stakeholders, while upholding regular, comprehensive communication is a critical part of the success of the risk management programme.

Typically, there is no formal communication plan in an organisation but the organisation needs to identify key stakeholders, consider how to consult with them and decide what information they should provide to them, and expect from them.

For example, it is important for a board to:

- have a clear understanding of the risk management outcomes they require;
- follow up this understanding with relevant information, including:
  - a draft policy
  - risk priorities
  - presentations on key risks and how they are managed.

The first step is to identify the stakeholders who are affected by the risk management process.

The second step is to develop a communication and consultation plan with each of the identified stakeholder groups.

The third step is to agree on the methods of communication the organisation will use in developing, implementing, and maintaining a risk management programme.

### *Establishing a Communication and Consultation Plan*

The communication and consultation plan determines the level of involvement for each stakeholder and the objective of the communication. The plan needs to address the following critical questions:

*What is the communication trying to achieve?*

At the very least, the plan should address the:

- objectives of the communication and consultation process
- nature of the stakeholder relationship (from the stakeholder map)
- stakeholder's perceptions and how they will be incorporated
- methods of communication and consultation
- evaluation of the process.

*Aims*

The stakeholder communication and consultation plan should aim to:

- identify each internal and external stakeholder group;
- define the roles and responsibilities of each group;
- identify the communication methods organisations should use to engage each group;
- define the level of interaction each group will have and the method for achieving this;
- document a process for identifying, resolving and escalating issues because of stakeholder management;
- identify how decisions are made and communicated.

*Plan Aspects*

The communication and consultation plan should consider the following aspects:

- the target audience
- key messages to be delivered
- communication strategies
- responsibilities and time frames
- resource requirements
- monitoring progress.

### *The Target Audience*

Ensure the communication and consultation strategy is appropriate for each stakeholder group.

For example, a simple memo regarding a significant change sent to those who have the greatest influence on a decision may be ineffective or insufficient and would not entail 'consulting' but solely 'informing'.

### *Key Messages to Be Delivered*

Organisations need to consider the key messages they want to deliver and the impact these will have on each stakeholder group.

For example, if a key message relates to a process change, how will this affect those who are involved in the process, or whom the process will affect?

Organisations should also identify the benefits or outcomes they expect to achieve because of this change and ensure they clearly communicate in a timely manner; furthermore, they should assess the potential benefits or 'costs' to the major shareholders.

### *Communication Strategies*

How the organisation relays the message, as well as the tools the organisation uses, depends on the nature of the stakeholder relationship.

**Self-Help Question 4.14**

Identify five methods for communicating and consulting with stakeholders (for example, staff meetings).

Answers to self-help questions are provided at the end of each section.

### *Responsibilities and Time Frames*

As with any planning exercise, the communication strategy involves carrying out specific actions. It is essential for the organisation to assign responsibilities to those involved with the decision-making process (for example, a project team) to ensure they carry out the desired actions within a certain timeframe.

### *Resource Requirements*

Organisations should also consider any resource constraints; for example, budgetary requirements for the development of a marketing campaign.

### *Monitoring Progress*

As with any plan, it is necessary to monitor the progress of the communication and consultation plan to confirm it achieves what it intends. The plan can be presented in a format like that in the following table.

**Communication and Consultation Plan**

| **Stakeholder** | **Stakeholder Relationship** | **Nature of Stake-Holding** |
|---|---|---|
| | For example, A, B, C or D from stakeholder map | For example:<br>• what potential influence does the stakeholder have on the project?<br>• what potential effect does the project have on the stakeholder? |
| **Communication methods** | **By whom** | **Timeframes** |

**Self-Help Question 4.15**

Using the following stakeholder map, place the following methods of communication and consultation in boxes A, B, C or D, as appropriate:

- staff meetings
- one-to-one meetings
- brainstorming sessions
- use of I.T. (for example, intranet, email or teleconference)
- advertising material (for example, posters or brochures)
- education sessions (for example, seminars or workshops)
- progress reports.

| | |
|---|---|
| **B. High consultation – low communication** | **A. High consultation – high communication** |
| **D. Low consultation – low communication** | **C. Low consultation – high communication** |

Answers to self-help questions are provided at the end of each section.

## Stakeholder Definitions

Stakeholders are any person or entity with an interest or concern in something.

**Activity | Definition**

Before continuing this section, refer to ISO 31000:2018 and review its definition of a stakeholder.

Stakeholders have a significant role in influencing and planning for organisational decision-making processes. Therefore, organisations should identify, understand, record and more importantly, address key stakeholder perceptions regarding the risks associated with key decisions (as well as the benefits).

### *Internal Stakeholders*

Internal employees are in the best position to know and understand the risks the organisation is taking to survive and prosper.

Examples of internal stakeholders include:

- the board and the departmental secretary
- the government and ministers in the relevant portfolio (in the case of a government organisation)
- senior management
- operational management
- staff.

### *External Stakeholders*

Examples of external stakeholders include:

- subcontractors
- suppliers
- key customer groups
- regulatory bodies
- industry associations
- special interest groups
- financial institutions providing funding or credit.

### *Stakeholder Groups*

Hanson et al. (2002) identified three separate types of stakeholder groups, each of which may influence decision making within the organisation. The following table defines and provides examples of these three stakeholder groups.

**Examples of Stakeholder Groups**

| Stakeholder Group | Examples |
|---|---|
| 1. Capital market | shareholders<br>capital investors |
| 2. Product market | customers<br>suppliers<br>unions |
| 3. Organisational | managerial staff<br>non-managerial staff |

*Interests, Needs, and Expectations*

Each stakeholder group has different interests, needs, and expectations in relation to the decisions the organisation makes. For example:

- shareholders expect a return on investment (ROI) and organisational growth;
- customers expect a quality product delivered at a reasonable price;
- staff expect:
  - rewarding and motivating work
  - a reasonable level of remuneration
  - optimal working conditions.

*Conflict*

Each stakeholder group's expectations may conflict with those of the other stakeholder groups. This conflict drives the need for effective stakeholder relations to ensure the organisation appropriately manages key expectations.

**Self-Help Question 4.16**

Categorise the varying stakeholder expectations in the following table by placing a checkmark against the most appropriate stakeholder group.

| | **Stakeholder Group** | | |
|---|---|---|---|
| **Expectation** | **Capital market** | **Product market** | **Organisational** |
| High dividends | □ | □ | □ |
| Compliance with safe practice standards | □ | □ | □ |
| Competitive prices | □ | □ | □ |
| Compliance with service delivery standards | □ | □ | □ |
| Professional development opportunities | □ | □ | □ |
| Sound corporate governance | □ | □ | □ |

Answers to self-help questions are provided at the end of each section.

### *Identification*

By identifying internal and external stakeholders, a manager can determine which stakeholders are critical to achieving organisational success. This diagram shows how stakeholders relate to organisational goals.

**Relationship of Stakeholders to Organisational Goals**

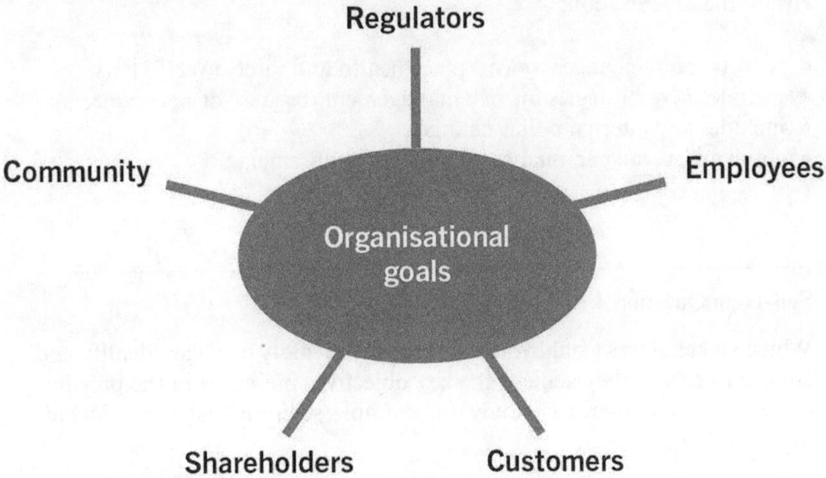


**Activity | Identifying key stakeholders**

Consider your own department (or a project on which you are working).

- Identify the internal and external stakeholders.
- Determine the stakeholder group under which your identified stakeholders can be categorised in the following table.

| | Stakeholder Type | |
|---|---|---|
| **Stakeholder group** | **Internal** | **External** |
| Capital market | | |
| Product market | | |
| Organisational | | |

***Case study – Construction Company***

The safety manager for a construction company is developing a communication and consultation plan as part of the strategy to review and implement a new safety management system.

The key objectives for revising the safety management system is to ensure the organisation:

- reflects recent changes to workplace health and safety (WHS) laws;
- includes new strategies for risk management (because of new projects);
- includes any internal policy changes;
- confirms overall compliance with safety requirements.

---

**Self-Help Question 4.17**

Which stakeholders would you recommend the safety manager identify and engage to ensure they achieve the key objectives presented in the previous construction company case study (for example, senior management, including the CEO)?

---

Answers to self-help questions are provided at the end of each section.

---

## Relations with Stakeholders

After identifying key stakeholders, it is necessary to identify the nature of the relationship the organisation needs to develop. Establishing and managing stakeholder relationships throughout the change process optimises the likelihood that the organisation can achieve the change objectives by:

- identifying the need for change
- planning for change
- implementing the change.

Stakeholder management involves gaining the support of those instrumental to achieving organisational goals. One key way to gain this support is through stakeholder engagement.

Stakeholder engagement requires managers to:

- share information regarding policies and decisions with stakeholders;
- involve all relevant stakeholders in the policy-making and decision-making processes.

Stakeholder management is one of the most difficult tasks in the management process as it relates to a manager's ability to ensure they appropriately identify and engage those:

- affected by organisational decisions and policies
- with a legitimate interest in the organisation.

***Benefits***

Effective stakeholder management benefits the management process by:

- including the perspectives of stakeholders, who can successfully influence planning for and attaining goals;
- engaging stakeholders from the beginning to increase the likelihood that they will support decisions (stakeholder buy-in);
- enabling a more efficient change management approach by:
  - anticipating and planning for any potential resistance
  - supporting and sharing information with those who may influence the outcome of decisions.

*Stakeholder Perceptions*

Stakeholders are likely to make judgements about the acceptability of a risk exposure based on their perception of that exposure. Since stakeholder views can have a significant impact on decisions, it is important for the organisation to:

- identify and record stakeholder perceptions of risk exposures;
- understand and address the underlying reasons for stakeholder perceptions of risk exposures within the risk management programme.

***Stakeholder Management***

Because of the importance of maintaining good relationships with stakeholders, risk managers need to fully understand their stakeholders. Therefore, after identifying the key stakeholders, risk managers should conduct a stakeholder analysis and produce a stakeholder map.

Each stakeholder influences decision-making and, ultimately, how the organisation achieves its goals and objectives in different ways. Understanding the power and influence stakeholders can have contributes towards ensuring organisations can use such influence positively and that they can effectively manage such resistance.

Organisations can use stakeholder analysis for a variety of purposes, including those described in the following table.

**Purposes of Stakeholder Analysis**

| Purpose | Description |
|---|---|
| Change management | As a precursor to buy-in analysis |
| Risk management | Threats are often uncovered (directly or indirectly) from an examination of stakeholders |
| Issue management | Stakeholder analysis is one of the most fruitful sources of key issues for a project |
| Project promotion and marketing | Knowledge of stakeholders helps focus marketing and promotional activities in support of the project |

### *Stakeholder Analysis*

Before engaging stakeholders, it is important to gain an understanding of their needs and expectations. Herein, organisations can ask several questions (either directly or indirectly) to determine the sort of influence stakeholders will have on achieving established goals and objectives.

**Activity | Stakeholder needs**

Rachel Thompson (2012) recommends asking the following list of questions to determine stakeholder needs. Consider one of your organisation's key stakeholders and fill in the following table that you may adapt to your specific circumstances.

| Question | Answer |
|---|---|
| What financial or emotional interest do they have in the outcome of your work? | |
| Is that interest positive or negative? | □ Positive □ Negative |
| What motivates the stakeholder most of all? | |
| What information do they want from you? | |
| How do they want to receive information from you? | |
| What is the best way of communicating your message to them? | |

| | | |
|---|---|---|
| What is their current opinion of your work? | | |
| Is their opinion based on good information? | □ Yes | □ No |
| Who influences their opinions generally, and who influences their opinion of you? | | |
| Do some of these influencers, for example, become important stakeholders in their own right? | □ Yes | □ No |
| If they are not likely to be positive, what will win them around to support your project? | | |
| If you do not think you will be able to win them around, how will you manage their opposition? | | |
| Who else might be influenced by their opinions? | | |
| Do these people become stakeholders in their own right? | □ Yes | □ No |

## Monitoring Key Stakeholder Relationships

Just as organisational changes influence risk exposures, so too can they influence the nature of stakeholder relationships.

### *Neglecting to Monitor*

Neglecting to monitor the relationship can result in a situation in which:

- the communication and consultation plans cease to be effective;
- individual stakeholders (or stakeholder groups) become detached or isolated from the decision-making process.

In relation to barriers to effective communication, neglecting to monitor key stakeholder relationships can result in:

- a lack of interest in, or understanding of, the importance of the communication;
- sending inappropriate (or untimely) information, which results in resistance;
- failing to manage hidden agendas, increasing the risk that goals will not be achieved.

In addition, this neglect affects immediate and ongoing relationships, which can be detrimental to future decision making or change management requirements.

This neglect may also cause an adverse result for the organisation if the stakeholder or stakeholder group is unaware of key changes, for example, to processes or protocols.

***Case study – Construction Company (continued)***

Continuing from the previous construction company case study on the review of a safety management system for a construction firm, the safety manager engages the identified stakeholders to review safety management system documentation.

### The communication plan

As part of the roll-out of the new system, the organisation implements the initial communication plan, which includes informing and educating all key stakeholders about required changes.

### Failing to monitor relationships

As time goes by, the safety manager fails to monitor the relationships they have established with the union representative group. The union representative group gradually becomes dissatisfied with their lack of involvement in implementing key changes.

### Stakeholder action

The union representative group believes the company is taking unsafe short-cuts and becomes concerned for the safety of their members. As a result, the union group organises a company-wide walk-off without consulting management. This protest results in significant delays for the company with regards to completing client work and jeopardises major contracts.

## Communication with Stakeholders

After identifying key stakeholders and determining the nature of the stakeholder relationship, the next step is to determine how to consult or communicate with stakeholders to:

- elicit information; and/or
- manage their resistance to change.

Organisations should apply the principles and types of communication explored earlier in this chapter to ensure effective organisational communication when determining communication and consultation strategies for stakeholder management.

Using the responses to the questions in the previous activity, organisations can categorise stakeholders to determine the required level of engagement. These groupings are based on a stakeholder's:

1. information contribution
2. resistance to change.

### *1. Information contribution*

It is rare for only one stakeholder to possess all the information necessary to identify the risks to an organisation (or even to an activity or project). It is important to identify a range of stakeholders who can assist in making this information complete.

Stakeholder consultation is the method by which organisations seek information from identified stakeholders to:

- gain their perspectives
- use their experience and knowledge
- provide information crucial to the decision-making process.

### *2. Resistance to change*

One of the most commonly encountered problems when implementing change is stakeholder resistance. There are many examples of an organisation's attempts to implement change failing, or perhaps not being as successful as first hoped due to resistance.

**Common Reasons Stakeholders Resist Change**

| Reason | Description |
|---|---|
| Self-interest | Perceptions of inconvenience or poor value for effort—what's in it for me? |
| Misunderstanding or lack of trust | Not fully understanding the purpose of the change or the intended outcomes |
| Differences in perceptions of the value of the change | As an example, those at the operations level may not fully appreciate the need for a change that is implemented at a strategic level |

### *Overcoming Resistance*

#### *A Communicative Approach*

A communicative approach can overcome resistance to change by establishing effective stakeholder relationships, whereby information is shared with the aim of:

- ensuring the organisation appropriately manages stakeholder perceptions (includes educational strategies)
- assisting stakeholders to understand how the change will benefit them
- engaging and involving stakeholders identified in the change process.

### *Other Methods*

Additionally, organisations can reduce the likelihood of resistance to change by:

- ensuring the organisation provides adequate levels of support – do not assume people can immediately cope with change; they need time to adapt;
- creating quick-wins by targeting areas that can lead to easy successes.

**Activity | Stakeholders**

1. List your organisation's internal and external stakeholders then prioritise them in order of importance by considering their relevance to the risk management process. You may find it useful to divide stakeholders into the following three categories, as demonstrated in the table:
   - highly relevant
   - relevant
   - marginal to no relevance.

   **Note:** The order does not need to be entirely correct.
2. List the types of information each stakeholder will be able to provide which may be of value to the risk process. For example:
   - an accountant would have an excellent perspective on the financial risks
   - a regulatory inspector would be able to provide information on the effectiveness of the programme and the underlying supporting legislation
3. Consider stakeholders' needs and the outcomes they require from the risk management process.

| | | **External stakeholders** | |
|---|---|---|---|
| | **High relevance** | **Relevant** | **Low relevance** |
| **Risk information** | | | |
| **Risk needs** | | | |
| | | **Internal stakeholders** | |
| | **High relevance** | **Relevant** | **Low relevance** |
| **Risk information** | | | |
| **Risk needs** | | | |

## Summary

Please keep the following points from this chapter in mind:

- The first key step in the risk management process is to establish communication and consultation channels with internal and, in some cases, external stakeholders.
- The organisation should maintain and utilise the lines of communication established in this initial phase throughout each subsequent stage of the risk management process to ensure:
  - it appropriately and effectively executes each activity
  - it clearly understands the relevant responsibilities, accountabilities and authorities.
- Understanding the needs and concerns of stakeholders, while upholding regular, comprehensive communication is a critical part of the success of the risk management programme.
- Stakeholders have a significant role in influencing and planning for organisational decision-making processes.
- Stakeholder engagement requires managers to:
  - share information regarding policies and decisions with stakeholders
  - involve all relevant stakeholders in the policy-making and decision-making processes.
- Effective stakeholder management benefits the management process by:
  - including the perspectives of stakeholders
  - engaging stakeholders from the beginning to increase buy-in
  - enabling a more efficient change management approach.
- Three stakeholder groups include:
  - capital market
  - product market
  - organisational.
- Organisations can use stakeholder analysis for:
  - change management
  - risk management
  - issue management
  - project promotion and marketing.
- It is important to identify a range of stakeholders who can assist in contributing as much complete information as possible.
- A communicative approach can overcome resistance to change by establishing effective stakeholder relationships.
- The stakeholder map documents essential stakeholder information and provides decision-makers with a profile to better understand stakeholder needs and concerns.

## Answers to Self-Help Questions

### Self-help question 4.1

Consultation processes may include:

- email/intranet communications
- newsletters or other processes and devices which ensure all employees have the opportunity to contribute
- mechanisms to provide feedback to the work team in relation to outcomes of consultation
- interviews/workshops
- brainstorming exercises.

### Self-help question 4.2

As the HR manager, the types of information you may share with managers across the organisation to aid in decision-making may include:

- equivalent full-time (EFT) staff data
- staff attendance statistics
- performance management data
- resource requirements (for example, current EFT vs expected EFT)
- WHS statistics
- employee cultural survey information
- anecdotal feedback from staff.

### Self-help question 4.3

By taking an integrated approach to risk management, the project manager responsible for introducing a new IT system should have:

- understood the broad areas of risk outside their own area of expertise;
- enhanced the planning for the project, which would have resulted in:
  - decreased project limitations
  - increased opportunities for achieving objectives
- increased the effectiveness of decision-making as a result of new system implementation;
- increased stakeholder satisfaction through enhanced communication processes.

### Self-help question 4.4

Reasons for top-down communication may include:

- defining organisational requirements;
- providing staff with information they need to fulfil requirements;

- passing on requirements from an external stakeholder; for example:
  - customer
  - regulator
  - insurer.

**Self-help question 4.5**

Examples of top-down communication may include:

- directives (verbal or written)
- job descriptions
- strategic plans
- business plans
- legislative requirements
- performance reviews.

**Self-help question 4.6**

Distorted top-down communication may be a result of:

- unclear/ambiguous messages
- overusing one or more communication mechanisms (for example, people receive so many emails that they often disregard those that are important)
- individuals who may be dishonest, or have a particular agenda for distorting or withholding information deliberately filtering information – information is often viewed as power.

**Self-help question 4.7**

Reasons for down-up communication may include the need to understand:

- operational performance (for example, progress, productivity, or quality)
- change requirements (for example, to environmental conditions and remuneration)
- material risks or unsolved problems that may prevent the organisation from achieving its objectives.

**Self-help question 4.8**

Examples of the types of down-up communication you may have experienced include:

- meetings between a subordinate and their supervisor (or manager)
- staff surveys
- grievance programs or other feedback mechanisms
- incident or occurrence reports.

**Self-help question 4.9**

Generally, down-up communication can become distorted as a result of:

- distrust, where the subordinate may filter or withhold information from a superior
- a subordinate altering the message (adding information) to increase the opportunity that their superior may respond favourably (for example, to gain a promotion, increased remuneration or recognition).

**Self-help question 4.10**

Examples of horizontal communication mechanisms may include:

- meetings (one-to-one or group)
- minutes and agendas for meetings
- reports
- emails
- telephone calls
- memos.

**Self-help question 4.11**

Barriers to effective horizontal communication may:

- include the development of a silo mentality, in which staff members either:
    - do not understand the importance of sharing information horizontally
    - are unaware of the need to do so.
- arise from departmental specialisation (Bartol et al., 2005), where a department focuses internally on their own work, rather than on the requirements of the organisation as a whole.

**Self-help question 4.12**

Informal communication channels can often be antagonistic towards the achievement of organisational goals, as the message may be distorted or the wrong message may be communicated. Without formal verification or context to an informal message, staff may form erroneous conclusions and dissatisfaction may result.

**Self-help question 4.13**

The channels of communication indicated in the case study included vertical (down-up and top-down) communication channels, as well as informal channels. The following table summarises these communication channels.

| Communication | Channel |
|---|---|
| Audit report | Down-up |
| Policy | Downward |
| Memo | Top-down |
| Supervisor meeting | Top-down |
| Discussion with colleague | Informal |

Examples of poor communication in this case study include the:

- informal discussion with Jane's colleague, which may have resulted in:
- uncertainty
- worry
- a decreased level of Jane's performance
- failure to successfully transmit the memo regarding audit changes, which resulted in an unsatisfactory audit report
- supervisor failing to:
  - enforce changes described in the memo; or
  - follow-up to ensure Jane had received the required information.

**Self-help question 4.14**

There are numerous ways in which organisations can consult and communicate with stakeholders depending on the nature of the relationship. These include:

- presentations
- briefing sessions
- education sessions (for example, seminars or workshops)
- brainstorming sessions
- marketing events (for example, a product launch)
- use of information technology (for example, intranet, fax systems or email)
- mail-outs
- advertising material (for example, posters or brochures)
- newsletters
- progress reports.

**Self-help question 4.15**

Communication and consultation methods can be categorised within the stakeholder map as follows.

| Consultation | Influence | Low Interest | High Interest |
|---|---|---|---|
| | | **B. High consultation – low communication** | **A. High consultation – high communication** |
| | *High* | One-to-one meetings<br>Progress report | Staff meetings<br>Brainstorming sessions<br>One-to-one meetings<br>Progress reports |
| | | **D. Low consultation – low communication** | **C. Low consultation – high communication** |
| | *Low* | Advertising materials:<br>Posters<br>Brochures | Use of IT (for example, intranet, fax systems, email and teleconference)<br>Advertising material (for example, posters and brochures)<br>Education sessions (for example, seminars or workshops)<br>Staff meetings |
| | | *Low* | **Interest** *High* |
| | | **Communication** | |

**Self-help question 4.16**

Stakeholder expectations can be assigned to specific stakeholder groups as follows.

| | Stakeholder group | | |
|---|---|---|---|
| **Expectation** | **Capital market** | **Product market** | **Organisational** |
| High dividends | ☒ | ☐ | ☐ |
| Compliance with safe practice standards | ☐ | ☐ | ☒ |
| Competitive prices | ☐ | ☒ | ☐ |
| Compliance with service delivery standards | ☒ | ☐ | ☐ |
| Professional development opportunities | ☒ | ☐ | ☐ |
| Sound corporate governance | ☒ | ☐ | ☐ |

**Self-help question 4.17**

In recommending stakeholders for the safety manager to identify and engage, you may have identified:

- project managers
- union representatives
- WHS representatives
- insurer
- contractors/suppliers
- clients.

---

Chapter 5

# Risk Monitoring and Reviewing

## Introduction

Monitoring and reviewing are integral to the effectiveness of the risk management programmes over time. Risk exposures are not static and, as circumstances change, programmes need to alter to reflect those changes. Consequently, the risk management process needs to be applied in an iterative and ongoing way within the risk management programme for the organisation.

The monitoring and reviewing of risk treatment plans is aimed at ensuring successful creation of execution of plans, and at providing assurance to stakeholders that risk is being managed appropriately.

No matter how well-planned and implemented a risk management programme is, the nature of risk exposures is such that they are unpredictable and unexpected events/losses will undoubtedly occur. Monitoring and reviewing the risk management process can reveal successes of the programme as well as changes necessary to further improve performance.

It is also possible that an organisation's commitment to risk management will vary over time. By utilising the outcomes of the monitoring and review process, the risk management programme can be adjusted to ensure that it remains viable and relevant, keeping the risk management programme up-to-date and on track.

Risk treatment plans provide an important performance measure for the risk management programme. The purpose of monitoring and review is to:

- review the effectiveness of the existing risk management programme;
- identify any changes in the context;
- identify any new and emerging risks;

**Risk Measurement and Monitoring, 81–113**

**Published under exclusive licence by Emerald Publishing Limited**
**doi:10.1108/978-1-83662-310-620251013**

- monitor risk exposures which have already been identified;
- review data sources used in analysis and revise/update the data;
- ensure risk treatment programmes are being adhered to.

This topic provides you with an overview of the monitoring and review process. Organisations should monitor the risk management process on an ongoing basis, which:

- includes supervising risk management process activities;
- examines each individual risk exposure to ensure changing circumstances do not alter the parameters under which the organisation has formulated:
  - risk strategies
  - priorities.

## Learning Outcomes

By the end of this topic, you should be able to:

- describe how to monitor and review the application of the risk management process;
- explain how to establish an event/loss reporting system;
- identify and review loss trends and changes in risk exposures;
- outline how to formulate and recommend appropriate risk and loss control measures;
- explain how to establish an event/loss reporting system;
- understand the importance of compliance review process and what is factored in the review.

## Monitoring and Review – An Overview

Organisations need to formally monitor and review individual risk exposures by asking the following questions:

- Has the risk changed?
- Are the controls we have established operating?
- Has the organisation executed our improvement plans?

In addition to asking these key questions, the organisation should also continually monitor and review each step in the risk management process.

Monitoring and review are critical elements in the effectiveness of risk management programmes because no matter how well an organisation plans or implements a risk management programme:

- risk exposures are not static;
- risk exposures are unpredictable;
- unexpected events/losses undoubtedly occur;
- specific actions need to be completed.

As circumstances change, organisations need to modify risk management programmes and apply the risk management process in an ongoing, iterative fashion.

The organisation should monitor and review all the steps in the risk management process on a continual basis to ensure it achieves the optimum risk management results.

## Monitoring

Section 3.8.2.1 of ISO/Guide 73:2009 Risk management – Vocabulary defines *monitoring* as:

> continual checking, supervising, critically observing or determining the status in order to identify change from the performance level required or expected
> **Note:** Monitoring can be applied to a risk management framework, risk management process, risk or control.

The basics of monitoring were covered in the previous book volume, which explored the questions:

- Why do organisations need to monitor?
- Who does the monitoring?
- What should be monitored?
- How should the monitoring be conducted?
- When should the monitoring be done?

This block will explore monitoring in a bit more detail.

### *Specific Tasks*

Monitoring involves continually maintaining and managing risk information by:

- recording and showing any risk profile changes;
- tracking the progress and completion of risk control actions;
- measuring an organisation's progress against the risk management plan;
- allocating and tracking the accountability for:
  - risk exposures
  - treatment measures
  - control actions

- triggering monitoring and assurance activity;
- providing a means for the measurement and reporting of:
  - risk management activities
  - general progress.

### *Fine-Tuning*

Organisations must continually monitor themselves and the environment in which they operate to keep abreast of changes that may affect their:

- risk exposure
- treatment and financing programmes.

Continual monitoring and review enable fine-tuning of a risk management programme to achieve the best possible outcome for the organisation from the risks to which it is exposed.

**EXAMPLE**

**Overseas Markets**

If an organisation starts selling products in new overseas markets, it is likely that the risks the company is exposed to will expand and change (for example, currency exchange risk exposures).

## Key Monitoring Questions

It is important to consider the following questions regarding monitoring.

### *Why?*

The following table outlines the most common reasons for monitoring.

**The Most Common Reasons for Monitoring**

| Reason | Description |
|---|---|
| Effectiveness of the programme | Organisations should review risk management processes to ensure they are effective and deliver value. Organisations should ask the following key questions:<br>• Have we adopted the right techniques?<br>• Are those techniques still relevant to the current organisational structure and activities? |

| | |
|---|---|
| The need of the board and executive to understand organisational risks | As the board/executive is ultimately accountable, the organisation needs to provide information/feedback:<br>• enabling the board/executive to monitor residual risk<br>• on whether the organisation is taking on too much or too little risk. |
| Identifying new/changed exposures | Organisations need to promptly identify and report new and changed risk exposures because:<br>• 'new' exposures continually arise<br>• some older exposures become redundant.<br>For example, an organisation may decide to:<br>• outsource the operation and maintenance of its motor vehicle fleet, thereby changing the nature and extent of motor vehicle risk exposures<br>• go into a new market thereby changing its market risk |
| Allocating funds | • There are considerable costs associated with risk exposures and a programme to manage those exposures.<br>Monitoring provides ongoing information to:<br>– enable such costs to be properly allocated<br>– justify the allocation of these costs<br>– prove the benefits of establishing a risk management programme. |
| Statutory reporting | Monitoring can provide statistics and data that may be required to satisfy statutory obligations. For example:<br>• workers compensation reporting<br>• environmental legislation. |
| Defending the risk management programme | Monitoring can provide the information needed to defend the organisation's actions if the organisation questions its risk management practices.<br>Areas an organisation must question include:<br>• exercising a duty of care<br>• contractual obligations<br>• legislative responsibilities. |

***Who?***

The following table outlines the key responsibilities of those involved in the implementation of a risk management programme.

**Key Responsibilities of Those Involved in the Implementation of a Risk Management Programme**

| Role | Responsibilities |
|---|---|
| Risk manager | Monitoring the quality of the risk management programme |
| All organisational employees | • Managing risk, with differences in assigned:<br>– scope<br>– breadth<br>– accountability<br>• Monitoring and reporting on key exposures (applies to all those with clear accountability, authority and resources for managing risk) |
| The executive/ board | • Monitoring the risk profile<br>• Ensuring that the risk process is functioning correctly according to organisational reports |

### *What?*

Organisations should monitor each activity in the risk management process.

The following are suggestions of what those responsible in an organisation should monitor:

- changes in structure, or activities or new projects that could alter the risk portfolio
- changes in the organisational context, such as new legislation
- changes to the risk profile
- risk mitigation action plan execution
- execution of internal audit programmes to ensure key controls are operating (the internal audit plan should link to the risk register)
- incidents with a focus on trends, including:
  - work accidents
  - near misses
  - machinery failure
  - security issues.

### *When and How?*

A risk management programme needs both informal and formal monitoring and review processes. Types and examples of these processes were covered in the previous book volume, along with information about when they should occur.

## Establishing a Monitoring and Review Regime

The most important aspect of establishing an organisation's monitoring and review regime is the independence of the person or group appointed to conduct that monitoring and review. The usual place for the monitoring and review function to reside in an organisation is either with the manager responsible for risk management and the risk management committee or with the manager responsible for internal audit and the audit committee. In either case, it is appropriate to avoid any potential for a conflict of interest by ensuring that the manager responsible for monitoring and review has not been closely involved in the development of risk treatments across the organisation.

In many organisations, risk managers work closely with business managers to identify risks and risk treatments. In this case, it is more appropriate for an internal audit manager to have responsibility for monitoring and review. In some organisations, internal audit and risk management responsibilities are combined, which requires some other means of ensuring independence in the monitoring and review of risk treatments; for example, through the use of external auditors or risk management contractors.

The monitoring and review regime of the independent party does not relieve the risk owner of responsibility for managing risk. The risk owner is in the best position to monitor and review the effectiveness of a risk treatment plan on a regular basis and to make changes as required. The independent party needs to monitor and review the risk owner's diligence in implementing a sound risk treatment plan and adapting the plan as needed. It is essential that the independent party has adequate expertise and experience to carry out such a review.

Assuming that a sound base for independence is established, a vital aspect of monitoring and review is senior management involvement. Senior management must receive monitoring and review reports to which they should respond. Business and line managers need to know that their risk treatment programmes are being monitored and supported at the highest level of the organisation. Otherwise there is a tendency to report less frequently and/or to reduce resources devoted to implementing risk treatments.

Finally, the monitoring and review regime must have clear responsibilities and timeframes for delivery, and those given the responsibility of monitoring and review must be given the authority to complete the task. This may include authority to audit risk treatment plans for:

- performance against stated objectives
- accuracy of reporting by risk owners to senior management on their progress with implementation.

### *Case Study – Insightful Insurance*

Insightful Insurance is a general insurance company operating in Continental Europe. Among other products, they underwrite commercial business packs, which provide a combination of insurance covers aimed at protecting small and medium enterprises (SMEs). It offers cover for property damage, business interruption, public liability, burglary and theft, and a number of other covers.

The division that underwrites commercial business packs is staffed by a small number of very experienced underwriters and a much larger number of less-experienced underwriters. In recent years, prices have been falling and the division is no longer profitable. There is anecdotal evidence that most other competitors are still making profits despite heavy price competition.

Senior management of Insightful Insurance requested Internal Audit to conduct a review of the performance of the division. The audit found that a major cause of the financial position of the division was a lack of underwriting skills in the less-experienced staff and the heavy burden placed on experienced underwriters to support them.

The ongoing non-profitability of the division is a major risk in the company's strategic risk profile. It was felt that the company may have to exit the SME market if the business could not be turned around, and that this would require many redundancies at a high cost to the company. The risk was rated as Extreme for the organisation and the CEO appointed his Chief Operations Officer (COO) to be responsible for the risk.

The COO consulted with the Risk Manager for Insightful and initiated a number of risk treatments including the following:

- Streamlining the underwriting process to allow more time for senior underwriters to supervise and generally guide junior underwriters. This part of the treatment was assigned to a senior business analyst.
- Narrowing of the business focus by reducing the number of industries that could be underwritten by Insightful. This allowed more time for senior underwriters to work with junior underwriters. This part of the treatment was assigned to the Chief Underwriter.
- Developing underwriter training programme specifically designed for junior underwriters of commercial business packs, with a heavy emphasis on risk assessment of individual risks. This part of the treatment was assigned to the Risk Manager because she was experienced in underwriting and had recently developed a training programme for staff on general risk management practices.

The treatments were documented in one risk treatment plan for the strategic risk of continued non-profitability of the division leading to exiting from the SME market. It included a monitoring and review regime and the following performance criteria:

- Streamlining underwriting process – The target was a 10% reduction in the average time taken to underwrite a file. A baseline was to be established by reviewing the past productivity of underwriting teams based on numbers of files underwritten per person day.

- Narrowing of the business focus – The target was a 10% reduction of quotations as a percentage of all business offered to Insightful. The baseline was already established because statistics were already available on the number of requests for quotation versus the number of quotations provided;
- Developing underwriter training programme – The target for the programme was to train 90% of underwriters within six months, with 95% of participants attaining a satisfactory assessment or better.
- Assessing profitability – The treatment should return the division to profitability within 18 months.

---

**Self-Help Question 5.1**

Answer the following questions about Insightful Insurance's monitoring and review regime for their risk treatment plan for the SME division.

1. Who should the COO report to regarding the progress of implementation of the plan?
2. Who would be best placed to monitor and review the progress of implementation – the Internal Audit Manager or the Risk Manager? Why?
3. Would the manager responsible for the monitor and review most likely have the authority required to assess progress of implementation? Why?

---

Answers to self-help questions are provided at the end of each section.

---

### *Organisational Performance Criteria for Monitoring Treatment Plans*

In addition to monitoring and reviewing specific risk treatment plans for performance against stated objectives, an organisation can establish broader performance criteria for monitoring and reviewing its overall performance in treating risk. Monitoring criteria might include the following:

- The quality of construction of plans – An organisation should periodically assess whether treatment plans are following organisational guidelines and if the level of detail in the plans is appropriate.
- The timeliness of implementation – Organisations should monitor both key and lesser risk treatments to identify whether timelines are being met. It is common for the risk treatments for lower rated risks to remain outstanding for many months or even years because of a lack of urgency associated with the risk level. By monitoring the level of risk treatments outstanding over time, management can

determine whether their urgency needs to be upgraded. Management also assesses the cumulative risk that accrues when many minor risks are outstanding.

- The overall effectiveness of plans – An organisation should also monitor risk treatments to identify their effectiveness in managing risk. This could be achieved by monitoring for:
  - lower-impact higher-frequency risk events, the number of risk events occurring
  - higher-impact risk events, identifying whether risk treatments were in place but were ineffective. Just because a risk event occurred, it does not mean failure by the organisation to manage risk – e.g. earthquakes cannot be avoided; however, the consequences can be reduced by pre-planning. In the event of an earthquake, a review of the effectiveness of pre-planning will provide the management with some insight into whether their investment in risk treatment prior to the event was money well spent or not.

---

**Self-Help Question 5.2**

1. Referring to the case study about Insightful Insurance, list at least two items that could be assessed during the monitoring and review process to assess the quality of construction of the COO's risk treatment plan for the unprofitable SME division.
   You may wish to review the previous book volume, Chapter 7 to remind yourself of the key issues to be addressed when preparing a risk treatment plan.
2. What is a major problem with assessing the overall effectiveness of the COO's risk treatment plan?

---

Answers to self-help questions are provided at the end of each section.

---

### *Statistics in Monitoring and Review*

The larger the organisation, the greater the need for a statistical approach to monitoring and reviewing treatment plans. Introducing basic statistics allows an organisation to randomly sample treatment plans for review and estimate the likelihood that the findings from the sample represent its entire population of treatment plans.

For example, if, from a sample of 50 risk treatment plans, five were found to be grossly inadequate in their effectiveness in managing risk, then it can be inferred that 10% (5 is 10% of 50) of all risk treatment plans in the organisation are grossly inadequate. The level of confidence is calculated statistically, based on the size of the sample and the variation of the results found in the sample. Typically, the confidence level will range from 60+ per cent to 99%. The larger the sample relative to the entire population and the less varied the results, the higher the confidence of the estimate for the entire population.

The issues that need to be addressed include the following:

- Identifying the entire population of risk treatment plans to ensure the statistical analysis is representative of the population of all plans – If all are in one system, the population is defined. If they are maintained on separate systems or by individual risk owners, there needs to be a method for identifying the entire population.
- Choosing a sample size relevant to the population size – Statistics dictate that the greater the sample size the more confident we can be that the results of the monitoring and review are representative of the population. However, more human resources are required to carry out the monitoring and review.
- Choosing a sampling method – The simplest is random sampling where, as an example, around 50 treatment plans are chosen by manually picking from a list. There are more advanced methods available including the use of random number generators and stratified random sampling where sampling occurs within packets of similar treatment plans. For example, there may be more concern over IT projects than in other areas of the business, so the sampling method can be slanted towards the IT projects using this technique, without losing overall confidence in the results for the whole organisation.

---

**Self-Help Question 5.3**

Why is it necessary to identify the entire population of risk treatment plans across an organisation when conducting a statistical analysis exercise?

---

Answers to self-help questions are provided at the end of each section.

---

### *Documentation*

Documenting the monitoring and review process is necessary for assuring stakeholders that the organisation is aware of, and is managing, its risks. The documentation should cover the following:

- details of the monitoring and review regime and how often it is being conducted
- outcomes of audits and statistical analysis of the results
- details of how the organisation acts on any findings from the monitoring and review phase.

### *Risk Financing Plans*

Risk treatment plans, both risk reduction and risk financing, use the same principles of monitoring and review; however, risk financing plans will have major repercussions if a risk treatment fails during a major risk event. This is because risk financing plans usually treat high impact events and, consequently, require a commensurate level of monitoring and review.

---

**Self-Help Question 5.4**

1. What are the most critical elements of a successful monitoring and review regime?
2. When building performance criteria for monitoring and review, what should an organisation be monitoring and reviewing with respect to the following?
   - the quality of treatment plans
   - the timeliness of implementation
   - the effectiveness of treatment plans.
3. What is the main reason for using statistics in monitoring and review?

---

Answers to self-help questions are provided at the end of each section.

### *Knowledge Management*

Knowledge management is a transdisciplinary approach to improving organisational outcomes and learning, through maximising the use of knowledge. It involves the design, implementation, and review of social and technological activities and processes to improve the creating, sharing, and applying or using of knowledge.

Knowledge was included as a resource in the 2015 update of *ISO 9001 Quality management*, along with other more tangible resources such as people, infrastructure and monitoring resources.

Monitoring and review of risk treatment and financing plans is essential to help guarantee organisational performance in managing risk. A key aspect of guaranteeing performance is ensuring the organisation learns from the outcomes of the monitoring and review programme.

It is usual for organisations to learn at the senior management level from monitoring and review reports, and for individual risk owners to learn from specific issues raised. What is less common is a knowledge management approach where the systems and documents used and generated during the process are used for organisation-wide awareness and learning about risk and compliance issues.

### *The Knowledge Continuum*

The process of gaining knowledge has been researched by a range of management practitioners, from information technologists to process engineers to psychologists. The notion of knowledge as a continuum stems from the process we follow to gain information and act on it. Consider the following.

- *Attention* – Before we can have knowledge, we must first be drawn to the need for knowledge. Human senses such as hearing and sight draw our attention to certain signals in our immediate environment.
- *Data* – Once we're paying attention, we need data. Continuing with the example of human senses, once our attention is drawn to a sound, for example, our brains demand data. How loud is it? How close is it?
- *Information* – Data alone are not information. Information comes when we have the data in a clear context. When we hear a sound, our brain takes the data it can gather and processes it. It will compare it with other sounds we are familiar with and try to identify it.
- *Knowledge* – To have 'knowledge', we also need to have the wisdom to act on the information gained. Fortunately for humans, our brains have evolved a strong survival instinct and from an early age we have the wisdom to know that frightening sounds are sufficient information for us to take precautionary action.

The knowledge continuum in the context of the monitoring and review process can be viewed as follows.

- *Attention* – The existence of the monitoring and review process draws our attention to the need for knowledge.
- *Data* – Collating risk treatment information, monitoring and reviewing plans and producing documents provides lots of data.
- *Information* – Establishing the context for the data for staff in organisations should occur in the development of the organisation's risk management policy and framework. The good or bad information generated from the monitoring and review process should have meaning for staff that have read and understood the policy and framework. They should be able to understand that the organisation's risk appetite is being maintained or exceeded. For any data to become useful information, they need to be analysed and summarised so that the key issues can be understood.
- *Knowledge* – The outcome of the monitoring and review process is knowledge that will identify both risk and opportunity that require action. Staff should understand who is responsible for action and when, and have the authority to act and use processes to refer risks and opportunities that cannot be actioned because of a workplace obstacle to management.

It is easy to see the 'attention' aspect is gained if a monitoring and review process is in place. It is also easy to assume there are sufficient quality data if the monitoring and review regime addresses all identified issues; less easy to assume in most organisations is whether sufficient staff have sufficient information and the skill to act. Organisations should ask the following questions:

- What information needs to be available to which staff and in what format?
- What guidance do we need to provide to staff to ensure they have the skill to act?

Each organisation will have very different answers depending on the industry and the type of staff that may need to act. An organisation of technical people will have very different information needs and different preferences for information format from those of staff in a cultural organisation such as an art gallery or museum.

Skill is gained using many pathways. People have a range of different preferences for how they learn and gain skill. Organisations should invest in understanding the different types of people in their organisation and how best they will gain the skill to act on information that management perceives as essential to the success of the organisation.

**Activity | Knowledge management**

Assess the knowledge continuum for the monitoring and review of risk in your organisation. Ask yourself the following questions.

- Is my attention gained? Am I aware there is a monitoring and review process?
- Do we have good data? Is it accessible and useable? Can it be analysed easily?
- Do I understand the risk management policy and framework of the organisation? Does it provide sufficient context for me to understand the results of any monitoring and review activity?
- Do I know what to do if I am presented with the results of a monitoring and review activity? Do I know how to action items and how and when to escalate issues?
- Is the monitoring and review regime located within the broader 'knowledge management' framework of the organisation?

## Internal Control Self-Assessment

While managers responsible for individual risks (for which they have documented controls) are primarily responsible for ensuring that the controls are in place and operating reliably, boards and audit committees often require greater assurance that an organisation is adhering to control plans.

Therefore, an internal audit team can often work very effectively with the risk management team by periodically undertaking reviews to confirm the documented controls exist and are operating.

Such a review is often known as an internal control self-assessment (ICSA), or simply a control self-assessment (CSA).

The ICSA is part of the regular risk management process, yet is a structured framework. It supports organisations to identify, document and manage their risk exposures and, importantly, supports managers and risk owners to assess the effectiveness of the controls that are in place. It differs from internal audits as the goals of the ICSA are determined by operational managers, rather than internal audit departments, and as transactions are not tested.

The goals of an ICSA vary depending on the organisation, but there are three shared objectives:

- To gain an understanding of the roles and responsibilities of all departments regarding a specific function, especially individual roles within each department.
- To determine acceptable levels of risk.
- To determine the acceptable cost-benefit ratios relating to new controls.

### *Other Techniques*

Other review techniques include:

- periodic management confirmations (or attestations) that the organisation is adhering to the risk plan
- a risk register which automatically:
  - surveys managers
  - confirms controls are operating
  - notes the field describing the responsible manager
  - automatically generates an email to the responsible individual.
- external reviews in key risk areas (such as WHS and treasury).

**EXAMPLE**

#### Example – Periodic Management Confirmation

A periodic management confirmation (or testimony) can usually be as simple as a manager stating the following:

I am satisfied we have:

- recorded the material risks in my area of responsibility in the risk system
- executed the documented controls consistent with the way they have been described.

Other than the following noted issues, we are developing documented control improvement plans according to the agreed schedule.

### *Risk Improvement Plans*

Risk managers typically monitor risk improvement plans directly to ensure the organisation is executing them. Depending on its sophistication, the organisation can use the risk register as a tool to:

- provide email reminders to responsible managers;
- schedule formal reviews of the change process.

### *Hazard Monitoring*

Monitoring systems for hazard-type risks are also important and may include:

- workers' compensation/accident compensation claims
- claims by third parties for faulty products
- property loss reports
- claims by third parties for bodily injury or property damage
- motor vehicle accident reports
- WHS reporting (for example, accident investigation reports)
- operating licence renewals (for example, dangerous goods storage and waste discharge).

### *Fundamental Information*

Recording the following information should form a fundamental part of any monitoring system as would any article in the press to be factually truthful, and provide answers to the following questions:

- Why? (causes)
- When? (time)
- Where? (place)
- Who? (persons involved)
- What? (quick description of the event)
- Consequences? (amount of losses for all parties involved)
- AND? (other information the organisation may use for analysing unexpected events/losses).

## Reviewing

The risk management system must remain relevant to the organisation always. As an organisation's circumstances are changing all the time, the regular review of previous risk management decisions is vital.

In addition to ongoing monitoring procedures, organisations should conduct regular formal reviews of risk management processes to assess and document:

- the effectiveness of:
  - the risk treatment plan
  - strategies

  - the management system
  - adherence to risk treatment measures
- the relevance of the risk management plan to the organisation's objectives
- factors which may affect the adopted likelihood and consequence measures
- board and management commitment to the risk management process.

### *The Board and Management*

The board and management should take responsibility for developing and implementing mechanisms to ensure the organisation undertakes a formal review of its risk management system (in accordance with the organisation's risk management framework) at regular intervals (for example, on an annual basis).

Including risk management reviews in the board calendar is one simple technique.

### *Review Questions*

The review of an organisation's risk management processes should attempt to answer the following questions:

- Are risk management objectives aligned with organisational performance objectives and values?
- Do risk management initiatives reflect the realities of the environment in which the organisation operates?
- Is the organisation able to effectively measure the outcomes of risk management?
- Do the risk management initiatives generate value for the organisation?
- Is clear and concise information provided for the management and the board's evaluation?
- Does the information allow senior management to make decisions about whether to increase or reduce resources/efforts in managing risk exposures?

***Case Study – The XYZ Planning Authority***

The XYZ Planning Authority established its risk management programme some years ago and reviews it on an annual basis.

As part of its annual review, the risk manager identifies changes in the context of the organisation as outlined in the following table.

Changes in the Context of the Organisation

| Change | Description |
|---|---|
| **Legislative framework** | The legislation underpinning the regulatory model has expanded to include additional organisations |
| **XYZ Planning Authority** | XYZ plans to replace its licensing system to:<br>• provide greater functionality<br>• improve communication with licensees |

| | |
|---|---|
| **The Board** | • There has been significant turnover in the board<br>• XYZ has appointed a new chair |
| **Management/organisational structure** | • Management has been relatively stable<br>• The organisational structure has not changed |
| **Executive meetings** | • Executive meetings were meant to have risk on the agenda<br>• A review of the minutes highlights this has not occurred |

**Self-Help Question 5.5**

Which of the previous factors should you consider when reviewing the risk management programme for XYZ?

Answers to self-help questions are provided at the end of each section.

## Trend Analysis

As part of the monitoring and review process, an organisation analyses event/loss information to reveal whether the loss experience is part of a trend. This trend analysis can provide information on:

- unexpected event trends associated with risk exposures
- the changing nature of risk exposures
- how the organisation might adapt the risk management programme to deal with changed exposures (for example, risk financing)
- how to fund risks with potential financial consequences
- specific loss information (for example, the days of the week or time of day in which motor vehicle accidents are likely to occur).

### *Design Before Implementation*

Keep in mind the following saying when considering trend analysis: 'What you measure is what you get'. Omitting relevant information from a trend analysis results in:

- an incomplete and inaccurate analysis
- incorrect/misinformed remedial decisions.

It is invariably too late to add extra analysis requirements to an analysis system once it has been running (even after only a few months). Organisations must therefore design such systems correctly and completely before implementation.

Organisations need to use valid and reliable statistical techniques to conduct a trend analysis. The types of statistical data an organisation uses to identify loss trends may include:

- time series analysis
- event frequency trend analysis
- seasonal effects/peaks
- value comparison
- trend projections.

### *Time Series Analysis*

Time series analysis is a collection of observations of data items obtained through repeated measurements over time.

A time series analysis:

- helps identify patterns and any trends developing over time
- highlights the following three areas:
  - long-term trends
  - seasonal movements/shifts
  - irregular fluctuations.

Depending on the type of organisation and the activity involved, a time series analysis could cover anywhere from a number of months to a number of years. For loss statistics, the time series analysis should cover at least five complete years, though ideally 10 years or longer.

### *Event Frequency Trend Analysis*

Event frequency trend analysis highlights whether a particular event is occurring on a regular basis. For example:

- Slippage accidents/incidents may be occurring on a factory floor on a regular basis due to inappropriate flooring or inadequate definition of walkways in a wet area.
- A spate of motor vehicle accidents may occur in the organisation's car parking facility.

### *Seasonal Effects*

A seasonal effect is a systematic and calendar-related effect. Seasonal effects or peaks help identify if there are certain times when an incident might occur. The following table presents some examples of seasonal effects.

Seasonal Effects

| Organisation | Seasonal Effect |
|---|---|
| **Clothing store** | A chain of clothing stores expects to achieve higher sales than normal during the weeks before Christmas. Coinciding increases in shoplifting may also occur. |
| **Fruit packing company** | A fruit packing company might experience a higher incidence of machinery breakdown claims during the summer fruit picking season. |
| **School** | Fires at schools may occur more often during holiday periods. |

Understanding seasonal effects, peaks and troughs allows an organisation to make seasonal adjustments to its budgets, forecasts, and activities.

### *Value Comparison*

Organisations can employ value comparison to compare event/loss values for the same types of risk exposures and determine why one event/loss might cost more than another.

### *Analysis of Risk Management*

A value comparison also provides a useful analysis of the effective management of unexpected events and losses; for example, was the loss amount/impact reduced in the second or third instance by employing risk management techniques?

### *Repairer/Supplier Costs*

Organisations can also employ value comparisons to review repairer/supplier costs to ensure the amount for a repair or provision of goods/services is reasonable.

### *Trend Projections*

Available information from several different sources could indicate a trend that may increase or decrease in the future. Examples of this kind of information could include client, insurer, and industry data.

Such trends may have an impact on an organisation's risk management programme, particularly the risk financing component.

**EXAMPLE**

**Motor Vehicle Insurance Premiums**

The following bar chart provides data regarding motor vehicle insurance premiums over a six-year period. The trend highlights to the organisation its increasing private motor vehicle insurance premium costs.

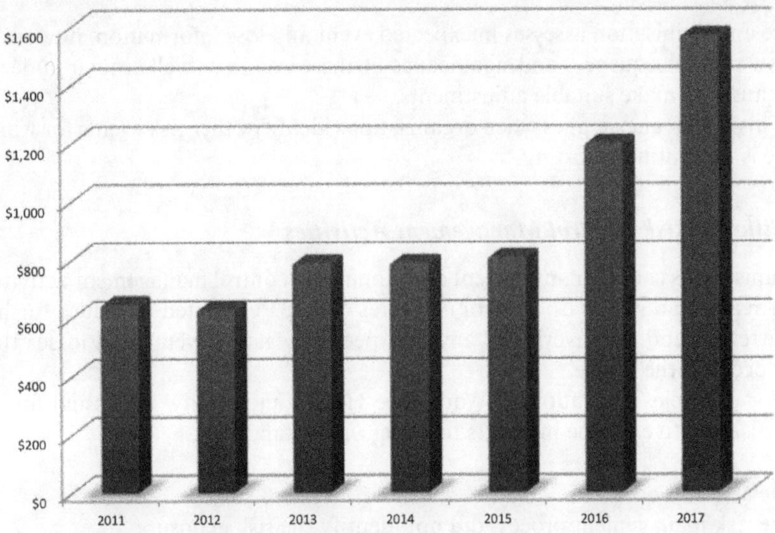


Private Motor Vehicle Insurance Cost Per Vehicle

**Activity | Trend analysis techniques**

1. Examine your organisation's loss report.
2. Consider the techniques your organisation uses to analyse any trends.
3. Did your organisation make any recommendations to reduce the likelihood and consequences of future events/losses?
4. If so, can you identify whether the incidence and severity of the risk event has reduced?
5. If there were no recommendations, can you identify the reasons why?

---

**Further References**

Refer to the following website to learn more about the methods described in this section for identifying and analysing trends:

- Eurostat – www.ec.europa.eu/eurostat

---

## Taking Action

Once an organisation assesses unexpected event and loss information, it needs to review the consequences and significance of these events, as well as their underlying causes to make suitable adjustments.

This review also applies when organisations identify other risk events for which there is no routine reporting.

### *Additional Risk Control Management Activities*

Organisations can often implement additional risk control management activities after realising a risk. Risk control measures can be formulated to reduce further occurrences and the severity of any unexpected negative events and losses that may occur in the future.

For example, in relation to Workplace Health and Safety, it is usual for an organisation to examine incidents to better understand why:

- the accident occurred
- the risk management process did not identify the risk exposure.

The following example further contextualises how an organisation can implement additional risk control management activities after realising a risk.

**EXAMPLE**

**Forklift Load Hazards**

If a stacked load fell from a forklift and injured the driver there are many questions the organisation could ask to identify how to prevent future recurrences. For example:

- Was the driver using the right forklift for the height of the warehouse?
- Did the forklift have a protective cage for the driver?
- Did the driver transport a load that was too heavy?
- Did the driver (or other employees) incorrectly stack the transported load?

### *Risk Management in Action*

Asking the types of questions presented in the previous example is risk management in action. While an organisation would hope the risk management process would prevent the incident in the first place, no process is perfect, so the organisation must analyse the underlying causes and take measures to prevent it in the future.

### *Frequency*

An organisation should monitor and communicate its event and loss experiences at regular intervals so it can take immediate action rather than at the end of the financial year or at the time when it renegotiates its renewal of insurance covers.

### *Documentation*

It is important for the organisation to carefully consider, document, and communicate any changes to its risk management programme (particularly risk control measures) resulting from loss reporting and trend analysis.

### *Risk Financing*

Regarding risk financing, the changes to an organisation's risk management programme may also provide the basis for premium incentives or penalties with respect to their insurance programme, and other risk financing techniques.

### *The Ultimate Goal*

The ultimate goal of a risk management programme is not just to treat and control an organisation's risk exposures but rather, to attempt to increase economic efficiency, i.e. profits in a for-profit company, while preventing losses (if possible).

---

**Self-Help Question 5.6**

GPG's risk management programme is now in place and management has stressed the importance of regular formal monitoring and review.

1. Review the information this module has presented about GPG as well as the information this section presented about event/loss reporting.
2. What information would a property loss/event report for GPG most likely contain?
3. What procedures could GPG implement to ensure the regular formal monitoring and review of:
   - individual risk exposures
   - the overall risk management programme?

---

Answers to self-help questions are provided at the end of each section.

---

### *Regular Reviews*

In addition to ongoing monitoring procedures, regular formal reviews of risk management processes and risk exposures should also be conducted to assess and document:

- the effectiveness of the risk treatment plan, strategies and management system
- the effectiveness of and adherence to risk treatment measures
- the relevance of the risk management plan to the organisation's objectives
- factors which may affect the likelihood and consequences of a risk exposure
- factors which affect the suitability or cost of treatment options
- board and management commitment to the risk management process.

Mechanisms need to be developed and implemented to ensure that regular reviews take place. The board and management of an organisation should take responsibility for making sure that a formal review of the organisation's risk management system, in accordance with the organisation's risk management plan, is carried out at regular intervals, such as annually.

The risk management system must remain relevant to the organisation at all times. As an organisation's circumstances are changing all the time, the regular review of previous risk management decisions is vital.

In reviewing each of the activities in the risk management process, it is essential that:

- the decisions made and the actions taken are checked to ensure that they are the most logical and effective;
- the actions taken (including any measures implemented) are working as expected and are bringing about the desired result;
- remedial action is taken to address those decisions or actions taken (including any measures implemented) that are not working or not having the desired effect – this remedial action should correct the situation.

To undertake a review of the management of risk, it is important to record details of:

- how often individual risk exposures and the risk management programme itself will be reviewed
- the outcomes of the review and any other monitoring procedures
- how review recommendations will be actioned.

### *Review Questions*

The review should ask the following questions:

- Are the risk management objectives aligned with the organisational performance objectives and values?

- Do the risk management initiatives reflect the realities of the environment in which the organisation in question operates?
- Are the outcomes of risk management able to be effectively measured?
- Do the risk management initiatives generate value for the organisation?
- Does the information provided allow senior management to make decisions about whether to expand or contract resources and effort in managing risk exposures?
- Is clear and concise information provided for evaluation by management and the board?

## Compliance Reviews

Companies also need to undertake a compliance review to assess the adequacy, effectiveness, and efficiency of an organisation's compliance culture, as well as the arrangements and measures designed to meet its legal and regulatory obligations. Ongoing compliance describes the ability of the compliance framework to enable compliance in the future at agreed levels and within agreed changes to the environment in which it operates. Past compliance describes a review of the compliance framework to determine whether it could ensure compliance to an agreed level over an agreed period.

A broad compliance review considers a company's overall regulatory framework, together with its business structure, culture, operational processes, supervision, and monitoring and reporting procedures. A compliance review may be requested by the board (or management) seeking to inform itself of the effectiveness of its compliance processes. Compliance reviews are often requested by regulators as part of enforcement activities, meaning that the standard required for reviews is high.

Compliance reviews often apply audit techniques, but they also differ from audits in several key ways.

*Audits* are performed by auditors in accordance with relevant legislation and regulations. They cover past events, determine the company's position at a specific point in time (such as 30 June) or over a specified period (such as the last financial year) and result in a written opinion in the form of an assurance being presented to the company for consideration.

*Compliance* reviews look at frameworks and processes the company has in place to comply with its legal and regulatory obligations going forward. They assess the compliance culture, the quality and effectiveness of the compliance processes and the effectiveness of the compliance programme and its interrelationship with the risk management and governance programmes.

Compliance reviews are not usually conducted at regular intervals and may be linked to quite specific issues, such as:

- regulatory enforcement – e.g. enforceable undertakings
- takeover due diligence
- contractual requirements – e.g. as part of a loan or outsourcing agreements.

Where there is legislation requiring audits be undertaken at times or at regular intervals, care must be taken to ensure this is done.

Compliance reviews may be commissioned by a company itself to test the effectiveness of its compliance programme or by a regulator seeking assurance that all agreed compliance procedures are in place and will remain effective going forward. The basis for the review is established in the review plan. Sometimes there is a requirement that the parties agree on a review plan that states the reason for the review and clearly defines what will be covered, the level of review and the reviewer's obligations in terms of a breach and the period to be covered by the review.

A compliance review should include in its final report the reviewer's observations in relation to:

- whether the company has in place the systems and resources to enable it to comply with the law
- whether the necessary elements of the compliance standard are being used for benchmarking purposes
- the nature of the corporate compliance culture
- the adequacy of compliance resources and systems
- the level of 'business ownership' for compliance
- the adequacy of supervision and monitoring
- the effective communication of the compliance policy
- the links between compliance, risk management, and governance
- the level of comfort in relation to whether the company's management knows what the company is doing and has a desire to improve
- the level of reliance on key staff
- the ability of the compliance programme to adapt to planned changes in the company's strategic direction or operations
- external factors that may impact on the company's ability to meet its ongoing compliance obligations in the light of changes to legislation or regulatory event.

Some regulators have issued their own position statements in relation to compliance reviews and the requirements.

**EXAMPLE**

**The Australian Competition and Consumer Commission (ACCC)**

The ACCC issued a position statement in relation to Trade Practices compliance reviews being carried out for the purposes of an enforceable undertaking.

The company requires detailed and comprehensive information on the performance of its compliance program, which may include:

- if, and to what extent, the trade practices compliance program includes all the elements required by the undertaking
- if, and to what extent, the company compliance policy includes all the elements required by the undertaking
- if, and to what extent, the trade practices compliance program covers the parties identified in an initial Trade Practices Act risk assessment conducted in accordance with the undertaking
- if, and to what extent, the trade practices training is carried out and is effective
- if, and to what extent, the Company's complaints handling system is effective
- if, and to what extent, the Company can provide confidentiality and security to whistle-blowers, and staff are aware of the whistle-blower protection mechanisms
- actions recommended by the reviewer to ensure the continuing effectiveness of the company's trade practices compliance program.

The ACCC requirements were for information that may include:

- details of the evidence gathered and examined during the review
- the name and relevant experience of the person appointed as the company compliance officer
- the reviewer's opinion on whether the company has complied with the Trade Practices compliance component of the undertaking
- actions recommended by the reviewer to ensure the continuing effectiveness of the company's trade practices compliance programme
- confirmation that any actual and potential inadequacies in the company's compliance programme have been brought to the attention of the compliance officer and the governing body
- confirmation that the reviewer has revisited any actual and potential inadequacies in the company's trade practices compliance programme identified in any previous review
- any reservations that the reviewer might have about the reliability and completeness of the information to which the reviewer had access in the conduct and reporting of the review; and
- any comments or qualifications concerning the review process that the reviewer, in his or her professional opinion, considers necessary.

As in the case of auditors, the person responsible for reviewing the compliance should be independent. This means that they:

- did not design or implement the compliance programme;
- are not an existing or past employee or director;

- have not acted and do not act for the organisation in compliance matters being reviewed;
- have not and do not consult to the organisation or provide other services on compliance related matters other than the compliance review;
- have no significant shareholding or other interests in the organisation.

## Summary

Please keep the following points from this topic in mind:

- The ongoing monitoring of activities, actions, systems, benefits and losses is a vital part of the success of the application of the risk management programme. People, products and activities are the focus of the monitoring process. A risk management programme needs both formal and informal monitoring and review processes.
- The most common reasons for monitoring the risk management programme are to:

  - ensure performance targets are met
  - properly allocate funds to the risk management programme
  - meet statutory reporting requirements
  - identify new and/or changed exposures to risk
  - defend the risk management programme
  - ensure performance targets are met
  - properly allocate funds to the risk management programme
  - meet statutory reporting requirements
  - identify new and/or changed exposures to risk
  - defend the risk management programme
  - review the performance of the risk management programme.

- Establishing and maintaining unexpected event and loss reporting programmes is an effective way to monitor and review incidences of loss. Reporting programmes provide valuable information on which future decisions about risk exposures and treatment and financing can be made.
- A loss report should include items such as:

  - details of individual losses
  - third party recovery action
  - claims outstanding and reasons why.

- Types of statistical data used to identify trends include:

  - time series analysis
  - event frequency

- seasonal peaks
- value comparison
- trend projections.

- Regular formal monitoring and review of a risk management programme is conducted to assess:
  - the effectiveness of the risk treatment plan, strategies and management system
  - the effectiveness of control measures
  - the relevance of the management plan
  - factors which may affect the likelihood and consequences of a risk
  - factors which affect the suitability or cost of treatment options
  - management commitment to the risk management process.

- A compliance review is the process undertaken to assess the adequacy, effectiveness and efficiency of an organisation's compliance culture, as well with its arrangements and measures to meet its legal and regulatory obligations.
- Compliance reviews often apply audit techniques, but they also differ from audits in several key ways.
- Compliance reviews may be commissioned by a company itself to test the effectiveness of its compliance programme or by a regulator seeking assurance that all agreed compliance procedures are in place and will remain effective going forward.

---

**Answers to Self-Help Questions**

**Self-help question 5.1**

Insightful Insurance's monitoring and review regime for their risk treatment plan for the SME division:

1. The COO should be reporting to the CEO regarding the progress of implementation of the plan because it is a strategic risk for the organisation.
2. ERM results and risk analysis must be an input for Internal Audit. The results of the ERM analysis can be integrated into the audit plan and used for the evaluation of Risk Management practices. If the audit shows a less than expected level of effectiveness, Risk Management should re-evaluate the final exposure as well as the related internal controls.
3. The Internal Audit Manager would most likely have the authority required to assess progress of implementation because they would not usually report to the COO and would report to a board audit committee or the CEO. They would also normally have the authority to follow up on the business's response to an audit finding.

→

→

**Self-help question 5.2**

1. Items that could be reviewed to assess the quality of construction of the COO's risk treatment plan include:
   - whether the plan considered the breadth of the target audience, which included both senior and junior underwriters
   - whether the plan was written in appropriate language
   - the inclusion of an appropriate cost–benefit analysis. For example, was there an analysis of the cost of narrowing the business base versus the impact on profitability? Similarly, was the cost of training considered against the likely benefits?
   - the clarity of the plan in articulating the baselines against which the plan would be measured
   - the method and frequency of reporting.

2. The major problem with assessing the overall effectiveness of the COO's risk treatment plan is that there are many other factors that can affect the profitability of the division. These include movement in costs in other areas of the division and changes in competition in the SME insurance market.

**Self-help question 5.3**

It is necessary to identify the entire population of risk treatment plans across an organisation when conducting a statistical analysis exercise so that the random sample is representative of the entire population and that the resultant estimates for the entire population based on the sample are as accurate as possible.

**Self-help question 5.4**

1. The most critical elements of a successful monitoring and review regime are the following:

   - independence of the monitoring and review function;
   - senior management commitment;
   - clear responsibilities and time frames for delivery, with those responsible having sufficient authority to deliver.

2. When building performance criteria for monitoring and review, an organisation needs to monitor and review the following:
   - the quality of treatment plans – by reviewing whether plans meet the organisation's policy on preparing plans and whether sufficient detail is included in plans
   - the timeliness of implementation – by reviewing the overall timeliness of implementation of plans across the organisation, not just individual plans
   - the effectiveness of treatment plans – by monitoring the number of risk events that occur before and after risk treatments are put into place.

→

→

3. The main reason for using statistics in monitoring and review is to minimise monitoring and review resources by randomly sampling risk treatment plans for review and using statistical methods to estimate the quality, timeliness and effectiveness of the entire population of risk treatment plans.

**Self-help question 5.5**

The following table lists the factors XYZ Planning Authority needs to consider when monitoring its risk management programme.

| Factor | Description |
|---|---|
| **Changes in the legislation** | • Will lead to new risks for XYZ in its regulatory role<br>• Management needs to examine the legislative changes and the associated risks<br>• Management also needs to assess and document these risks and the related controls in the risk register |
| **Licensing system replacement** | • IT change programmes are notoriously risky, often failing to deliver on functionality and in accordance with the original budget<br>• The risk manager should sponsor a project risk assessment to identify and document:<br>– the project risks<br>– how to manage these project risks |
| **Board Turnover** | • Board members are one of the most important stakeholder categories<br>• The new board may have different:<br>– needs from the risk management process<br>– risk appetites to that which the previous board agreed<br>• The risk manager needs to meet with the chair to:<br>– determine a process to address these issues<br>– review the risk reporting the organisation is providing to the board to ensure it is relevant and timely |
| **Management stability** | • No action other than to routinely review the risk profile |
| **Executive meetings** | • Managements review of the risk profile should address this issue in terms of the currency of the risk data<br>• The risk management review should also discuss the issue with the CEO to:<br>– understand why it has fallen off the agenda<br>– agree to either revert to including risk management on the agenda; or<br>– agree on an alternative technique to ensure the executive is regularly monitoring the risk profile |

→

→

**Self-help question 5.6**

GPG's risk management programme is now in place and management has stressed the importance of regular formal monitoring and review.

1. GPG's property event/loss report might contain some of the following information:

   - the specific insurance policies applicable
   - brief details of the item/property insured and claims deductible (if applicable)
   - the date and time of the event
   - associated loss or damage
   - the specific location of the event (including loss/damage), including the precise location of any machine/plant item that may be involved
   - the cause of the event/incident and how the loss/damage occurred
   - the amount of loss/damage
   - if the item/property was repaired or replaced
   - who is undertaking the repair/replacement and the time frame
   - details of any third parties and associated damage (if applicable)
   - if third parties may be responsible for the loss/damage and what recovery action can be taken against these parties
   - details of the notification of the incident/event to police
   - any remedial action taken to avoid similar incidents
   - other parties involved (for example, a finance company may have a commercial interest in a plant item)
   - consequential interruption to the organisation or other parties
   - details of external reports (for example, coronial inquiry)
   - review of contractual liabilities arising from the incident/event
   - names and details of any government authorities involved in the incident/event.

2. Individual risk exposure monitoring techniques GPG could implement include:

   - incident/accident reports
   - a copy of the insurance company claims reports
   - property/liability surveys (industry reports/statistics)
   - monitoring compliance with statutory reporting requirements (for example, accident reporting requirements under various WHS Acts)
   - technical information.

→

→

*GPG can monitor the overall risk management programme by:*

- developing a formalised plan which should include regular meetings to:
- discuss any changes in the risk profile or the organisation's operations
- ensure the organisation undertakes any necessary or recommended actions
- developing a board/management risk management policy statement
- training key managers/personnel
- conducting an organisational risk exposure review
- developing reporting and monitoring systems.

# Chapter 6

# Risk Reporting

## Introduction

The previous section described the importance of organisational structure and communication channels in effective decision-making. The section also examines the vertical flow of information in a down-up direction.

This section describes the importance of management reporting with respect to the down-up communication of information, including the purpose and benefits of reporting from a business and legal perspective. This section also addresses the what, why, when, and how of reporting on risk management strategies.

## Learning Outcomes

After completing this section, you should be able to:

- define corporate governance;
- understand the integral role reporting plays in the management process and decision making;
- identify the different reporting methods and types;
- describe the importance of a risk reporting framework.

### *Internal Reporting*

Bartol et al. (2005) state that a report is essentially the result of transforming data into information useful for:

- planning
- decision-making
- coordination
- control.

**Risk Measurement and Monitoring, 115–140**

**Published under exclusive licence by Emerald Publishing Limited**
**doi:10.1108/978-1-83662-310-620251015**

**Self-Help Question 6.1**

Record a few of your ideas regarding why information is important to senior management. Focus specifically on what information allows senior management to do (for example, compliance with regulatory and statutory requirements).

Answers to self-help questions are provided at the end of each section.

Reporting is an essential component of the management process and forms a key element of formal down-up communication. Reporting provides key decision-makers with crucial information to help steer the organisation towards its objectives and goals. Reporting is essential because the executive management team and the board are ultimately accountable for the performance of the organisation and need to fully understand existing material risks and how they are being managed.

Although reporting is integral to the entire management process, it sits most comfortably within the management controlling function, which relates to obtaining information about the effectiveness of the entire management process. This information-gathering focuses on addressing the following question:

> Are the tasks that we are carrying out, because of the direction provided by our plans, effectively achieving the organisation's goals?

Managing the reporting process is a crucial element in the organisation's overall information system. Without managing the process, the organisation would fail to use the information the data provided for effective management and achieving organisational goals.

The more common reporting methods include:

- risk profile reports summarising all the risks in excess of an agreed threshold (usually risks exceeding an agreed combination of likelihood and consequence);
- reporting on the status of control improvement plans;
- presenting individual and material risk exposures;
- risk alerts when risk events exceed a pre-determined threshold;
- separate reports on risks requiring close monitoring (such as major projects or WHS).

The level of detail required in reports varies as different organisations have different complexities and individuals receiving reports have their own views on the level of detail required.

**Activity | Reporting**

1. Consider your organisation's risk reporting.
2. Summarise the reports your organisation prepares for the executive and the board.
3. Consider whether this information provides an effective overview of risks and how the organisation is managing the risks.
4. Could the format be improved?
5. Is there clarity involving when to report the risks and risk thresholds?
6. Does your organisation provide this information on a regular basis?
7. Document your critique of your organisation's risk reports and any ideas that could improve these risk reports.

| Criteria | Evaluation | Improvement opportunity |
|---|---|---|
| **Content** | | |
| **Timeliness** | | |
| **Format and quality** | | |
| **Relevance** | | |
| **Accuracy** | | |

### *Management Report Types*

There are many different reports a manager may need to prepare, which depend on the purpose of the reported information. For example, there may be requirements to report:

- within a department
- down-ups to another hierarchical level
- horizontally to another department within the same hierarchical level
- externally; for example, to:
  - regulatory bodies
  - funding bodies
  - economic partners (customers and suppliers)
  - shareholders.

Management reports can be categorised by the following main functions:

- maintaining corporate governance
- planning and executing strategy
- reporting against business requirements.

### *Maintaining Corporate Governance*

Company directors are accountable for ensuring the organisation is compliant with legislation. This compliance is designed to mitigate corporate failures and criminal acts.

Depending on the organisational structure, it is rare for senior managers or the board to have direct access to the information required to make decisions about:

- running the organisation
- the organisation's strategic direction.

The organisation needs to develop a reporting system to facilitate the comprehensive flow of information so the senior management team and board of directors can ensure they are meeting their legislative obligations.

#### *Benefits*

A reporting system can ensure the organisation:

- understands its compliance requirements;
- fulfils any legal requirements to report externally (for example, to report OHS incidents);
- can monitor performance against organisational goals (including the impact of key individuals on these);
- understands its key areas of risk and any existing mitigation strategies;
- can assess if the existing mitigating controls are fulfilling their requirements.

---

**Self-Help Question 6.2**

List five types of reports your organisation uses to fulfil its internal reporting requirements (for example, staff appraisals).

Answers to self-help questions are provided at the end of each section.

---

**Self-Help Question 6.3**

List three examples of external stakeholders to which your organisation needs to report (for example, funding bodies).

Answers to self-help questions are provided at the end of each section.

---

### Planning and Executing Strategy

An important element of planning is the ability to monitor the success of the plan and its effect on organisational change with respect to achieving the organisation's established goals.

#### KPIs

Implementing and monitoring a management plan requires the organisation to establish key performance indicators (KPIs). The organisation monitors the plan against these associated KPIs.

KPIs may refer to measures for monitoring (or evaluating) the efficiency or effectiveness of a system. Organisations may use KPIs to demonstrate accountability and to identify areas for improvement.

KPIs are usually very specific in nature; for example:

> To increase sales by 20 per cent within a 12-month period.

#### Progress Reports (Project Updates)

A manager can easily report on the progress against KPIs (like the previous example) to:

- show how quickly the target is being reached;
- identify any obstacles preventing the target from being achieved.

Reports in this category are usually known as progress reports or project updates.

---

**Self-Help Question 6.4**

Record your ideas on what you believe a progress report would typically contain (for example, progress against established KPIs).

---

Answers to self-help questions are provided at the end of each section.

---

#### Benefits

In summary, the benefits of management reporting with respect to strategic planning and execution include:

- enabling key decision makers to monitor the plan implementation progress;
- ensuring the direction, the organisation takes is consistent with its established goals;
- assisting the organisation to make decision/s regarding the need to change course.

**Activity | Progress reporting**

Access a management report in your organisation that is designed to report progress against a pre-established plan. This may be for a specific project, or an operational report against a business plan or strategic plan.

Using the suggested contents of the progress report listed above, review the report and identify whether there are any:

- key information missing
- additional information that may be useful to the intended audience.

### *Reporting Against Business Requirements*

In addition to monitoring progress against the planned implementation of strategy, there are many reasons for management to report against standard business requirements.

Although these requirements affect the organisation's ability to achieve its organisational goals, they are separate from monitoring progress against an organisational plan.

This information is crucial for the executive managers of the organisation to ensure the business is running effectively.

**EXAMPLE**

**Sufficient Business Funding**

The chief financial officer (CFO) is responsible for ensuring the organisation has sufficient cash in the bank to meet its ongoing financial requirements, including accounts payable and staff remuneration requirements. This is a business requirement (not a strategic requirement) but could have a significant effect on the organisation's ability to achieve its strategic goals.

**Self-Help Question 6.5**

Managers are required to provide reports on a regular basis against standard business requirements (for example, financial performance). List five other business requirements.

Answers to self-help questions are provided at the end of each section.

There are many benefits associated with such business requirement reporting, including:

- providing day-to-day information required to manage and coordinate the organisation;
- ensuring the company's product or service meets market demands.

### *Variation Reporting*

Another major part of monitoring and review is the establishment of a *variation reporting programme* to provide detailed information about the nature of variations from the expected that an organisation has experienced over a particular period of time.

Variation reporting is only suitable for risk events an organisation can easily define and measure, for example:

- Workplace Health & Safety (WHS) incidents
- compliance breaches
- vehicle accidents.

#### *Loss Reporting Programmes*

In loss reporting programs, organisations need to capture details of *near miss* and *below the retention* loss events. They analyse these details to form a complete picture of the success of the risk management programme.

Details regarding near miss and below the retention loss events enable an organisation to:

- learn from all past incidents;
- determine if risk management is having a positive effect on the organisation through reducing the number of incidents and severity.

### *Event/Loss Reports*

An organisation must establish an effective event/loss reporting programme to monitor and review its loss incidents. An effective event/loss reporting programme informs the organisation about the risk exposures that have resulted in a negative impact over a particular period.

Event/loss reports provide valuable information about the:

- nature of unexpected events and associated consequences
- likelihood and the consequence of an event
- underlying causes.

The organisation can use this information to determine:

- trends
- the future requirements of the organisation's risk management programme (particularly its risk treatment plans)
- any risk financing arrangements.

Before implementing an event/loss reporting programme, the organisation needs to determine the following factors so it can easily analyse associated information at a later date:

- categories of required information
- the reporting formats.

### *Reporting Programme Requirements*

The programme should be:

- comprehensive
- reliable
- accurate
- electronically accessible
- user friendly.

A comprehensive loss reporting programme should:

- pinpoint specific risk exposures which have resulted in a loss
- provide valuable information about:
  - trends
  - considerations for lessening (and possibly eliminating) the effects of such risk exposures in the future.

### *Mandatory Event/Loss Reporting Obligations*

Mandatory event/loss reporting obligations may also be a necessary part of operating a business in a particular industry. As such, some organisations may already have established event/loss reporting systems to report losses or incidents such as electrical breakdowns and workplace injuries.

**Activity | Event/loss reporting**

1. If possible, access your organisation's event/loss report.
2. Answer the following questions:
   - Who is responsible for the loss reporting programme?
   - What is the standard content and circulation of the report?
   - How does your organisation maintain/update the loss reporting as required?
   - How does your organisation tailor the loss reporting facility to meet the needs of particular departments/business units?
   - What are your organisation's follow-up procedures to ensure it actions identified problem areas?

### *Managing and Analysing Reports*

The manager has the following two key roles in relation to the management report, both of which involve applying skills of analysis:

1. preparing a report for down-up communication
2. reviewing and analysing received reports.

**1. Preparing a report for down-up communication**

A report is a mechanism for communicating information. The manager must ensure the information is suitable and that it appropriately communicates the intended message. The information must also be useful and appropriate, otherwise it may send the wrong message or confuse the recipient, which may lead to incorrect decision making.

***Four characteristics of useful information***

Davidson and Griffin (2003) theorise that information should align with the four characteristics outlined in the following table to be useful.

**Four Characteristics of Useful Information**

| Characteristic | Description |
|---|---|
| **Accurate** | • the information must provide a valid and reliable reflection of reality to be of value to a manager |
| **Timely** | • does not necessarily mean speediness; it means information needs to be available in time for the appropriate managerial action<br>• what constitutes timeliness is a function of the situation |
| **Complete** | • information must tell a complete story for it to be useful to a manager<br>• if information is less than complete, the manager is likely to get an inaccurate or distorted picture of reality |
| **Relevant** | • information must be relevant if it is to be useful to managers<br>• relevance, like timeliness, is defined according to the needs and circumstances of a particular manager:<br>– operations managers need information on costs and productivity<br>– human resource managers need information on recruitment needs and turnover rates<br>– marketing managers need information on sales projections and advertising rates |

The previously defined characteristics clearly indicate the role of the report-writing manager in ensuring they report information to achieve reporting requirement objectives.

*Case Study – Information Characteristics*

## The quarterly HR reports

Anish, a HR manager of a small retail chain, is responsible for quarterly reporting to the executive team and the CEO regarding:

- staffing requirements for the company
- any major staff management risks that may affect the company's ability to achieve its sales targets.

The report is predominately a verbal report, with any associated data provided in a written summary format.

## Greta's replicated report

Anish takes compassionate leave due to the sudden death of a close family member and the HR department consequently operates without a manager for most of June. A few days before the HR quarterly report is due, the CFO approaches Greta (one of the senior HR officers) to request that she present the HR quarterly report at the end of the month.

Unaware of what the report should include, Greta attempts to replicate an old report with data from the previous quarter. The HR staff and retail outlet managers provide her with the required information. Greta forwards the report to the executive committee, confident she has appropriately completed her task.

## Unresolved staffing issues

Some weeks later, one of the retail outlets reports they are understaffed due to several their casual employees. This remaining understaffing will significantly affect the sales figures of that outlet for the coming months, until the organisation can employ and train new staff.

Another outlet reports that their levels of staff do not meet the increased volume of customers they are experiencing because of a new marketing programme.

The executive team's investigation reveals several unresolved staffing-related issues emerged during May and June, leading to staff frustration and dissatisfaction.

## The June report review

A review of the June report reveals there were several discrepancies in the data, including:

- no mention of potential industrial relations issues concerning casual employees
- no recommendations for increased staffing levels to meet expected increases in demand.

Greta was unaware of the planned marketing campaign and was not in a position to provide a recommendation for staffing levels. In addition, Greta was unaware of the requirement to identify and report potential industrial relations issues, which Anish usually reported verbally.

**Self-Help Question 6.6**

1. List the issues with the case study HR report in terms of the four characteristics of useful information.

| Characteristic | Issues |
|---|---|
| Accurate | |
| Timely | |
| Complete | |
| Relevant | |

2. How could this situation have been improved?

Answers to self-help questions are provided at the end of each section.

## *2 Reviewing and analysing received reports*

As previously described, the overall purpose of a management report is to provide key information needed for decision-making. It is essential that the manager receiving the report is aware of the need to process the information in the report and to act on it as required.

Managers at all levels of an organisation are required to make decisions based on received information. This decision may simply be to escalate the information to the next line of management, or may require more complex levels of decision-making in relation to organising, leading and control.

Regardless of the report type, there will be a requirement for the manager to effectively analyse the presented information and to determine what actions (if any) need to be taken.

**EXAMPLE**

**A Progress Report Against a Project Plan**

A progress report against a project plan may identify that the project is at risk of exceeding the budget. The role of the manager responsible for the project (the project sponsor) is to act on that information to determine why the project will exceed the budget and how that can be prevented, or possibly to seek commitment for more funding. The manager needs to communicate this outcome back to the project team so they are aware of their requirements in relation to the changing circumstances.

***The manager's role***

The role of the manager in analysing a management report involves considering the:

- characteristics of the provided information
- required key information for decision making
- required actions
- distribution of findings.

***Characteristics of the information provided***

Before taking any action, the manager receiving the report needs to assess if any elements of the report do not appear consistent with expectations. The manager should look for specific indicators or ask those responsible for preparing the report a series of questions to confirm the provided information is reliable and accurate. For example, the presented data should have a stated time frame and specify the report authors. In addition, the manager may seek clarification on the source of the data and the extraction and collation methodology.

***Required key information for decision-making***

The manager needs to analyse the report information to determine the critical elements required for decision making (the indicators alerting the manager action needs to be taken). For example, the report may include a comparison of data against pre-determined benchmarks or KPIs.

The information required for decision making may be part of the report or it may be a manager's responsibility to conduct this comparison on receipt of the report. The manager may intuitively be able to identify these indicators or they may be documented as part of the report.

***Required actions***

After analysing the information, the manager must determine:

- *where* they need to act
- *what* those actions are
- *who* is responsible
- *when* the actions need to be taken.

> **EXAMPLE**
>
> **Operational Performance Variation**
>
> Because of a variation in operational performance, there may be a need to modify an operational process. The impact this variation has on overall organisational success determines if this action is critical.

It is essential that the organisation assigns responsibility for ensuring they act and specify a time frame.

### *Distribution of Findings*

After identifying management actions, it is essential for the organisation to communicate this information to those affected. This may require using down-up, top-down, and horizontal communication channels, as explored in Chapter 1.

- *Top-down communication:* The person responsible needs to understand what is expected, so top-down communication may be required.
- *Down-up communication:* The action may also be communicated down-up to inform decision-makers higher in the hierarchy about the decisions that have been made and on what basis.
- *Horizontal communication:* Horizontal communication may need to take place because other departments (e.g. human resources or finance) may also be affected by the actions.

---

**Self-Help Question 6.7**

What would be the potential effects of a manager failing to communicate the findings of the management report analysis?

---

Answers to self-help questions are provided at the end of each section.

## Risk Management Reporting

As discussed, reporting is essential for management process success. As an integral component of effective management, the organisation must establish requirements for reporting risk.

Previous sections in this module briefly described the risk reporting framework. This subsection explores the framework in more detail, specifically addressing the requirements of managers in reporting risk.

### *Risk Reporting Framework*

The reporting framework provides the infrastructure required for escalating risk information throughout the organisation. This can be diagrammatically presented as shown in the following figure.

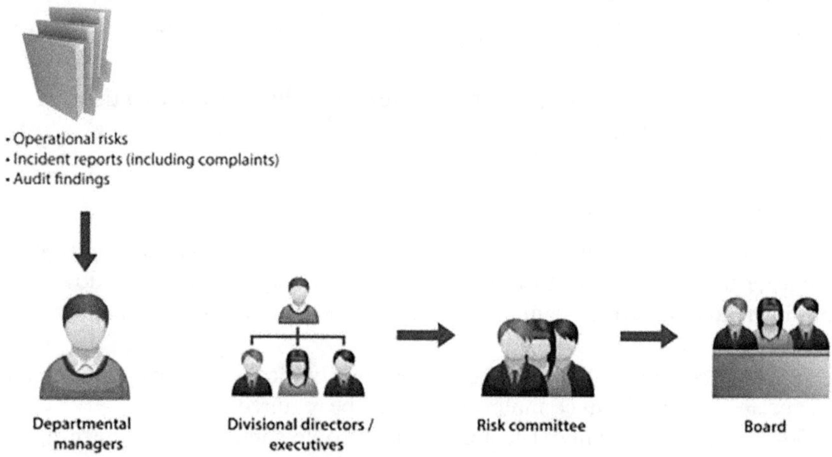


**Example – Risk Reporting Framework**

### *Down-Up Communication*

The risk reporting structure involves the down-up flow of information regarding risk. This down-up information flow provides key decision makers with the information required to effectively make decisions about how the organisation conducts its business, in the context of the risks to which the organisation is exposed.

Risk reporting enables a strategic view of risk to be gained, and risk-based information to be used in the decision-making process.

The risk reporting process involves identifying risk at the operational levels of the organisation, and reporting these risks up through the hierarchy, in accordance with the risk management framework. The level to which risks are reported depends on the risk management accountability framework, which dictates:

- the owner of the risk
- those with the authority to make decisions regarding the control techniques applicable to the risk.

EXAMPLE

**Organisational Unit Managers**

Organisational unit managers may be able to decide to tolerate low levels of risk exposure on behalf of the organisation, but higher levels of risk should be reported to senior management or even the board before a decision can be made to either:

- tolerate a risk
- reduce the risk to a level that can be managed.

### *Frequency of Risk Reporting*

Organisations may conduct an exercise to profile risk and report across the organisation on an annual (for example) or more frequent basis.

This is not the only time that staff members should report risk. Risk reporting is an ongoing requirement, which is integral to the overall management reporting system.

### *Risk Reporting Requirements*

The responsibility and accountability framework should clearly identify that risk management is the business of all those involved in the organisation. This framework should show that all staff members are responsible for identifying and reporting risk, as well as having a role in managing risk effectively.

### *Potential Sources of Risk Reporting*

Risk reporting does not just include reporting risk management implementation plans or documenting risks in a risk register. Risk reporting can take several forms, and managers need to be aware of where risks can be reported to ensure these are captured and communicated effectively.

The following table lists potential sources of risk reporting.

**Potential Sources of Risk Reporting**

| Source | Purpose |
|---|---|
| Operational management reports | May identify specific areas of risk pertinent to the day-to-day management of the business |
| Incident reports | Often link to an existing identified risk, but may also be linked to a risk that had not previously been identified |
| Project progress reports | Can identify risks associated with not achieving project goals |
| Staff performance reports | May identify specific staffing risks |

| | |
|---|---|
| Exit interview reports | • Often contain information regarding risk<br>• For example, if a person has left due to dissatisfaction, they may discuss the cause of their dissatisfaction in their exit interview rather than raising it earlier (such as poor management styles, bullying, or poor safety conditions) |
| Client contracts | • Contain various areas of risk about which the organisation will need to be aware |

The number of potential sources of risk reporting highlights why it is essential that the risk management implementation plan is integrated within the entire management process and management systems. This is so organisations capture, analyse, and evaluate risk-based information before acting.

**Self-Help Question 6.8**

What are some of the negative consequences of failing to capture risks reported by the various management reports described within the risk management implementation plan?

Answers to self-help questions are provided at the end of each section.

**Activity | Risk reporting requirements**

Access your organisation's risk management policy and associated guidelines or framework document.

- Have the reporting requirements for risk been clearly identified?
- What additional information could you recommend for reporting risk within your organisation?

### *Analysing Risk Management Reports*

Whether the manager is analysing an operational report, or a report specifically designed to report risk (for example, a risk management implementation plan), they need to ensure that:

- the information provided is consistent with the previously highlighted information characteristics;
- the risk management implementation plan identifies and captures any risks.

Regarding analysing specific risk management reports (such as the risk management implementation plan), questions the manager may ask to identify the specific characteristics they need to consider could include those in the following checklist.

**Checklist to Identify Specific Risk Management Report Characteristics**

| Question | Yes | No |
|---|---|---|
| Is the context of the risk management implementation plan and risk assessment clear? | □ | □ |
| Have the external and internal contexts been described? | □ | □ |
| Is the risk management context appropriate? | □ | □ |
| Is it clear that the report has been written for the appropriate audience? | □ | □ |
| Have the appropriate stakeholders been identified and engaged? | □ | □ |
| Is a communication log provided? | □ | □ |
| Is the methodology clearly stated? | □ | □ |
| Is this appropriate for the context of the risk assessment? | □ | □ |
| Does the report identify any limitations encountered as part of the risk assessment exercise – for example, time constraints, availability of key stakeholders? | □ | □ |
| Does the report identify any assumptions that need to be made in reading the report – for example, that the information provided during the risk assessment was accurate? | □ | □ |
| Are the risks presented in an appropriate format – for example, consistent with the templates provided? | □ | □ |
| Do the risks appear appropriate for the context? Are there any obvious exclusions or inclusions? | □ | □ |
| Have the risks been worded appropriately – are they objective in nature and provide an indication of causal factor and impact? | □ | □ |
| Have the risks been rated in context of existing controls? If not, is it clear that the risk rating is the 'inherent' risk? | □ | □ |
| Are the risk ratings consistent with the tool provided, and are they appropriate? | □ | □ |
| Have existing controls been identified? | □ | □ |
| Is there a recommended risk treatment plan provided? Is it clear how the decisions regarding these recommended treatments were made – for example, cost–benefit? | □ | □ |
| Does the risk treatment plan clearly state the action required, the person responsible for the action, and a timeframe for the action? | □ | □ |
| Has the methodology for monitoring and reviewing the risks, existing controls and the treatment required been documented? | □ | □ |

The requirements of the risk management implementation plan determine the level of provided information (for example, the purpose of the report or its intended audience). Managers should analyse reports with these pre-defined requirements in mind.

**Activity | Analysing risk management reports**

Locate a risk assessment report, either from within your organisation or on the internet.

Analyse the report to determine whether the information is accurate, timely, complete, and reliable using the previous list of questions about analysing characteristics of risk management reports.

## External Reporting

External reports are financial statements that organisations prepare for public consumption. Depending on the organisation, they may or may not differ from internal reports. The key is for the reports to present a complete and accurate picture of the organisation's financial position so that investors and stakeholders can easily understand it. Reports can be considered a global decision-making tool for boards and external stakeholders.

External reporting leads to increased transparency, which leads to more and better information being published, which leads to better decision-making. It is known that analysts, scientists and investors base their analyses on publicly available information, so that information should be as accurate and comprehensive as possible. Better analyses lead to better understanding, which leads to better outcomes.

Better outcomes are at the forefront of current discussions, with the Paris Agreement designed to improve climate change outcomes and the CSR initiatives listed in Chapter 3 designed to improve environmental and human rights outcomes. They are also behind the recent legislative amendment establishing requirements for non-financial reporting.

### *Legislation*

Directive 2014/95/EU, an amendment to Directive 2013/34/EU, requires public-interest companies with more than 500 employees to publish non-financial statements covering specific information. This information must be disclosed annually from 2018 onwards. The intention is to provide investors and shareholders with a more complete picture of their position and to encourage such companies to develop their approach to CSR.

The non-financial statements required by this Directive are reports that cover an organisation's development, performance and position, as well as the effects of its activities in relation to:

- environmental protection
- social responsibility and treatment of employees

- respect for human rights
- anti-corruption and bribery
- diversity on boards.

The report must include:

- a brief description of the organisation's business model
- a description of organisational policies, including due diligence processes
- the outcomes of organisational policies
- principal risks faced by the organisation and the risk treatment measures in place
- non-financial KPIs
- where applicable, explanations of amounts reported in financial statements.

In June 2017, the European Commission published guidelines to the Directive 2014/95/EU to support companies in the preparation of this non-financial statement. Although they do not refer specifically to enterprise risk management (ERM), the Guidelines mention concepts of risk management.

The guidelines do not add any legal requirements to the NFR directive, nor are they mandatory. They do not prescribe reporting guidelines or standards but they recommend a few of them, such as the UN Guiding Principles on Business and Human Rights, ISO 26000, or the German Sustainability Code.

They also consider the 2015 UN COP21 Paris Climate Agreement, with the disclosure of information on the actual and potential impacts of the organisation's activities on the environment, especially regarding the reduction of greenhouse gas emissions.

The guidelines recommend the use of scenario analyses and appropriate assessments of likelihood. These concepts were not present initially in the 2014/95 Directive.

A second set of guidelines on reporting climate-related information was issued on June 2019. They consist of a new supplement to the existing Non-Financial Reporting Guidelines. They provide companies with recommendations on how to better report the impact that their activities are having on the climate and the impact of climate change on their business.

They explicitly recommend businesses to:

- Categorise the principal risks of climate change on the financial performance of the company according to whether they arise from the transition to a low carbon economy (policy, legal, technological, market, and reputational), or physical risks from the direct effects of climate change (acute and chronic).
- Disclose any risk mapping that includes climate-related issues.
- Provide definitions of risk terminology used or references to existing risk classification frameworks used.
- Describe links between principal climate-related risks and key financial performance indicators.

While the basic content of the statements has been described, the way organisations prepare their reports has been left to their individual discretion. The basic obligation is that an organisation either complies with a Standard or explains why they cannot.

There are several guidelines available to assist organisations to produce their statements. These include:

- the European Commission guidelines on non-financial reporting
- the UN Global Compact (refer to CSR section)
- OECD guidelines for multinational enterprises
- ISO 26000.

Read more about non-financial reporting on the European Commission's website (search for non-financial reporting).

**Activity | External reporting and CSR**

If you work for a large company, consider the above reporting requirements in connection with your organisation.

- Do you already track the required data?
- Would you need to change the way you develop internal reports to suit these requirements?
- Which of the available guidelines do you think would best suit your organisation's reporting needs?

## *The Role of Risk Managers in External Reporting*

Although it is not explicit in the new Directive or the guidelines, the risk manager has a fundamental role to play in external reporting, especially given the new non-financial requirements. FERMA outlined the role in its Position Paper of 15 April 2016, 'Response to the European Commission consultation on non-financial reporting guidelines', and its position is referred to throughout the following section.

### *ERM and External Reporting*

Before exploring the risk manager's role in non-financial reporting, it is useful to revisit what ERM is. As defined in ISO 31000:2018, the ERM model is the framework:

> that integrates the process for managing risk into the organisation's overall governance, strategy and planning, management, reporting processes, policies, values and culture.

It is a framework that operates across an entire organisation, and that is present in every department. A sound risk management framework should have identified, analysed, and evaluated all risks facing an organisation, including social, environmental and political threats, and have devised ways to either reduce or remove the risks. It should have also determined who the relevant stakeholders are, how to best communicate and consult with them, and have established monitoring and reviewing regimes.

Three of the risk management principles spelled out in ISO 31000:2018 state that risk management should:

- *create value*
  Risk management should contribute to the demonstrable achievement of objectives and improvement of, for example, efficiency in operations, environmental protection, financial performance, corporate governance, human health and safety, product quality, legal and regulatory compliance, public acceptance, and reputation.
- *be an integral part of organisational processes*
  Risk management should be part of the responsibilities of management and an integral part of the normal organisational processes as well as of all project and change management processes. Risk management should not be a stand-alone activity or be separate from the main activities and processes of the organisation.
- *be transparent and inclusive*
  Appropriate and timely involvement and inclusion of stakeholders and decision-makers at all levels of the organisation, should ensure that risk management remains relevant and up-to-date. Involvement also allows stakeholders to be properly represented and to have their views considered in determining risk criteria, stakeholders' perceptions and levels of tolerable risk.

Bearing all this in mind, it should be clear that an organisation with a sound ERM framework should be in a strong position to meet the non-financial reporting requirements.

- Relevant environmental and human factors should already have been analysed as potential threats and, if needed, considered for treatment, with a rationale as to why each treatment was chosen.
- Sound corporate governance and risk management strategies minimise the potential for corruption and bribery – and, as discussed, the global financial crisis demonstrated the need to tighten these measures.
- The ERM framework requires risk managers to have an understanding of the organisation's strategic vision and business model so they can effectively identify, prioritise and treat risks.
- Organisational policies and outcomes will likely have been analysed as part of the holistic risk assessment step, and should have been documented.
- KPIs are often considered when establishing KRIs to minimise overlap and to ensure that the KPIs are supported. Additionally, KPIs are a key component of the business strategy, so they are considered during the risk management process.

Risk managers are responsible for implementing the ERM process: they collect information from across the organisation, and interact with staff from all levels, from line managers to CEOs, and from all departments. As such, the risk manager is in a unique position to lead the non-financial reporting initiative, using their existing risk management skills to obtain and analyse the data, to determine what information can safely be disclosed and what would unduly expose the organisation, and to communicate the conclusions to internal and external stakeholders and regulators.

FERMA recommends that the report be developed as follows:

- Design a risk map, including a risk matrix (see Chapter 6, the previous book volume), to assess the likelihood and consequences of non-financial risks.
- Consider adverse impacts according to likelihood and consequence ratings.
- Assign each adverse impact into one of two main categories of risk treatment measures: prevention measures and protection measures (see Book Volume).

The final report should also address:

- *comprehensibility*
  Most staff members should be able to understand the language and format of the report.
- *relatability*
  High-quality, current, and accurate data should be collected.
- *comparability*
  KPIs, risk treatment outcomes and policies should be monitored and reviewed regularly to ensure they remain appropriate and effective.

### *ERM and Communication*

A key stage of the risk management framework is to communicate and consult.

FERMA argues that a key element of external reporting is that the report is comprehensible, not only to external parties but also to internal ones. The reports are intended to provide decision-makers with more information on a broad range of topics to enable them to make better informed decisions. Once the decisions are made, it is essential that they are implemented, and implemented well. Therefore, it is crucial that internal personnel understand the report so that any recommendations, strategies or targets can be effectively implemented.

The risk manager is required to communicate and consult with all stakeholders regularly, and therefore is practised in explaining connections and requirements in simple and educational ways that can be understood by all personnel.

### *ERM and Disclosure*

Lastly, but importantly, disclosing information can be a risky practice. A potential issue with external reporting is that confidential information may be disclosed that could harm the organisation. For example, if something is reported that alters a stakeholders' perception of the organisation, they may withdraw their support or funding. Accordingly, FERMA states that the main criterion for deciding what information to disclose should be 'the potential impairment of the organisation objectives on value and trust'.

## Summary

Please keep in mind the following points:

- A report is essentially the result of transforming data into information useful for:
  - planning
  - decision-making
  - coordination
  - control.
- Reporting is an essential component of the management process and forms a key element of formal down-up communication. Reporting provides key decision makers with crucial information to help steer the company towards its objectives and goals.
- Management reports can be categorised by the following main functions:
  - maintaining corporate governance
  - planning and executing strategy
  - reporting against business requirements.
- The manager has the following two key roles in relation to the management report, both of which involve applying skills of analysis:
  - preparing a report for down-up communication
  - reviewing and analysing received reports.
- Information should be accurate, timely, complete and relevant to be useful.
- The role of the manager in analysing a management report involves considering the:
  - characteristics of the provided information
  - required key information for decision-making
  - required actions
  - distribution of findings.
- The reporting framework provides the infrastructure required for escalating risk information throughout the organisation.
- Potential sources of risk reporting include:
  - operational management reports
  - incident reports
  - project progress reports
  - staff performance reports
  - exit interview reports
  - client contracts.

## Answers to Self-Help Questions

### Self-help question 6.1

Information is important as it provides senior management with the ability to:

- meet external reporting obligations (such as to shareholders or regulatory bodies);
- monitor strategy implementation;
- provide appropriate resources for the day-to-day operations of the company.

### Self-help question 6.2

For internal reporting requirements, the types of reports identified within this category may include:

- compliance reports (for example, audit and self-assessment reports)
- performance reports
- competency checks (or other background checks, such as police checks)
- risk assessments
- risk management implementation plans
- incident and near-miss reports
- investigation reports (for example, workplace accident investigation or root cause analysis reports)
- customer complaints.

### Self-help question 6.3

Examples of external stakeholders to which your organisation needs to report include:

- accreditation bodies
- other regulatory bodies
- customers/clients (for example, through a quality or performance report)
- shareholders (for example, through an annual report)
- insurance companies
- suppliers.

### Self-help question 6.4

A progress report may contain information regarding:

- limitations or key risk areas encountered during execution of the plan
- strategies used to address key risk areas or limitations
- reasons/recommendations for modifying the plan
- environmental changes.

**Self-help question 6.5**

The reports managers need to provide against standard business requirements may include:

- financial performance
- staffing requirements
- other resource requirements
- customer requests
- environmental reports
- operational statistics, such as:
  - productivity rates
  - processing volumes
  - running costs
  - staffing costs.

**Self-help question 6.6**

1. Referring to the characteristics of useful information, the problems with the HR report include those listed in the following table.

| Characteristic | Issues |
|---|---|
| **Accurate** | Greta did not have the training to identify where information was inaccurate |
| **Timely** | • Greta did not have a great deal of time to prepare the report<br>• a greater lead-in time may have allowed Greta to discuss the report with the executive team to determine their expectations |
| **Complete** | It was difficult for Greta to prepare a complete report as Anish would normally:<br>• deliver the report verbally<br>• write a brief summary of data provided in a written report |
| **Relevant** | It was difficult for Greta to understand the relevance of the provided information due to her:<br>• inexperience<br>• lack of understanding of the executive committee's expectations |

2. This situation could have been improved by:

   - clearly documenting reporting requirements across the organisation, including enforcing the need for information that is essential for decision making to be presented in a written report
   - mitigating the risk of knowledge loss through appropriate succession planning
   - involving the team in the development of the report, which would have acted to:
     - spread the workload
     - provide staff with an insight into how the report is developed.

**Self-help question 6.7**

The potential effects of a manager failing to communicate the findings of the management report analysis may include:

- actions not being implemented (for example, risks not being mitigated)
- major delays
- customer dissatisfaction
- increased risk exposure in other parts of the company (if actions are not communicated horizontally).

**Self-help question 6.8**

It is important to capture reported risks by the various management reports described within the risk management implementation plan, because failure to capture them may result in:

- increased areas of risk exposure because of viewing risks in silos – by not communicating risks across the organisation, it is difficult for the organisation to gain a holistic view of risk;
- over or under-resourcing, as a result of failing to understand the level of risk – failing to analyse and rate the risk in accordance with the risk management implementation plan and evaluate it against the organisation's appetite for risk;
- failing to provide a corporate memory bank for future decision making – failing to document risks and decisions made in relation to managing those risks;
- failing to gain a holistic understanding of existing controls to manage risk.

Chapter 7

# Operational Risk Management

## Introduction

## Learning Outcomes

By the end of this chapter, you should be able to:

- define operational risk management;
- identify operational activities that occur in modern organisations;
- recognise the risks associated with siloing;
- identify the fundamental organisational components and group them by inputs, organisation and outputs (IOO);
- develop a risk assessment structure;
- identify and assess compliance and financial risks.

## Definitions

Operational management is the tier of an organisation's hierarchy that:

- leads and organises operational activities to meet outcomes defined in strategic and operational plans;
- plans the necessary operational tasks;
- organises and controls the day-to-day elements of operations, ensuring there are adequate resources to meet expressed goals or objectives.

### *Operational Activities*

An organisation's operational activities vary significantly from industry to industry, as well as from organisation to organisation. Nonetheless, organisations essentially all engage in a series of activities or tasks that produce, sell and distribute their outputs to customers, that may be end users/consumers or

**Risk Measurement and Monitoring, 141–183**

**Published under exclusive licence by Emerald Publishing Limited**
**doi:10.1108/978-1-83662-310-620251017**

other organisations. Each organisational activity is interrelated (dependent on other operations) and works together to contribute to the overall success of the organisation.

---

**Self-Help Question 7.1**

List five typical operational activities in modern organisations (for example, research, design, and development).

---

Answers to self-help questions are provided at the end of each section.

---

### *Operational Managers*

Operational managers have a multi-faceted role; whether they are responsible for a discreet task or a wide range of activities, an operational manager must perform numerous functions. Essentially, operational managers are responsible for converting the organisation's strategic, tactical and operational goals into actual deliverables to ensure the business has a profitable and sustainable future.

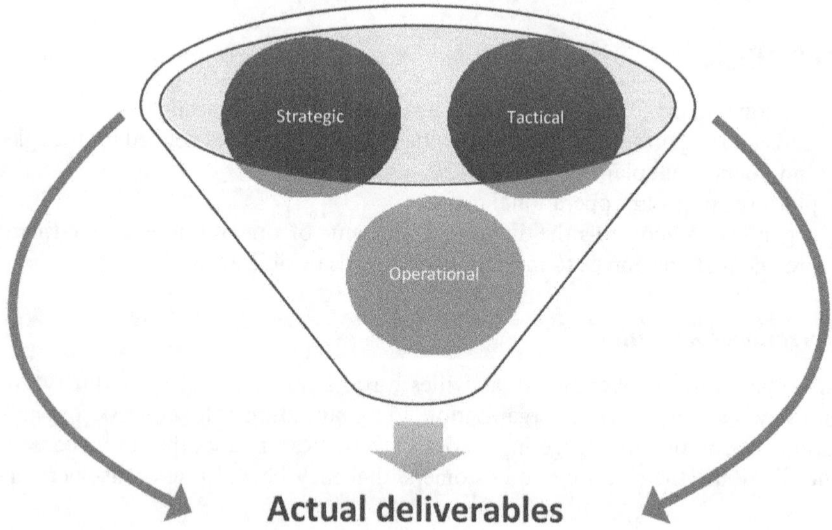


Converting Goals into Deliverables

**Activity | Identifying operational areas**

1. Reflect on an organisation you work for (or that you are familiar with).
2. Identify services or products the organisation sells or delivers.
3. Compile a list of operational activities that contribute to delivering the product or service (feel free to use ideas from the list you created in the previous self-help question).
4. What internal organisational resources would you use to compile your list?

### *Operational Structures*

An organisation's operations can be numerous and, depending on the requirements of the business, can be structured or organised in different ways.

**Self-Help Question 7.2**

The following table lists some common methods of organising operations. Record what you believe to be some example organisations or organisational activities aligning with these methods.

Common Methods of Organising Operations

| Method | Description | Example |
|---|---|---|
| **Functional** | Grouping operations into units that undertake similar tasks or activities. | |
| **Customer** | Organising operations in a way to interact with specific customers or customer groups. | |
| **Location** | Grouping operations based on defined geographical sites or areas. | |
| **Sequence** | Grouping operations based upon some sequence of actions or customers. | |

Answers to self-help questions are provided at the end of each section.

### *Operational Interdependence*

Regardless of how operations are structured or organised, all operational units must recognise how they interconnect with and complement each other. Individual operations are a part of a larger machine and must interconnect as smoothly as possible, working in unison to meet the deliverables set out in the business plan. Furthermore, units that are in contact with external partners, upstream and downstream, must be aware of the threats and opportunities they may bring to the organisation through them (see Chapter 8 Supply Network Risk Management).

### *Disconnection*

Problems develop quickly when diverse operating groups no longer recognise or prioritise their interrelationships. Sometimes the structures themselves can contribute to this disconnection; for example, organising operations by the location structure may result in employees never seeing or meeting members of other operational units. This lack of engagement may easily result in a disconnection of operations and a failure to understand the role of other parts of the organisation. If left unresolved, this disconnection can further lead to a failure to meet strategic objectives.

#### ***A Silo Mentality***

A disconnected operation may simply focus on its own role, regardless of the effect it has on the other interconnected operations. Employees may have little interest in how their activities affect other interdependent operations so long as their activity appears to be working well. This is known as the 'silo mentality'.

The following case study highlights the operational and other risks to an organisation in not addressing such disconnection.

***Case Study – National Water Filters***

**A new product line**

National Water Filters is preparing to undertake a significant expansion into new domestic water filter technology by releasing a new line of products. The organisation needs to:

- help facilitate the proposed growth with the assistance of new employees;
- quickly fill any vacancies in the Research and Development (R&D) operation, because employee levels in that unit are critical for the release of new products.

**HR**

The Human Resources (HR) unit is responsible for the recruitment process for new employees for the organisation. The HR unit views its operational objective as filling vacancies as quickly as possible for all operational areas (with a priority for the R&D unit).

The HR unit takes great pride in being able to have replacements begin work within two weeks. While the HR unit believes it is operating effectively to meet the R&D employee needs, it is in fact impeding R&D's effective operation.

**Impeding R&D's operation**

The new R&D employees are poorly trained or lack the basic knowledge, skills and ability to function efficiently in the R&D unit. As a result, R&D has had to slow down its operations to train the new employees in research methods. This training:

- affects R&D's development schedules;
- causes growing frustration and resignations from the company;
- creates more vacancies, which are again filled with other insufficiently qualified and inexperienced employees.

---

**Self-Help Question 7.3**

1. Identify the differences between the operating objectives of National Water Filters' HR unit with that of the R&D unit.
2. Could you recommend an alternative operating objective for the HR unit?
3. What would be the overall impact to National Water Filters if the HR unit did not modify its objective?

---

Answers to self-help questions are provided at the end of each section.

---

**Siloing and risk**

In the National Water Filters case study, siloed operational units created significant risks for other units, seriously jeopardising the organisation. By only examining their day-to-day activities and objectives and not how the unit affected interconnected operations, the HR unit exposed the organisation to serious risks that affected its expansion plans.

Each operational area depends on others for information and resources to perform its respective activities. When operational units act as silos, organisations can experience significant systemic problems. For operational managers/designated risk managers, identifying and successfully managing risks is critical to an organisation's success.

**Self-Help Question 7.4**

Reflecting on the organisation you reviewed in the first activity (identifying operational areas), reconsider its operational activities. Try to develop an operational impact table by working through the following steps:

1. Place your identified list of operational activities in the *operational activity column* of the following table.
2. Identify and record up to four of the most important internal operational areas (units and divisions), which those operational activities service in the key internal operations serviced column.
3. Record three possible areas of failure for each listed operational activity in the possible activity failures column.
4. Record two consequences from any of the possible activities failing in the significant business consequences column.

| Operational Activity | Key Internal Operations Serviced | Possible Activity Failures | Significant Business Consequences |
|---|---|---|---|
| | | | |

Answers to self-help questions are provided at the end of each section.

## The Organisation

Effective operational risk management relies on:

- understanding key components of an organisation;
- understanding how operations are managed;
- applying a risk management model to operational risks.

In its simplest form, an organisation is a group of two or more people working together in a structured fashion to attain a set of goals. This subsection examines aspects that can be used to define organisations, including their types and attributes.

### *Effective Application of the Principles and Practices of Risk Management*

A key challenge for the line or operational manager is to apply the principles and practices of risk management within the existing wide range of organisations.

To do this effectively, the operational manager must identify and understand:

- organisational types
- common organisational attributes
- a typical organisational model
- operational control in organisations.

### *Organisational Types*

There are many types of organisations, but the most common ones fall into the following categories:

- private
- public
- not-for-profit organisations (NGOs)
- government.

---

**Self-Help Question 7.5**

Match the following descriptions with the *most appropriate* organisational type.

| Organisational Type | | Description |
|---|---|---|
| 1 Privately held | A | Created by legislation or by the direction of elected officials to meet some type of public need or deliver some type of public good |
| 2 Publicly traded | B | • Established to administer funds to meet a defined objective other than making a profit or creating wealth for its owners<br>• Examples include organisations dedicated to finding cures for diseases, or charities to support the work of those who serve the needy and poor of the community |
| 3 NGO | C | Large groups of people (such as shareholders) own these types of organisations and have the right to share in the profits of the organisation |
| 4 Government | D | Individuals or small groups of individuals entitled to the profits of the organisation |

→

→

Answers to self-help questions are provided at the end of each section.

### *Common Organisational Attributes*

The types (and structures) of organisations can be quite varied but most organisations share similar characteristics, which means they also share common operational risk exposures. The first step is to understand the common attributes of an organisation.

Common attributes of organisations are that they:

- are artificial creations
- are separate legal entities
- perform some purpose
- convert inputs to outputs
- seek success.

#### *Artificial Creations*

The following table describes the formal or informal ways in which organisations can be artificially created.

Formal/Informal Ways in Which Organisations Can Be Created

| **Creation method** | **Description** |
|---|---|
| Formal | Through legal recognition (for example, incorporation or registration with regulating bodies) |
| Informal | An agreement between people who have some common interest and have decided to establish a structure under which this common interest can be mutually pursued (such as a club or society) |

#### *Separate Legal Entities*

Organisations are usually defined as companies and have a separate legal entity to their owners. More specifically, a company:

- can enter into contracts in its own right;
- can sue and be sued;
- is responsible for contracts and actions it undertakes in its own name.

***Company types***

Companies can be divided into the two legal types defined in the following table.

**Two Types of Companies**

| Company type | Description |
|---|---|
| **Privately held** | no more than 50 members<br>no ability to make public capital raisings<br>no obligation to hold an annual general meeting (AGM)<br>can pass resolutions without a meeting<br>does not need to prepare an annual financial report or a directors report (unless legislation states otherwise) |
| **Publicly traded** | owned by shareholders who purchase shares in the company<br>no limitation on the number of shareholders<br>can exchange and raise capital by offering shares to the public |

*Perform Some Purpose*

Organisations are created to fulfil some specific purpose, which:

- varies from organisation to organisation;
- may change over the life of the organisation (depending on changing market conditions).

*Convert Inputs to Outputs*

Regardless of the class or type, an organisation operates to convert resources (inputs) into a set of final products or services (outputs) for a surplus (profit for companies).

*Seek Success*

Organisations operate to deliver a profitable return to shareholders/stakeholders.

**Note:** Measures of success are different for government agencies and NGOs, in which they usually measure success in terms of a social good or a community service.

***The Typical Organisational Model***

Line or operational managers with direct day-to-day responsibility for the management of risk work in:

- different types of organisations (from small private businesses, to large and complex government agencies)
- organisations with different operational structures.

*Fundamental Organisational Components*

While all organisations differ in type and structure to some extent, they all comprise three fundamental (or universal) components. The three fundamental components of all organisations are the:

- inputs (including resources)
- organisation itself (its systems and processes)
- outputs (products or services).

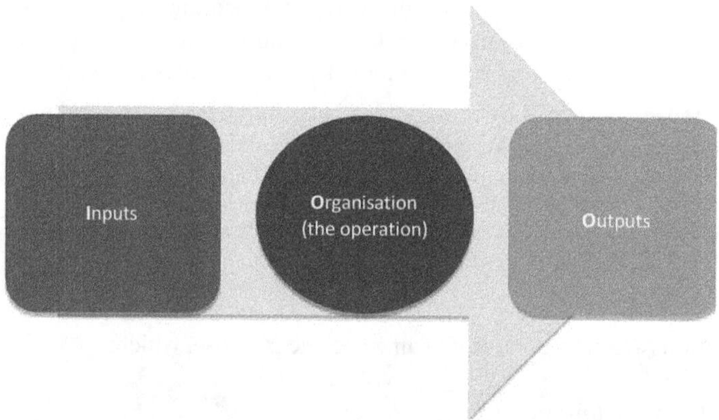


Fundamental Components of an Organisation – IOO

*The Sequential Business Process*

The previous figure lists the fundamental organisational components, which can be recalled with the **IOO** acronym. The graphic illustrates how these components operate by following a sequential business process of:

1. collecting and organising inputs
2. channelling those inputs through systems within the organisation
3. transforming inputs to the kind of outputs the organisation is designed to produce.

*The Inputs*

Organisations may have different levels of reliance on inputs, but all require some external resources, which are critical to the successful operation of the organisation. Disrupted or interrupted access to these inputs would seriously undermine the ability of the organisation to produce outputs and meet its objectives.

***Typical Inputs***

While there can be a multitude of inputs, they generally fall into well-recognised categories that are almost universal in their application in all organisations. The list of inputs can vary from organisation to organisation, but most organisations require similar kinds of inputs (including resources)

---

**Self-Help Question 7.6**

The following table provides examples of typical inputs major operational areas require. List some examples of these inputs in the *examples* column.

| Inputs | Examples |
|---|---|
| **Personnel** | |
| **Financial** | |
| **Physical** | |
| **Technological** | |
| **Legal** | |
| **Reputational** | |

---

Answers to self-help questions are provided at the end of each section.

---

**Self-Help Question 7.7**

**Stan's books**

Stan's Books is a newly opened corner bookstore located near a residential train station in the suburb of a major city. Stan's Books sells new books to customers and helps in locating hard-to-find, out-of-print editions of old books.

**Objectives**

The objectives of Stan's Books are to:

- earn a 30% profit on all sales
- become the largest bookseller in the region.

→

→

**Key Inputs**

For new book sales to be profitable (outputs), what inputs do Stan's Books require to be able to meet its organisational objectives? Describe the purpose of each of these inputs.

| Inputs | Purpose |
|---|---|
| | |

Answers to self-help questions are provided at the end of each section.

*The Organisation Itself*

The organisation is the series of systems, processes, and procedures created and adopted to convert or transform inputs into outputs.

While this section suggests that all organisations vary in size and scope, a line or operational manager's role is to:

- ensure the organisation procures its necessary inputs;
- direct these inputs via systems, processes and procedures to create required outputs.

Systems, processes, and procedures are similar in different organisations; however, most organisations customise standard processes and procedures to:

- accommodate their unique characteristics;
- gain efficiency in operations.

***Purpose of Systems, Processes, and Procedures***

An organisation uses a wide variety of critical day-to-day operational systems, processes, and procedures to:

- meet its business objectives;
- process inputs into outputs;

- enable management to understand if:
  - the organisation is correctly applying financial resources
  - the organisation is maintaining output quality
  - there are reliable sources of inputs
  - employees are adequately skilled
  - the organisation is meeting customer needs.

**Self-Help Question 7.8**

What are three examples of systems, processes, and procedures you can identify in the case of Stan's Books? Briefly describe their associated purpose.

| System, process or procedure | Purpose |
|---|---|
| | |
| | |

Answers to self-help questions are provided at the end of each section.

*The Outputs*

Identifying an organisation's objectives for outputs is a very effective method by which to understand the breadth of operational risks. This is because all operations are designed to assist the organisation in reaching its output objectives.

Organisations may create outputs:

- to meet a specific or emerging need in the market, such as the public demand for mobile phones
- for non-commercial or non-consumption purposes, such as to respond to emergencies or to ensure public health objectives are met.

The following table describes the types of categories an organisation may use to group organisational outputs.

**Categories for Grouping Actual Outputs**

| Category | Description |
|---|---|
| **Products** | Tangible items that can be used by:<br>individuals<br>consumers<br>other organisations |

*(Continued)*

(*Continued*)

| Category | Description |
|---|---|
| **Services** | Intangible outputs which hold a value for the end-user, such as:<br>expert advice<br>professional or technical knowledge, used in the creation of other goods and services |
| **Profits** | The return received on a business undertaking after meeting all the operating expenses that can be re-invested back into the business or distributed to shareholders as a dividend |
| **Information** | Knowledge that organisations sell to customers to use in their own organisations (for example, demographic or financial information) |
| **Public goods** | Products or services delivered by government organisations (for example, water and sewerage services) |
| **Regulation** | Output in the form of:<br>legislation<br>codes<br>licensing requirements |

**Self-Help Question 7.9**

List three typical organisational output objectives (for example, making a profit for the owners or shareholders).

Answers to self-help questions are provided at the end of each section.

**Self-Help Question 7.10**

1. How difficult would it be for Stan's Books to succeed if it lost its employees?
2. How difficult would it be for Stan's Books to succeed if it lost its complete inventory of new books?
3. Could Stan's Books continue to operate profitably if it lost its franchise to distribute certain books? What might be its options?

Answers to self-help questions are provided at the end of each section.

*Organisational Components: Summary*

The following diagram summarises the different categories that fall under the three organisational components.

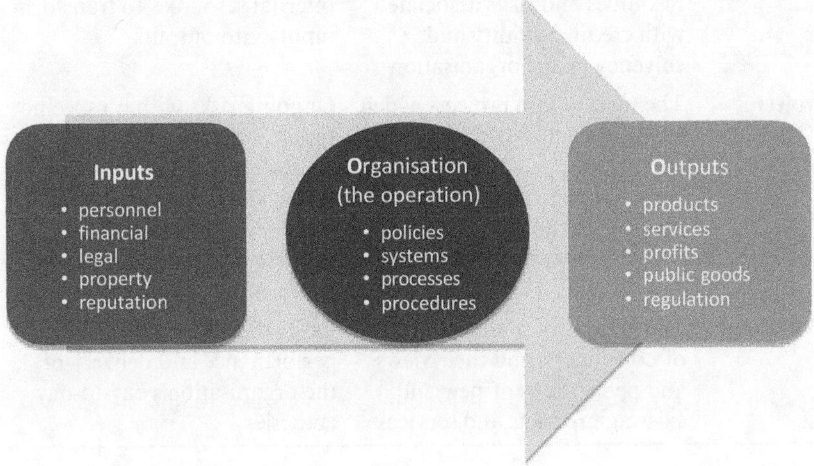


***The Internal Environment/Context***

The internal environment of both an organisation and an operational unit is the structure, policies, systems, processes and procedures that work together in the pursuit of the organisation's goals and objectives.

A useful way to understand the internal operational risk environment for operations is to consider how organisational risk differs from other operational risks, such as:

- strategic
- financial
- project
- marketing risk.

The following table describes how organisational risk differs from these other operational risks.

**How Organisational Risk Differs from Other Operational Risks**

| Risk | Organisational Relationship | Organisational Relationship |
|---|---|---|
| **Strategic** | The long-term goals and objectives of the organisation as it operates in its environment over time | The day-to-day goals and objectives through which the operation eventually meets the organisation's strategic goals |

(*Continued*)

(*Continued*)

| Risk | Organisational Relationship | Organisational Relationship |
|---|---|---|
| **Financial** | Using corporate financial resources and risks associated with credit, liquidity and solvency of the organisation | Effectively and efficiently using internal resources to transform inputs into outputs |
| **Project** | The risks within projects which have a specific beginning and end.<br>**Note:** Some risks may be initially unknown if the project is new and innovative | Ongoing risks with no specific timeframes; they exist as long as operations continue.<br>**Note:** These risks tend to be more familiar and known because an organisation has experience of its own operations |
| **Marketing** | The actions of a large number of consumers, and their views and perceptions of new and existing products and services | Risks that affect the efficient performance and delivery of the organisation's day-to-day activities |

***Case Study – East Coast Oil***

**Company profile**

East Coast Oil is a regional independent oil retail company, with a network of 50 company-owned petrol stations in rural regions along the eastern seaboard.

**Ewen's new managerial role**

Ewen Daley has just accepted a new position as the manager of an East Coast Oil 'fuel farm' facility.

Ewen needs to manage East Coast Oil's fuel farm facility, which is the company's depot for storing and distributing refined:

- leaded petrol
- unleaded petrol
- diesel fuel.

Ewen will be the operational manager responsible for transporting and storing refined petroleum products from the refinery to the individual East Coast Oil petrol stations. Ewen is also wholly accountable for implementing operational risk management within the fuel farm operation.

**The fuel farm's operations**

The fuel farm directly purchases refined product from a nearby refinery. Two large tanker trucks pick up fuel at the refinery and transport it to the fuel farm, where is it stored in large tanks. When East Coast Oil needs to move fuel to the 50 petrol stations to replace inventory, a fleet of smaller tanker trucks load and deliver the fuel to the 50 petrol stations.

**Ewen's challenge**

Ewen must rapidly identify the operational (sub-organisational) model (consisting of inputs, policies, systems, processes, procedures and outputs) underpinning how East Coast Oil runs the fuel farm. He is also accountable for high-level operational risk management responsibilities, so he needs to review the fuel farm's operational risk management plan to determine internal and external environmental factors that may impact East Coast Oil's business.

**Self-help question 7.11**

Imagine you are Ewen, the fuel farm's operational manager.

Review the fundamental components of an organisation in the following diagram.

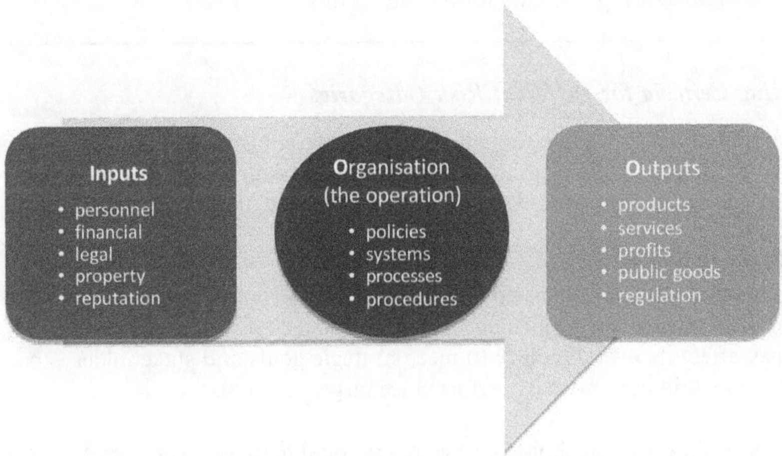


Using the fuel farm's sub-organisational model (Ewen's internal risk environment), fill in the following table with information about areas in which operational risks may arise.

| Inputs | Organisation | Outputs |
|---|---|---|
| Personnel | **Policies, systems, processes and procedures** | Products |
| Financial | | |
| Legal | | Services |
| Property | | |

→

→

Answers to self-help questions are provided at the end of each section.

**Activity | The internal environment**

- Identify an operational group or area in your organisation.
- Identify key operational inputs and outputs.
- Consider how a specific type of risk (for example, personnel, legal, information security or fraud) could affect these inputs and outputs.
- Assess whether the operational area has:
  - a written policy addressing this type/s of risk
  - a set of procedures or guidelines addressing this type/s of risk.
- If there is a written policy/set of procedures or guidelines, who has the designated responsibility for managing this risk?

### *Setting Criteria for Different Risk Categories*

Operational risks within an organisation are different from the broader organisational risks. The difference is that operational risk occurs in the day-to-day activities of an operation, particularly in terms of how the organisation:

- monitors and controls these risks;
- is impaired by the associated losses;
- may fail to meet its performance targets or goals;
- may affect its overall ability to meet strategic goals and stakeholder expectations by failing to meet its performance targets or goals.

Consulting key stakeholders helps operational managers categorise risks into enterprise wide or unit specific types.

#### *Security*

Security breaches can seriously disrupt day-to-day operational activities. Because of the severity and frequency of the risk, organisations devote significant resources to assessing and treating security risks.

The following table lists some of these security risks.

***Security Risks***

| Security Risk | Example | |
|---|---|---|
| **Crimes against people** | • abduction/kidnap<br>• assault | • murder<br>• robbery |
| **Crimes against property** | • arson<br>• burglary<br>• deception | • vehicle theft<br>• inventory theft<br>• other similar destructions |
| **Crimes relating to information protection** | • communication interception<br>• copyright infringement | • data interception<br>• intellectual property (IP) theft |

***Assessment criteria***

Criteria for assessing tolerable levels of exposure to security risk may include:

- the size of a maximum possible security loss
- the typical sizes of historic losses
- the typical sizes of industry or community losses.

***Financial requirements***

When determining the financial requirement to treat security risks, stakeholders may be able to advise on adequate levels based on their industry-related experience.

*Fire*

The threat of fire is very familiar to operational managers, because its impact on operations can be so significant. The following table lists common assessment methods.

***Fire Risks***

| Cost | Examples |
|---|---|
| **Expected risk to life** | the cost of human losses in a fire incident |
| **Indirect human costs** | costs associated with:<br>• lost productivity<br>• employee turnover<br>• treatment for injured employees |
| **Direct economic costs** | • physical loss of assets<br>• inventory cost of clean-up overtime<br>• cost of insurance excess payments |
| **Indirect economic costs** | • loss of productivity<br>• loss of business data<br>• loss of reputation<br>• delays in operational schedule<br>• possible failure in meeting contractual obligations |

***Assessment criteria***
The criteria for assessing such fire exposures can be the sum of all these costs, including both the direct and indirect costs.

***Financial requirements***
Stakeholders may be able to advise on typical expected costs.

*Occupational/Workplace Health and Safety*

For almost all operations, the people who work to transform inputs to outputs are the most valuable operational asset.

---

**Self-help question 7.12**

List three serious risk exposures relating to the health and safety of personnel.

---

Answers to self-help questions are provided at the end of each section.

---

Organisations typically use frequency or consequence measures for assessing occupational/workplace health and safety exposures. The following table provides some examples.

**Frequency and Consequence Measures**

| Frequency Measures | Consequence Measures |
|---|---|
| lost work days | medical costs |
| number of incidents per hour worked | cost of lost wages |
| number of injuries per annum/size of workforce | **cost of productivity losses** |
| **numbers of deaths per annum/size of workforce** | |

***Critical Stakeholder Background***
Stakeholders with knowledge of the various state workers compensation regimes, legal obligations, medical treatment plans, as well as industrial workplace safety will be of assistance in determining occupational/workplace health and safety risks.

*Equipment/Technology*

Equipment or technology failure can pose a significant disruption to operational areas and if severe enough, may completely halt production. Any assessment of equipment/technology risk requires an analysis of:

- the probability of failure
- the impact or level of any expected interruption.

**Self-help question 7.13**

List three types of assessment criteria the organisation would typically review for equipment/technology.

Answers to self-help questions are provided at the end of each section.

***Critical Stakeholder Background***

Stakeholders with engineering or equipment-specific knowledge can assist the operational manager to identify areas of vulnerability and prepare a risk treatment strategy.

**Self-help question 7.14**

Identify and record two typical fuel farm risk exposures for the following risk categories.

Suggest one key stakeholder for each risk (either internal or external) who could help Ewen Daley establish the criteria by which to assess these risks.

| Risk Category | Typical Risk Exposures | Key Stakeholder |
|---|---|---|
| **Security** | 1. | 1. |
| | 2. | 2. |
| **Fire** | 1. | 1. |
| | 2. | 2. |
| **Occupational/workplace health and safety** | 1. | 1. |
| | 2. | 2. |
| **Equipment/technology** | 1. | 1. |
| | 2. | 2. |

Answers to self-help questions are provided at the end of each section.

***Performance Targets and Risk Criteria***

To ensure the organisation meets its overall goals and objectives, there needs to be close interaction/coordination between the various sub groups who undertake operations. Difficulties can emerge when the sub group is measured only based on meeting its individual operational performance targets.

*Objectives Alignment*

When implementing a risk management process, the operational manager must ensure the sub-group's objectives are aligned with the organisation's objectives. Operational managers also need to understand how well their operational performance targets relate to the organisation's goals.

***Case Study – East Coast Oil Stakeholders***

Ewen identifies a network of internal and external stakeholders for the fuel farm to assist him in understanding the levels and types of risk the depot's operations face. These stakeholders assist in both identifying the risk and assessing the potential range of impacts on the operation.

**Quantifiable measures of risk**

Ewen and his stakeholders use common quantifiable measures of risk, which are grounded in performance targets, to set criteria for assessing broad operational risks to the fuel farm. Such criteria include:

- levels of protection in the operation
- costs of protection
- costs of losses, such as:
  - *direct* cost of losses – for example:
    - buildings
    - infrastructure
    - insurance company payments (an expense)
    - personal injuries
    - other similar costs
  - *indirect* cost of losses – for example:
    - lost trade or customers
    - employee replacement owing to resignations
    - loss of potential clients
    - employee trauma counselling
    - accident investigation time
    - increased insurance payments
    - alternative supply costs.

**Risks difficult to quantify**

Ewen recognises it is difficult to quantify some measures of risk, because of either a lack of data or the nature of the risk.

**Example**

If there were a fatality (resulting from a fire) at the fuel farm, part of the loss's impact on the operation would be quantifiable in terms of the direct and indirect costs to the operation; however, the impact of the resultant decline in employee morale would be more difficult to measure.

### *Reporting on Difficult to Quantify Risk Exposures*

The impact of difficult to quantify risk exposures may be revealed in risk-sensitive management controls and indicators, which report on operational efficiencies, such as:

- KPIs
- operational objectives, reflecting the desired outcomes of the operational process relating to levels of output and quality of outputs.

#### *Case Study – Measuring Fuel Delay Risk Through KPI Targets*

Ewen has set a KPI to have fuel delivered to a petrol station within 24 hours of the station's product request. This 24-hour performance target is:

- an output objective – it helps Ewen schedule and manage his operation
- a sensitive measurement of the risk exposures that could affect this objective.

**Calling in sick**

A delivery driver contacts Ewen one hour before the start of his shift claiming that he is ill and cannot come to work.

A driver cancelling their shift one hour before obviously impacts Ewen's 24-hour KPI more than a driver calling in by the policy-defined eight hours.

With a much earlier call-in, Ewen would be able to locate an alternative driver to:

- uphold the original, agreed-upon schedule
- minimise the risk of late delivery or non-delivery.

**Operational targets and objectives**

Ewen can measure the impact of the driver's late call-in in terms of operational targets and objectives. This is because the fuel farm's targets and objectives are tied to other East Coast Oil operational objectives.

**Expectations of East Coast Oil's Operating Manager**

Shuchi Morris, East Coast Oil's Operating Manager, in charge of co-ordinating East Coast Oil's 50 petrol stations requires fuel at the stations within 24 hours of ordering to prevent a:

- loss of sales
- failure to meet the company's revenue performance targets.

Repeated failure of the retail operation to meet these performance targets could:

- result in cash flow problems for East Coast Oil;
- possibly threaten the current strategic objective of expanding into suburban markets (and other states) through purchasing additional petrol stations.

**Activity | Performance targets in your operational area**

Examine your working environment and identify performance requirements relating to your position. Possible sources may include:

- position descriptions
- competency standards
- employee annual performance review forms
- documented business processes
- work methods statements.

For each identified performance requirement, decide which operational risks you believe the performance requirement was designed to address and reduce. Evaluate your conclusions through discussion with your colleagues.

## Assessing and Prioritising Broad-Based Risks

After consulting internal and external stakeholders, the operational manager will be able to compile a list of potential operational risk exposures. Generating a list may seem daunting but assessing such risks will provide clear prioritisation for future assessment and treatment.

### *The Risk Assessment Process*

The risk assessment process needs to measure:

- the possible likelihood (or probability) of the risk
- the range of potential consequences (if the risk should manifest).

In addition, the risk assessment process aims to identify:

- key expectations (operational outcomes and objectives) of operational unit stakeholders in the risk management process

- the most significant areas of loss to the operational unit, such as:

  - property loss and its impact
  - human resources loss
  - environmental impacts
  - reputation impacts.

### *Developing a Risk Assessment Structure*

Recognising that not all risks affect an operation equally, the operational manager should be able to answer the following questions at the end of the context-establishing process.

**Questions to Ask at the End of the Context-Establishing Process**

| Question | Answer | |
|---|---|---|
| What are the most significant risks to the operation/s? | | |
| Would most stakeholders agree with this list? | ☐ Yes | ☐ No |
| Are these risks ranked from the most extreme to the least likely? | ☐ Yes | ☐ No |
| Which risks present a significant threat to the operational unit? | | |
| Which risks are within the scope of my activities to control? | | |
| How will I prioritise my time and effort to treat the identified risks? | | |

Answering the questions in the previous table requires the operational manager to structure and document a risk assessment process which prioritises a later evaluation of risks and determines whether current risk controls are:

- *adequate* in terms of level of protection
- *efficient* in terms of cost of protection from risks.

### *Creating a Hierarchy of Risks*

Once the first iteration of the systematic method of operational risk assessment is complete, the operational manager develops criteria by which they can determine a hierarchy of risks with input from stakeholders. The *hierarchy of risks* does not determine the importance of risks but rather demonstrates the spread of the risk and how many organisational resources may be required. The lower the risk in the hierarchy, the more of the organisation it affects and the more resources will be needed to address it.

Creating criteria for a hierarchy of risks can be a useful tool when examining operational risks because day-to-day operational matters drive operational goals, objectives, targets, performance levels and quality outcomes (for example) and risks still contribute to the overall strategic direction of the organisation.

The risk hierarchy tool allows an operational manager to focus accurately on identified risks within the control of the operating unit.

The following figure shows a typical organisational risk hierarchy, which includes some of the broader risk categories.

*Hierarchy of Risks*

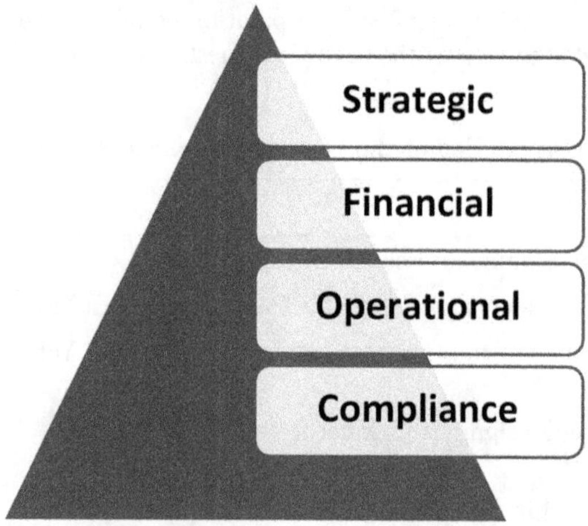


***Important***

Placing risk into hierarchies does not imply some risks are more important than others or have a lower risk profile.

Rather, the pyramid suggests risks lower in the hierarchy, e.g. compliance, have a broader organisational spread and may require more organisational resources to address/resolve.

*Risks Affecting Strategic Directions*

Some risks affecting strategic direction may indirectly affect operational issues. Even though an operational manager cannot control these risks, being aware is an important part of the manager's contextual helicopter view. An operational manager should still recognise higher-level risks that others need to address.

*Risk Categories*

The previous hierarchy of risks highlights that organisations can broadly categorise risks as strategic, financial, compliance and operational. Other risks, like project and marketing risks, are further categorised as risks that cross category boundaries.

An operational manager should be sufficiently familiar with relevant strategic, financial, compliance and operational risk exposures to be able to identify:

- how these risks may impact their operational activities;
- when these risks are irrelevant.

***Operational Risk***

The operational risk category includes additional, broad-based risks including:

- legal
- personnel
- property
- regulatory (compliance)
- reputational
- technological.

**Self-help question 7.15**

Complete the following table by identifying two typical risks for each category that may impact the East Coast Oil's fuel farm operation.

| Risk Category | Typical Risks |
|---|---|
| Strategic | 1. |
| | 2. |
| Financial | 1. |
| | 2. |
| Operational | 1. |
| | 2. |
| Compliance | 1. |
| | 2. |

Answers to self-help questions are provided at the end of each section.

## Non-Compliance Risk Assessment

Compliance risks can impact organisations at a number of levels, since organisations may be governed by:

- a complex web of regulations
- legislation
- industry codes
- corporate policies.

Organisations do not directly manage all compliance risks at the operational level. For example, the legal department or the board may directly manage some of these risks at a group level.

Compliance risks are located at the base of the hierarchy of risks because they are fundamental to the organisation's risk profile. These risks pose a challenge to the operational manager because of the time and resources required to ensure the operational unit is complying with its legislative (and other) obligations.

**Self-help question 7.16**

Identify two consultation methods by which organisations can identify compliance risks.

Answers to self-help questions are provided at the end of each section.

***Case Study – East Coast Oil Ensures Fuel Farm Compliance***

To Ewen Daley, operational compliance concerns:

- meeting and exceeding regulatory responsibilities
- preserving the fuel farm's legal ability to operate.

| Regulation | Purpose |
|---|---|
| Occupational/ workplace health and safety | Ensures the state government does not close the fuel farm because it is regarded as an unsafe workplace |
| EPA | Ensures the regulator does not revoke the fuel farm's permit to store and transport hazardous goods |
| Road traffic authority (RTA) | Ensures truck drivers are licenced to operate the tanker trucks and that the vehicles are legally licenced to operate in the states to which fuel needs to be transported |

The following table details some of the fuel farm's legislative and regulatory obligations.

The penalties for failing to comply with legislative obligations or the risk of losing a critical licence could seriously affect the fuel farm's ongoing operations.

**Activity | Consequences of compliance risks**

Based upon your current (or a previous) employer's operational requirements, create a list of the legislation or regulations with which your operation is required to comply.

From this list:

- identify five key compliance risks your operating unit currently faces
- categorise each compliance risk as:
  - an internal policy or procedure
  - an industry practice or code
  - a legislative or regulatory requirement

  or

  - a community expectation
- for each identified risk:
  - identify a typical consequence to your operating unit if it fails to comply
  - discuss how you can identify this risk with a colleague
  - identify who in your organisation is responsible for addressing this compliance risk.

### *Different Compliance Risks Impact in Different Ways*

Different compliance risks affect distinct operating groups in unique ways. All organisations must ensure they comply with all relevant legislation.

***Case Study – Fuel Farm Dangerous Goods Transport and Storage***

The fuel farm transports and stores dangerous goods, so it must be compliant with the legislation regulating such activities.

On further investigation, Ewen discovers the fuel farm has already developed standard operating policies, processes, and procedures to meet its legislative obligations. Ewen needs to ensure these documents are current and relevant.

*Tools for Assessing Non-Compliance Risk*

A diagnostic questionnaire is a useful tool for an operational manager to record the various compliance-related risks. The following table includes some typical questions.

**Diagnostic Questionnaire**

| | **Acceptable?** | |
|---|---|---|
| **Risk** | **Yes** | **No** |
| Is compliance management on the board's agenda? | ☐ | ☐ |
| Is compliance management on the operational management's agenda? | ☐ | ☐ |
| Do senior and operational management understand the link between compliance and reputation? | ☐ | ☐ |
| Do the organisation's IT systems play a significant role in meeting compliance management needs? | ☐ | ☐ |
| Is management accountability for compliance management clear to all operating managers? | ☐ | ☐ |
| Does internal or external audit monitor compliance risks? | ☐ | ☐ |
| Does the organisation have a systematic approach to identifying all new legislation which may have an impact? | ☐ | ☐ |
| Does the organisation use a standard compliance framework? | ☐ | ☐ |
| Does the organisation manage contracts and their compliance requirements effectively? | ☐ | ☐ |
| Do operational performance objectives include compliance criteria? | ☐ | ☐ |

## Financial Risk Assessment

Financial risks are enterprise-wide concerns and as such are located above operational risks in the hierarchy. Equally, the way organisations identify and analyse risks at the operational unit level has strong financial implications.

As organisations derive tactical and operational goals from strategic goals, financial resources are allocated according to higher level financial objectives. Therefore, financial indicators are always essential at all levels in the organisation.

*Assessing Financial Risk*

It is important that the risk professional understands common financial terms and their impact on operations. Understanding relative financial impacts of risk also assists in ranking and rating these risks, which allows managers to focus on risks which most seriously threaten the organisation or operation.

### *The Cost-Benefit Analysis*

The other important issue is to understand the cost of the treatment to control or mitigate the identified risk. Organisations often use a cost-benefit analysis to select the best treatment available from a range of treatment options. The cost-benefit analysis attempts to guide the organisation in selecting the treatment option that represents the optimal use of the organisation's resources.

### *The Cost-Benefit Analysis Process*

The cost-benefit analysis process requires the decision maker to undertake the following steps.

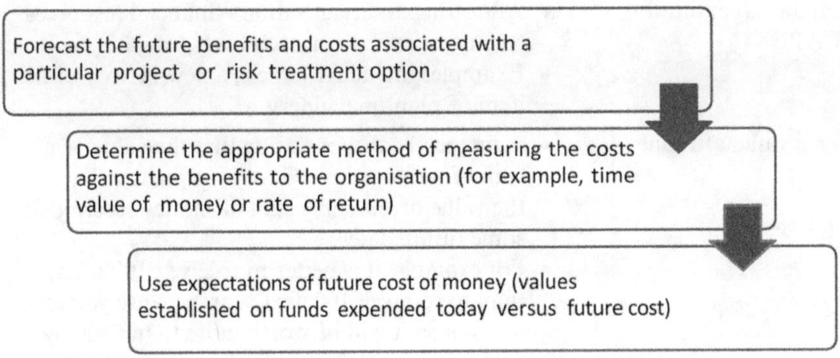


The decision maker examines the cost of capital and the expected return on funds used elsewhere in the organisation (for example, a market portfolio or increased investment in the organisation to produce an improved rate of return).

Using the cost of money and expected return on funds criteria, the decision maker determines if the risk treatment option delivers a greater financial benefit to the organisation than other applications of the same funds.

The organisation can express this determination in financial terms such as financial targets a risk treatment proposal must meet to obtain the necessary board or senior management financing and support.

*For more on cost-benefit analyses, read 'Cost-benefit analysis' in this book volume, Risk treatment I.*

### *Common Financial Terms*

A cost-benefit analysis requires some knowledge of common financial terms. The following table provides definitions of some common finance terms relating to financial risk identification and assessment.

**Common Terms Relating to Financial Risk Identification and Assessment**

| Term | Definition |
|---|---|
| Net cash flow (NCF) | • Capital investment-generated cash revenue minus the cash expenses the investment requires<br>• For example, the cost of purchasing and setting up a new production line compared to the increase in output revenues the production line generates |
| Capital budgeting | • A decision-making process evaluating alternative capital investment proposals<br>• The objective is to finance capital expenditures that meet the organisation's objectives, and to plan or budget for meeting those objectives |
| Capital expenditure (CAPEX) | • Allocating an organisation's financial resources to buy an asset with a relatively long life<br>• Examples include a vehicle, a new factory or an item of plant/machinery |
| Time value of money | • A financial concept stating that the value of a sum of money received today is greater than the value of the same sum of money received at some future date<br>• For example, it is better to receive €100 today than to receive €100 next year, because you can invest it so it will be worth more than €100 by next year |
| Cost of money | • The average interest rate at which money can be borrowed |
| Rate of return | • Net investment-generated income, expressed as a percentage of the amount invested |
| Cash inflow | • The capital investment-generated revenue or cash savings |
| Cash outflow | • The required cash expenditures for capital investment |
| Net present value (NPV) method (further details in Chapter 2, Book volume 3) | • A method of analysing a proposed investment in which an organisation has set a predetermined rate of return that all investments must meet<br>• The organisation computes the cost of capital used to make the investment over time (recognising the time value of money) and the net cash inflows and cash outflows. |

(*Continued*)

(*Continued*)

| Term | Definition |
|---|---|
| | • It then discounts the cashflows using as rate the cost of capital (DCF), compares the DCF with the initial investment and accepts the investment if the NPV is equal to the DCF – I is positive.<br>• The investment then meets the minimal rate of return, required as an organisation has other options for its finances, such as investing |
| Statement of financial position | • A standard financial statement showing the organisation's financial position, with three main elements:<br>1. assets<br>2. liabilities<br>3. owner's equity |
| Statement of financial performance | • A financial statement summarising the trading activity of the company during a specified period<br>• Classified as revenue less expenses to obtain the net profit or loss<br>• Previously called a profit and loss (P&L) statement |
| Asset | • Organisation-owned items of economic value expected to contribute to future earning capability |
| Capital | • A financial account of an owner's claims against the assets of the business |
| Net income | • Revenues minus expenses<br>• For example, the remaining amount when you subtract sales revenue from expenses (such as salaries and overheads) |

## Summary

Please keep the following points from this chapter in mind:

- Operational management is the tier of an organisation's hierarchy that:
  - leads and organises operational activities to meet outcomes defined in strategic and operational plans

  - plans the necessary operational tasks
  - organises and controls the day-to-day elements of operations, ensuring there are adequate resources to meet expressed goals or objectives

- Operational managers are responsible for converting the organisation's strategic goals into actual deliverables to ensure the business has a profitable and sustainable future.
- Each operational area depends on others for information and resources; when operational units act as silos, organisations can experience significant systemic problems.
- Effective operational risk management relies on:
  - understanding key components of an organisation
  - understanding how operations are managed
  - applying a risk management model to operational risks.

- There are many types of organisations, but the most common ones are categorised as private, public, not for profit (NPO/NGO) or government.
- While all organisations differ in type and structure to some extent, they all comprise three fundamental (or universal) components. The three fundamental components of all organisations are the:
  - inputs (including resources)
  - organisation itself (its systems and processes)
  - outputs (products or services).

- Operational risks within an organisation are different from the broader organisational risks. The difference is that operational risk occurs in the day-to-day activities of an operation, particularly in terms of how the organisation:
  - monitors and controls these risks
  - is impaired by the associated losses
  - may fail to meet its performance targets or goals
  - may affect its overall ability to meet strategic goals and stakeholder expectations by failing to meet its performance targets or goals.

- The operational manager should be able to structure and document a risk assessment process that prioritises a later evaluation of risks and determines whether current risk controls are adequate and efficient.
- Compliance risks are fundamental to the organisation's risk profile. These risks pose a challenge to the operational manager because of the time and resources required to ensure the operational unit is complying with its legislative (and other) obligations.
- It is important that the risk professional understands common financial terms and their impact on operations as this will assist them to rank and rate these risks, allowing them to focus on risks that most seriously threaten the organisation or operation.

## Answers to Self-Help Questions

### Self-help question 7.1

Typical operational activities in modern organisations include:

- research and design
- manufacturing and production
- client management, call centres, sales and marketing
- packaging, shipping, distribution and supply chain
- human resources
- building maintenance
- training and development
- accounting and finance
- support services
- fleet maintenance
- quality control and testing
- IT support.

Although this list is far from exhaustive, it illustrates the diversity of operational activities across an organisation.

### Self-help question 7.2

| Method | Suggested Example |
|---|---|
| **Functional** | An organisation may combine its IT, finance, accounting, and marketing operations into one functional group because all require extensive databases and IT resources to operate |
| **Customer** | The banking sector tailors' operations to deal with specific customer groups such as:<br>• business customers;<br>• customer mortgages; or<br>• agricultural customers |
| **Location** | • Many national manufacturers (especially in the agricultural industry) have plants in several states designed to service customers in their specific region<br>• Many large organisations operate round-the-clock shifts to ensure 24/7 operations on a global basis and divide operations by time zones |
| **Sequences** | Large insurance companies sometimes divide customer operations based upon the first letter of the customer's last name. One operational group may deal only with customers whose last names start with A–G, while another would deal with all customers with names beginning with H–Q |

→

→

**Self-help question 7.3**

1. The objective of the HR unit is to recruit, induct, and put new employees in place within a timeframe. The objective of the R&D section is to quickly develop new products to facilitate the growth of the organisation (not training new employees).
2. It would be wise for the HR unit to establish its objectives in terms useful to its customers. Incompetent and ineffective employees may prevent National Water Filters from meeting its goals. The objectives of the HR unit should be based upon an understanding of what output of the HR activity the internal customer (such as R&D) needs. This can be accomplished through:

   – understanding the needs of the internal customer via consultation and a needs assessment;
   – drafting contracts of performance, such as memorandums of understanding or service level agreements (SLAs);
   – developing mechanisms to monitor and audit whether performance is in accordance with agreements.

3. If the HR unit continues to fail to meet the needs of the R&D section, it is likely that valuable resources will be diverted. If more time is required by R&D to train the new employees recruited by HR, there will be less resources to develop the new products upon which the company is reliant. Failure to deliver new products on time can result in a loss of key customers or reputation in the market, which could seriously damage National Water Filters' organisational sustainability.

**Self-help question 7.4**

The following table provides a sample response for this question

| Operational Activity | Key Internal Operations Serviced | Possible Activity Failures | Significant Business Consequences |
|---|---|---|---|
| **Human resources** | Research and development | Failure to provide new applicants on time | Delay of the release of new products |
| | Production | Failure to recruit qualified applicants | Customers upset over delay in new products |

→

**Self-help question 7.5**

| Organisational Type | | | Description |
|---|---|---|---|
| 1 | Privately held | D | Individuals or small groups of individuals entitled to the profits of the organisation |
| 2 | Publicly traded | C | Large groups of people (such as shareholders) own these types of organisations and have the right to share in the profits of the organisation |
| 3 | NGO | B | • Established to administer funds to meet a defined objective other than making a profit or creating wealth for its owners<br>• Examples include organisations dedicated to finding cures for diseases, or charities to support the work of those who serve the needy and poor of the community |
| 4 | Government | A | Created by legislation or by the direction of elected officials to meet some type of public need or deliver some type of public good |

**Self-help question 7.6**

| Inputs | Examples | |
|---|---|---|
| **Personnel** | • employees<br>• contractors | • consultants<br>• other subject matter experts |
| **Financial** | • money<br>• investment opportunities<br>• access to credit | |
| **Physical** | • buildings<br>• plant<br>• equipment<br>• computers | • vehicles<br>• utilities<br>• inventory<br>• other facilities |
| **Technological** | • information<br>• databases<br>• hardware | • software systems<br>• business-specific knowledge |

→

| Inputs | Examples |
|---|---|
| **Legal** | The ability to:<br>• conduct operations<br>• occupy premises<br>• use certain products or logos<br>• enter into binding contracts |
| **Reputation** | A general public estimation or perception of the company |

**Self-help question 7.7**

The following table provides some examples of the inputs Stan's Books requires.

| Inputs | Purpose |
|---|---|
| Personnel | • to meet the needs of customers who come to the store to purchase books<br>• behind-the-counter employees (sales)<br>• support employees who work in the back-room handling purchasing, accounting and financial duties for the company (non-sales) |
| **Money** | • access to money in the form of credit to allow the business to purchase an inventory of books to sell and pay employees<br>• paying operating expenses such as rent, utilities and store repairs |
| **Premises** | • a place from which to operate<br>• requires shelving and fixtures to hold books for sale<br>• might require a vehicle for transporting books and tables, desks and chairs for workers, as well as office equipment such as computers, phones and fax machines. |
| **Specialised information** | • knowledge of the bookselling business<br>• information on what the books are about and where to buy them<br>• knowledge of competitors and the market<br>• an understanding of the shop's 'demographic' (for example, the tastes and interests of their potential customers, as well as their income levels) to understand what books customers can reasonably afford to purchase |

→

→

| Inputs | Purpose |
|---|---|
| **Special legal rights** | • needed to conduct business (for example, a business licence from a regulatory body or a franchise agreement from book publishers) |
| **Books to sell** | • an inventory of offerings that can be converted to outputs |
| **Reputation in the community** | • an ivmportant component to the success of the company<br>• potential customers and key stakeholders need to feel confident that Stan's Books will properly serve and meet their needs |

**Note:** If Stan's Books is unable to obtain any of these inputs, it will jeopardise its ability to meet its objective of making a profit.

**Self-help question 7.8**

The following table provides some examples of systems, processes, and procedures for Stan's Books and their associated purpose.

| System, Process, or Procedure | Purpose |
|---|---|
| **Inventory control system** | On-demand books are made readily available to sell |
| **Accounting system** | Recognises and reconciles the purchase price of the books with cost to ensure a profit |
| **Employee roster** | Ensures there are adequate sales employees to meet customer needs |
| **Sales or advertising plan** | Helps the store attract more customers |
| **Payroll system** | Ensures employees receive the correct pay in a timely manner |
| **Management system** | The owner ensures all the other systems work properly to meet the organisation's objectives |

→

→

**Self-help question 7.9**

Typical objectives for organisational outputs may include:

- providing services to a community, which support the growth of the business over time;
- creating strong brand recognition or customer goodwill;
- successfully promoting a public agenda or issue;
- enabling a national organisation to be competitive in global markets;
- stimulating R&D.

**Self-help question 7.10**

1. It would be very difficult for Stan's Books to succeed if it experienced a prolonged loss of employees. While customers could assist themselves in locating books, a consistent employee level would be required for the bookstore to succeed in a competitive environment. Casual or temporary employees could undertake the responsibilities of lower-skilled positions (for example, cashiers and pricing clerks) but the store relies on knowledgeable, personal service to succeed. A stable employee base is therefore critical.
2. If Stan's Books lost its complete inventory of new books, it may still be able to operate on a limited level. Depending on arrangements between the owner and the new book suppliers, it could supply a limited amount of new stock quickly (for example, using air transport and courier delivery). Stan's Books could also minimise the reputational impacts of such an event by informing its customers of the loss and offering to deliver ordered books as soon as possible.
3. Losing a franchise arrangement could be extremely damaging to Stan's Books, depending on how reliant they are on the franchising organisation's products, services and marketing.

   Stan's Books would have to quickly replace these products or services, and possibly re-brand their store to establish their own identity. The organisation would hope customer loyalty would be sufficient to maintain revenue continuity while it re-branded and searched for new products.

→

→

**Self-help question 7.11**

The following table provides some examples of the inputs Stan's Books requires.

| Inputs | Organisation | Outputs |
|---|---|---|
| **Personnel**<br>• drivers<br>• technicians<br>• maintenance employees<br>• mechanics<br>• administration employees<br>**Financial**<br>• budget<br>• petty cash<br>• credit<br>**Legal**<br>• permits<br>• licences<br>**Property**<br>• vehicles<br>• depot<br>• storage tanks<br>• site office | **Policies, systems, processes, and procedures**<br>• inventory control<br>• maintenance schedules<br>• standard operating procedures<br>• inspection programmes<br>• training programmes | **Products**<br>• unleaded petrol<br>• leaded petrol<br>• diesel fuel<br>**Services**<br>• fuel storage<br>• fuel transportation<br>• inventory regulation |

**Self-help question 7.12**

Serious risk exposures relating to the health and safety can include:

- employee, contractor or visitor death
- employee, contractor or visitor disability, because of illness or injury
- lost productivity because of a workplace accident
- legal action.

**Self-help question 7.13**

- Assessment criteria for equipment/technology typically include a review of:
- failure probability

→

→

- dependency of the operation on the equipment
- dependency of equipment on external sources of power or fuel
- operational consequences of equipment failures
- current maintenance levels
- replacement costs or arrangements.

**Self-help question 7.14**

| Risk Category | Typical Risk Exposures | Key Stakeholder |
|---|---|---|
| Security | 1. Burglar steals vehicles garaged overnight at the fuel farm | 1. Security expert |
| | 2. Hijack of full tanker | 2. Police department |
| Fire | 1. Fire originating in fuel farm pumping system | 1. System manufacturer |
| | 2. Vehicle fire after collision | 2. Fire brigade |
| OHS | 1. Back injuries of maintenance crews | 1. Industry experts |
| | 2. Injuries in vehicle collisions | 2. Ambulance service |
| Equipment/ technology | 1. Loss of data from computer system failure | 1. Computer system contractor |
| | 2. Brake failure while the tanker is travelling at a high speed | 2. Tyre manufacturer and/ or consumer information groups |

**Self-help question 7.15**

| Risk Category | Typical Risks |
|---|---|
| Strategic risks | 1. Poor sales slow East Coast Oil's plan to expand to suburban markets |
| | 2. East Coast Oil's investment portfolio grows more slowly than anticipated, slowing plans for expansion to other states |
| Financial risks | 1. The cost of refinery products increases so dramatically that East Coast Oil is no longer competitive |
| | 2. Interest rates increase to such a level that East Coast Oil has difficulty obtaining credit to buy refined product |

→

→

| Risk Category | Typical Risks |
|---|---|
| Operational risks | 1. Injury of employee due to an industrial accident<br>2. Theft of vehicles parked at the fuel farm's garage |
| Compliance risks | 1. Failure to conform to EPA licensing requirements, resulting in fuel farm depot shut down<br>2. Failure to meet OHS/Work Cover requirements, resulting in mandatory improvement notices being issued |

**Self-help question 7.16**

Organisations can identify compliance risks in consultation with:

- legal advisors and other subject matter experts (SMEs)
- relevant members of industry associations
- the relevant regulator/s.

# Chapter 8

# Supply Chain Risk Management

## Introduction

Whereas the world is getting more and more complex and interconnected, the risk of supply chain disruption has become one of the most challenging risks that organisations must meet; this is a threat that practically all sectors must manage due to a global and increasingly interdependent economy.

Supply chains are often exposed to threats brought by natural or man-made disasters. In addition, these challenges are becoming more dynamic as organisations are increasingly interconnected through global networks. While a wider outreach can be beneficial, as it provides more options for choosing materials, employing talent and reducing costs, such growing complexity can also mean increased vulnerability to disruptions. Hence, it is important to maintain a resilient supply chain to keep performances at high levels.

As a matter of fact the term 'chain' is misleading when the network has become a real web in which each organisation is but one node. The web resilience depends on the weakest link and this means that organisations must consider managing third party risk. As evidenced in recent world events like tsunamis in Asia and volcanic eruptions, many organisations do not have a clear idea of the frontier of their dependency network: it is like a cloud with blurred limits.

However, for consistency with most academic and professional usage, we will adopt here the commonly used expression: supply chain risk management (SCRM).

The topics to be covered when considering SCRM include but are not limited to:

- What are the key risks to supply chains currently, including potential impact on brand and reputation?
- What are the connections with CSR activity, including consideration of impact on the environment?

**Risk Measurement and Monitoring, 185–202**

**Published under exclusive licence by Emerald Publishing Limited**
**doi:10.1108/978-1-83662-310-620251019**

- How are these risks best managed and by whom?
- Who do risk managers need to work with to make sure these risks are effectively identified, assessed, managed, and treated (including insurance covers)?
- What are the latest tools and methodologies available to help more accurately identify and measure supply chain risks?
- What level of insurance coverage is available, does it meet buyers' needs and is it fairly priced?
- Where are the coverage gaps and how can they be filled?

The challenge of supply chain or procurement risk is not a risk manager's challenge but impacts a broad range of disciplines – business continuity managers, supply chain managers, purchasing managers, quality specialists, lawyers and also insurers, reinsurers, brokers and claims experts, not to mention other specialist professional service providers.

As many surveys – too many to be mentioned here – evidence, there is a real and growing awareness of the importance of supply chain risk and the urgency for it to be properly identified, managed, reduced, and – when and where possible – transferred in a structured and professional manner to partners (when it is to be reduced) or insurers (when it is to be financed).

As already mentioned in other topics in all rimap® blocks, there is also a growing recognition that this is one more enterprise-wide risk that cannot be managed in silos. No single individual, department or profession owns this risk and it needs to be shared and collectively managed. However, any risk needs a defined owner in an organisation, therefore authority and responsibility will have to be assigned to different members of the network depending on the identified causes and effects.

As evidenced in social media entries, one aspect that stakeholders are very attentive to is CSR issues, not to mention global warming! Not only global corporations but also all their partners up and downstream must be aware of these issues. Therefore, it is particularly important for global corporations to ensure that its supply chain partners do not directly or indirectly fund modern slavery.

This is a striking example of the complexity of this risk and how it not only doesn't fit neatly into the realms of traditional silos but requires a new way of thinking. Complexity theory helps us understand the social behaviours of teams and networks of people involved in and around organisation and their procurement network.

It remains quite puzzling how many serious multinational companies do not really seem to know exactly who is supplying their key components beyond tier one, how reluctant they appear to be to share this knowledge when it exists, and what few practical contingency plans appear to be in place to deal with disaster when it inevitably strikes, as in Thailand in 2013 and Tianjin a couple of years later.

The BCI Supply Chain Resilience Report 2018 shows that, as with cyber, there remains a huge gap between the understanding of the scale of this risk and the relative reluctance of organisations towards the adoption of more advanced solutions in the supply chain, with only 38% saying they employ technology to predict, monitor, record, measure, and report on disruptions. Furthermore, the insurance market does not seem to be truly willing and/or able to truly face up to this risk, that is, to properly manage and insure critical elements of it.

The following topic will concentrate on the specifics of SCRM and will not repeat the general aspects mentioned in previous blocks for holistic risk management, including ISO 31000:2018's three wheels (principles, framework, and process), although these also apply to this area of risk.

## Learning Outcomes

At the end of this chapter, you should be able to:

- define 'supply chain' and associated terms;
- design a supply chain taxonomy;
- describe the complexity of supply chain risk and the problems that this complexity poses;
- outline the cyber component of supply chain risk;
- simplify supply chain risk information for a board.

## Definitions

### *Supply chain*

Investopedia provides the following definition:

> A supply chain is a network between a company and its suppliers to produce and distribute a specific product to the final buyer. This network includes different activities, people, entities, information, and resources. The supply chain also represents the steps it takes to get the product or service from its original state to the customer.
>
> Source: Investopedia

A supply chain can be divided into five steps:

1. *Plan* – The process that evaluates supply and demand to best meet requirements for production, sourcing and deliveries.
2. *Source* – The process of procuring goods/services to meet planned or actual demand.

3. *Make* – The process that transforms products into a finished state to meet actual or planned demand.
4. *Deliver* – The process that brings the finished goods or services to the end customer to meet actual or planned demand.
5. *Return* – The process that handles customer-returned products.

***Supply chain management***

Supply chain management (SCM) oversees materials, information, and finances as they move from supplier to manufacturer to wholesaler to retailer to consumer. It even covers disposal of products at the end of their useful life.

The three main flows of the supply chain are the product flow, the information flow and the finances flow. SCM involves coordinating and integrating these flows both within and among companies.

***Supply risk***

A supply risk is a threat arising from the inability of your organisation to supply its current and/or future customers.

***Supply chain risk management***

SCRM is an organisation's efforts to identify, monitor, and reduce threats to supply chain continuity and profitability.

Threats to supply chains include cost volatility, material shortages, supplier financial issues and failures, and natural and man-made disasters. SCRM strategies help an organisation predict potential threats and adapt to them as quickly and efficiently as possible. It can even help organisations respond to unforeseeable threats.

## A Taxonomy

There are many structures to tackle supply chain risks, and professional literature offers several ways to breakout the field. A very simple way would be to look at risk factors according to where they appear:

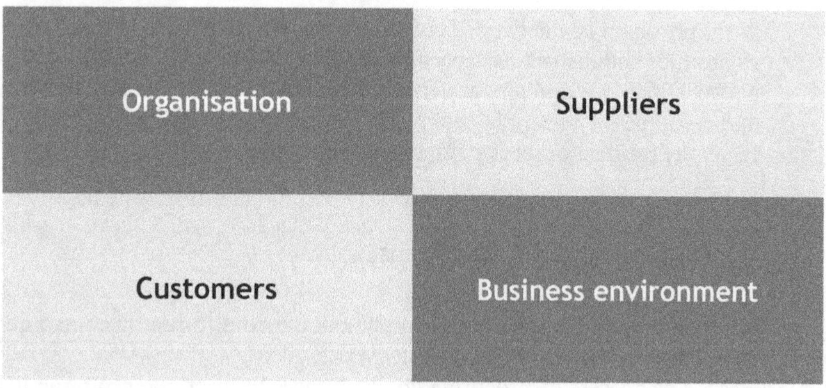

The four quadrants can then be expanded.

- Organisational (internal) risks

  – Plant explosion, earthquake, windstorm
  – An employee strike, pandemic, terrorism
  – Supply and demand forecasting error
  – Lean manufacturing/no inventory
  – Reputation
  – IT resiliency

- Supplier risks

  – Capacity/capability/quality
  – Intellectual property/technology
  – Financial stability
  – Their suppliers
  – All other risks considered internal risk (explosion, earthquake, windstorm, an employee strike, pandemic etc.)

- Customer risks

  – Changes in demand, tastes and technology
  – Availability of distribution channels
  – Quality/product recalls

- Business environment risks
  – Domestic regulatory changes
  – Foreign country and political changes
  – Market and foreign exchanges
  – Availability of credit

Another way to tackle the issue is to recognise that in every supply chain, risks lurk constantly and they can materialise from anywhere, including financial missteps, unresolved litigation, cyber attacks and outright fraud. All directors and officers must make sure their organisations proactively navigate these threats.

Let us review briefly the four main categories of risk.

- *Financial risk:* The financial condition and compliance practices of vendors as well as customers and distribution channels can pose a serious risk to supply chain. Some warning signs of poor financial health include deteriorating quality, late shipments, inconsistent statements, requests for early payments and lack of compliance.

- *Legal risk:* Pending lawsuits, patent disputes, trade wars and similar legal issues can seriously impair an organisation's future. It is essential to ask the right questions, such as:

  - Could negative public sentiment about a potential supplier or customer affect an organisation's reputation?
  - Will a vendor still be able to fill an order or will a customer accept delivery in spite of higher tariffs?

- *Cyber risk:* Cybercrime is increasingly relevant as industries digitise, and suppliers may be putting an organisation at risk. The questions to ask include:

  - Does your organisation know what safety measures its suppliers use?
  - Do your service contractors comply with relevant cyber security practices?

- *Fraud risk:* 'Many organisations are trapped in a pay-and-chase model for fighting supply chain fraud', says Mark Pearson, Deloitte Advisory Principal, Deloitte Financial Advisory Services LLP. This way of managing fraud risk could add up quickly and cost your business money.

To see an example of a detailed taxonomy, see the appendix.

## Managing Risk in Complex Systems

As the business world expands and become more integrated, supply chains become more complex. Manufacturers and distributors face a variety of potential disruptions ranging from natural disasters, fires and cyber threats to equipment breakdowns, counterfeit materials and supplier delays. However, with such complex supply chains, addressing these disruptions can be challenging, leaving businesses vulnerable to interruptions and potentially liable for faulty products.

To keep their supply chains running smoothly, manufacturers and distributors must closely manage supply chain partner relationships and company-specific operations.

- *Supply chain partner relationships:* Every supply chain consists of numerous players ranging from suppliers, manufacturers and distributors, to dealers and retailers. These players will each have a unique role in producing a final product or service.
- *Company-specific operations:* A business must also consider its own operations, including:

  - owned and public infrastructure, such as buildings, utilities, roads, vehicles, and machinery
  - technology, such as computers, software, and servers
  - staffing and the processes that employees use to get work done.

In a successful supply chain operation, all aspects of the chain work together so that each member of the network can deliver its products or services on time and on budget.

### *Proactive Planning for a Competitive Advantage*

Supply chain disruptions can affect a business in a variety of ways. If a supplier doesn't make a delivery, a business may be unable to fill orders. If a product component fails to meet quality standards, a business could face a product recall or legal or regulatory violations. These and other disruptions can also damage a business's customer relationships, reputation, market share and profitability.

However, a business that proactively plans how to mitigate supply chain disruptions may have a competitive advantage and be better positioned to grow its customer base and revenues. The following practices can help manufacturers and distributors minimise potential supply chain disruptions.

#### *Have a Formal Business Continuity Plan*

Business continuity plans are critical for minimising disruptions during an emergency and helping to protect the business, its employees and customers. In addition, a company's ability to quickly recover and resume operations after a disaster, whether as a result of a hurricane, fire or other event, is vital to maintaining its customer base and stakeholder trust and confidence and therefore its reputation.

The following steps will produce efficient plans:

- Conduct a risk assessment of the geographic area involved and operations to identify the most likely interruptions. It is essential to consider also technological disruptions such as data breaches and cyber attacks.
- Investigate and establish alternative business operations by identifying temporary facilities, backup suppliers, critical manpower needs, reroutes for shipments and access to inventory and equipment.
- Form a cross-functional recovery team that can help the business recover and get operations up and running.
- Secure important data, such as customer and employee records, business contracts, inventory, accounts payable/receivable and other financial information.
- Establish protocols for communicating with employees, customers, community and government agencies, and the media.

#### *Know Your Partners (And Their Partners) Well*

An organisation must understand the operations and supply chains of the suppliers, manufacturers, distributors and any other partners it works with – particularly when working with foreign companies. In today's economy, a business can no longer just be familiar with tier 1 partners (ones that are 'one up' and 'one down' in its supply chain). For example, if one of the suppliers works with tier 2 or 3 partners, the organisation must analyse how a disruption to these operations would affect its business. To protect their own operations, there are some additional questions that organisations need to consider during the exchanges with its partners, which include:

- What specifications do you use during development?
- Do you follow internationally recognised safety codes and consensus standards?
- How do you check the quality of the final product?
- Do you have business continuity plans in place? For what scenarios?
- How do you manage cyber security and protect intellectual property?
- Do you have a strong track record, and are they financially stable?

*Build in Contingencies*

Even in the world of lean and just-in-time processes, having contingency plans and access to extra inventory and equipment is critical. This includes the need to:

- diversify suppliers across geographic regions, and not rely solely on foreign sources that could be impacted by catastrophes or political instability;
- formalise relationships with alternative partners throughout the supply chain, including suppliers, distributors, and transporters, so replacement parts, equipment, and inventory are readily available;
- establish multiple facilities in different geographic areas so locations can support affected operations if needed;
- back up electronic files via the cloud and/or a secure, off-site location daily.

*Make Product Safety a Priority*

Making product safety a business priority helps protect customers and your business against product liability lawsuits and product recalls, which can cause major disruptions to any supply chain and operations. Therefore, it is recommended to:

- use a systematic evaluation process to qualify and select suppliers;
- create and follow a written design review process that identifies relevant safety codes, quality specifications, and consensus standards that should be met by partners throughout the supply chain;
- consult with customers to understand design specifications and final applications of products
- perform regular audits to confirm quality is consistent with expectations and that there are no safety issues;
- consider independent product testing;
- review instructions, user warnings, maintenance manuals and any other marketing, sales or technical communications developed to support the product;
- retain all documentation of processes and decisions throughout the product life cycle;
- establish formal product recall procedures so affected inventory is quickly identified and removed from the supply chain.

*Reduce Risk Through Contracts and Insurance*

A company's risk management, financial and legal teams should establish formal contracts with supply chain partners and review insurance needs with the company's insurance broker and carrier.

The process needs to include the following steps.

- Detail terms and conditions, roles, responsibilities, and service expectations and assign liability appropriately.
- Define the process for resolving known or suspected product safety risks. Clarify which parties will respond and in what manner if product defects arise.
- Review the company's and partners' insurance programmes to minimise the risk of coverage gaps. Consider coverage such as general liability, product liability and recall, equipment breakdown, cyber liability and umbrella, and confirm limits are sufficient.
- Verify that supply chain partners include the business as an additional insured on their general liability policies.

Advances in technology, evolving customer preferences, and the entry and exit of business partners are driving changes in the global economy and supply chain. Those companies that establish and follow robust risk management plans for their supply chains will be in the best positions to respond to these changes and recover from interruptions.

## Cyber Risk Issues

Like cyber risks, supply chain risks do not have borders. Effective vendor/supplier/provider cyber risk management is essential to ensure that the use of external services and goods does not generate potential adverse events (business disruption, security, and/or privacy breaches) that could negatively impact the company's business performance.

Cyber risk in supply chains is illustrated by what happened to Maersk and Merck. Both were hit by the NotPetya attack and cyber security analysis has identified their tax accounting software, MedDoc, as the access point for the malware.

Traditional vendor/supplier/provider risk management deals essentially with the suppliers' political and financial risk (including credit quality and liquidity). Digitalisation is impacting every component of supply chains. Nowadays, many small companies provide cloud services as needed as it is more economical.

The ability to identify critical vendors from a cyber security standpoint is crucial. Establishing a dedicated cyber risk governance team is a necessary step with a first mission to define the scope of specific risk assessment for cyber risk in the supply chain. Then, security, privacy and business requirements can be addressed in the request for proposals (RFP) or tender process.

As with any contractual activity, legal function will play a key role for the selection of the most appropriate requirements and wording to cope with the organisation's specific circumstances. However, the processes for reviewing vendor cyber risks on an ongoing basis are a demanding task. The level of screening should be tailored to the criticality of the service or process provided and/or outsourced by each vendor and the vendor's position along the supply chain.

Cyber risks require rethinking of the traditional mitigation strategies implemented for years in the procurement process. These solutions were based on diversifying sources to cover defects and secure alternatives.

But all suppliers can be subject to similar cyber threats, hence usual mitigation strategies can prove useless. Therefore, it is essential to look at layers, not just alternative suppliers. Individual suppliers should not be viewed in isolation; a holistic approach should assess the correlations and causalities within a supply chain.

From a cyber liability standpoint, the issue of transfer throughout the supply chain is highly challenging. Here are some of the reasons for this:

- There are few court precedents as of now, therefore few indications as to how such situations would or should be handled.
- It is difficult to prove that the lack of security was violating market standards. Also, who would be defining these standards?)
- Not all suppliers are able to implement industry best practices concerning security and due care.

The following can result:

- An inability to solve cyber liability issues can sometimes be a deal breaker.
- Organisations are potentially over-insured because they are uncertain about where liability lies and where coverage needs to be.
- Suppliers and cloud providers may begin to interact negatively; for example, some cloud service providers can carve out the liability element in an infrastructure provider service level agreement because they sit on a bigger cloud infrastructure provider (e.g. AWS).
- Difficulty in convincing supply chain partners to accept liability for cyber events (only for the recovery on some costs of services, cyber insurance).
- Lack of clarification of exposures to cyber liabilities (role of the regulators).

### Practical Examples

As part of the procurement process, Organisation A has a mandatory security policy that every supplier must accept to be selected. This policy includes the provision that suppliers can be subjected to audits. The policy is currently implemented but needs to be challenged to ensure it is up to date. It includes no requirements regarding cyber insurance thus far.

There is an idea to co-develop cyber insurance products with insurers so suppliers can have a tailored coverage validated by Organisation A.

Security policy requirements, evaluation process to assess the providers, different levels of assessments based on the risks, an addendum to the contract: outcome of the assessment (commensurate with the requirements, gaps, remediations be implemented) and Mandatory cyber insurance requirement and Privacy evaluation (compliance with GDPR), become part of the contract.

There are some key considerations:

- How does digitalisation affect the exposure of an organisation to supply chain risk?
  - How does it affect mitigation strategies (correlation dimension among the suppliers)?
  - How does it affect liability?
- What cyber incident scenarios should be developed to assess the suppliers and quantify their exposure?
- In a multi-layered supply chain, how can an organisation assess the impact of interdependency between suppliers?
- How does one supplier impact another? If there is a weakness in the supply chain, what does it mean to the overall risk profile? What signals should be looked for?
- How is cyber liability distributed in multi-layered supply chains?
- How can an organisation ensure that suppliers are handling data properly and in a secure manner?
- Should it be the role of regulators to clarify exposure to cyber liabilities?
- Overall, can the cyber liability risk be quantified and transferred though insurance or other products?

The management of cyber risk in supply chain implies that the risk manager should:

- consider cyber risks in the evaluations of third parties and especially the following:
  - new and cutting-edge procurement practices, adaptations in the recent years and showcase current practices
  - evolution of risk management strategies to take cyber risks in supply chains into account
  - expertise to determine the range and bounds of cyber liability.
- set-up an exchange or discussion/conversation group with possibly a final paper to be shared with a broader audience.

## Impact on Reputation

At the June 2019 Airmic Conference, Paul Goulding, head of insurance at Heathrow Airport, described the effect supply chain risk can have on reputation and used Heathrow Airport as an example. His presentation is summarised in this section.

Threats to reputation are increasingly dangerous within the supply chain. Reputational risk from supply chain failures is now a greater threat than that posed by supply chain inefficiencies to production, because of its long-term impact on the organisation and, in addition, a comparative lack of adequate insurance covers to mitigate the reputational risk.

Conducting checks to ensure good practice among suppliers is not enough to cover the risk. The question is, how far back up the chain do you go to know that you aren't reliant on some little outlet in China and exposed to all sorts of reputational damage? It is essential to take it as far up the chain as needed to protect the strategic goals of the organisation.

Furthermore, when it comes to risk financing, it is important to decided what kinds of insurance it is important to try and purchase to make sure that the chain is secure. Technically it is possible be fully covered, but the question is always how many resources should be put into insurance; what is financially responsible?

For organisations with few suppliers, managing supply chain resilience might be an easier task. But for organisations with hundreds of suppliers, such as major retailers, serious efforts are needed to establish a level of prioritisation in assessing the risk.

In the retail industry, it was usual to have people that would regularly visit key suppliers, but some industries do not have an army of people to do that, so there must be some level of prioritisation. In some respects, as bigger suppliers are likely to be more established and well-known, it's the smaller ones that are potentially going to be a source of problems.

This prioritisation is evident at Heathrow Airport. Paul revealed that relatively little supply chain risk assessment is conducted of major airlines because they are largely open and transparent in how they work. However, where the airport outsources work or hires companies on construction projects, analysis is undertaken at multiple layers of the supply chain.

The airport outsources several activities, and if they were outsourced to someone who is adopting unfair practices then the airport would suffer the damage to reputation.

Said Paul:

> *We have things that we do to try and validate what we insist our suppliers comply with and we use a number of contractual conditions in what we do and try and monitor that the best that we can. It's how far do you go and whether that is appropriate for the level of input that you put into these things.*

A good example is the London Living Wage: Heathrow Airport is trying to drive that through so that everyone, including contractors and suppliers, complies with that.

Some resources liaise with suppliers to find out what their arrangements are and to make sure they comply with requirements, but again it's how they push that back up through their supply chain and back into those multi-layers and levels that must be worked through all the time.

*What we don't want to be doing XYZ properly, only for their supply chain to be letting us down on that. So, it's important that we partner with the right people and establish that they are doing things in the way that you want.*

Reducing the number of suppliers is an option to save money and to make supply chain risk analysis more complete. But doing so requires a more in-depth multi-level analysis to understand the implications if one of these suppliers were to let you down. KFC provides a good illustration of how over-reliance on a single supplier can lead to general trading losses and reputational damage: the fast food chain ran out of chicken last year, when a supplier failed to deliver. The decision by KFC to radically overhaul its UK supply chain system, which ultimately forced it to temporarily shut down some 750 of its 900 UK outlets because chicken deliveries failed to turn up in February 2019, underlines the importance of SCRM.

*The KFC supply breakdown has had a serious impact on many people: the franchisees, the employees, as well as the brand as a whole. Immediate lost revenues, huge amounts of management time, damaged shareholder value and hordes of regular customers who tried a different fast food outlet. So lessons need to be learned.*

(Professor Richard Wilding, Chair in Supply Chain Risk Management at Cranfield School of Management, UK)

A few years ago, there was a move to reduce the number of suppliers, but when looking at it from a resilience perspective, it is easy to understand that if everything goes through one component it is essential to appreciate the implications of the loss of that part on the business.

To illustrate the point, one can consider the risk manager versus the supplier manger until they work together on long-term resiliency.

## Modern Slavery Risk

There are several cases where an organisation's reputation can be tarnished when the organisation does not take enough precautions to make sure that no member of its supply chain is in breach of CSR principles and ethics.

| Supply manager | Risk manager |
|---|---|
| • Reduce inventory | • More inventory |
| • Reduce supply base | • Multiple suppliers |
| • Minimize excess capacity | • Need excess capacity |
| • Use subcontractors | • TPMs are additional risks |
| • Reduce overall costs | • Balance costs & risks |

*Source*: Presentation at ERM seminars organised in France by Carm_Institute.

**Activity | Modern slavery risk**

Read the following two articles to learn more about modern slavery risk and to read about an example of a well-managed risk.

- 'Modern slavery index reveals depth of supply chain risk' from *Commercial Risk*. www.commercialriskonline.com/modern-slavery-index-reveals-depth-of-supply-chain-risk
- 'Adidas reaps reputational rewards for best-in-class modern slavery strategy' from *Commercial Risk Europe*.

http://edition.pagesuite-professional.co.uk/html5/reader/production/default.aspx?pubname=&edid=fd34b341-ae79-42aa-ad45-236970ddeba9

## Keeping It Board Simple

Managing supply chain risk is no easy task and demands an enterprise-wide response, but how is this best achieved? Risk managers need to involve all the necessary stakeholders, including strategy, and obtain the wide range of information needed to properly get a grip on this risk. However, there is also a need to keep things simple when reporting to the C-suite and the board.

Tackling supply chain risk requires an enterprise-wide risk management (ERM) approach. The risk is simply too large and complicated to lend itself to a silo approach as it involves many different business functions. The risk-management team needs to be aware of all the different risks and business units linked to the supply chain and then join the dots. The team's role is to ensure that risk is being managed holistically across the whole of the organisation.

To make that happen it is essential to be aware of what the different business units need to achieve and then adapting the process to work with them, without losing sight of the overall principals of the framework used.

### *Align Framework*

As is clearly suggested in the ISO 31000:2018, risk managers are to align the ERM framework with other processes led by units such as procurement, and then lean on them to help get the message across. ERM is about ensuring that risks, including those in the supply chain, are not managed in silos.

ERM dashboards that allow easy flow of information and, crucially, reports for top management and the board that are easy to understand and act upon. Too much information can cause board members to rush for answers to questions that aren't really going to be a problem. Too little information means the risk manager does not tell the board and C-suite about things that they need to be told about, which they then must tell them later. Identifying which information is essential is difficult; it is all about relating it to the things that matter, which is why involving strategy in the discussions is very important.

*Data Integrity*

Getting appropriate information on third parties can be very difficult. There are issues with data privacy, for example, and trusting the integrity of that data. So that can present some real challenges about what information can be presented to top management with reasonable assurance.

***Involve All Stakeholders (Internal and External)***

Engaging with the whole business on SCRM is essential; if doing otherwise, risk management runs the risk of things falling through the gap. So, the real question is: who would not be involved? The whole extended company (including customers and suppliers) must be engaged both on the operational and strategic side. Every stakeholder must be involved at a given point in time. Even focusing in on who are the most important people to work with can prove quite dangerous. Whatever the size of an organisation, there will always be stakeholders who must be identified across the enterprise.

It is also critical that the ERM team ensures that ownership of risks lies with those in the front line while ownership of activities must lie with those people who are managing relationships with stakeholders, third parties and operations involved.

Risk committees are very important when tackling complex threats such as those in the supply chain. The risk committee can give very clear and precise information to the board after taking a more in-depth look at the issues; boards simply do not have the time to do all that work. When it comes to the supply chain risk board, their reports must focus on opportunities as well as threats. It is necessary to ensure both sides of the risk equation are considered and to stress that ERM can provide upside benefits, as well as manage downside risk.

## Pitfalls

To ensure resilience and to manage the supply chain risks that are lying in the network of partners the organisation should be wary of the following pitfalls:

1. Disregarding the financial strength of non-listed suppliers
   *Tip to avoid it:* Review the financial health of private suppliers.
2. Neglecting the political context
   *Tip to avoid it:* Analyse geopolitical forces to identify third-party network vulnerabilities before they turn into real problems.
3. Neglecting to monitor early warnings for quality, consistency, and reliability
   *Tip to avoid it:* Monitor early warnings for quality, consistency, and reliability.
4. Misjudging the capacity constraints of technological suppliers
   *Tip to avoid it:* Identify where supplier constraints and material shortages could impact the third-party network.
5. Assuming all suppliers work at the same speed
   *Tip to avoid it:* Use real-time data to better understand your third-party ecosystem and gain a competitive advantage in a radically shifting supplier landscape.

6. Using brute force not collaboration
   *Tip to avoid it:* Have processes in place to monitor and manage suppliers that are struggling with quality, consistency or delivery; communication, coordination, and collaboration can head off future disruptions.
7. Considering cyber security to be an IT problem
   *Tip to avoid it:* Recognise that cyber security is not just an IT risk. It can create the same sort of third-party network exposures as a natural disaster (See 'Cyber risk issues' above).
8. Re-creating an in-house vendor intelligence network
   *Tip to avoid it:* Implement a system to monitor, evaluate, and identify vulnerabilities with high-impact vendors.
9. Isolating the supply chain from other client-facing business elements
   *Tip to avoid it:* Make sure you can assess third-party network exposures in a fully integrated business, from product development to point-of-sale and beyond.
10. Living in the dark
    *Tip to avoid it:* Visibility is key to third-party network management. The value of third-party intelligence to inform smart decisions is clear. Ultimately, with enough data and intelligence, third-party network management can become more aware and more responsive.

**Activity | The top 10 third party management mistakes**

Read Part 2 of the KPMG report 'Top 10 third party management mistakes' to learn more about these pitfalls and their related vulnerabilities.

https://institutes.kpmg.us/content/dam/institutes/en/manufacturing/pdfs/2018/top-10-third-party-management-mistakes.pdf

## Third-Party Network Threats and Opportunities

Everyone knows a natural disaster can wreak havoc on third-party network management. But not every disruption appears with the force of a hurricane or tsunami. For large manufacturers managing hundreds of third-party vendors, sometimes the dynamics playing out below the surface can change the course of even the most well-orchestrated third-party network. The surprise bankruptcy of a closely held service provider, a labour action on the other side of the world or the discovery of counterfeit components might be all it takes to bring your production to a grinding halt.

Understanding your third-party network ecosystem can help you identify vulnerabilities to your own production and product development – and anticipate which third-party risks could have the greatest impact on your day-to-day operations and strategic priorities.

In its broadest sense, third-party vulnerability is any threat to your third-party network or weakness within your vendor base. However, a third-party network ecosystem is a complex, dynamic network; therefore, identifying vulnerabilities requires technology that is not only able to highlight vulnerabilities but also to anticipate potential consequences to your production cycle.

Global supply chains are irreversible, as are the supply-chain risks that globalisation has brought with it. Experience suggests that it is critical for organisations to build robust programmes for managing both known and unknown supply-chain risks. Leaders should also recognise that risk management is not merely about setting up processes and governance models, but also entails shifts in culture and mind-sets. By employing these approaches, organisations increase their chances of minimising supply-chain disruptions and crises, while capturing the full value of their supply-chain strategies.

## Summary

Please keep the following points from this chapter in mind:

- A supply chain is a network between a company and its suppliers to produce and distribute a specific product to the final buyer.
- A supply chain can be divided into five steps: Plan, Source, Make, Deliver, and Return.
- SCM oversees materials, information, and finances as they move from supplier to manufacturer to wholesaler to retailer to consumer.
- A supply risk is a threat arising from the inability of your organisation to supply its current and/or future customers.
- SCRM is an organisation's efforts to identify, monitor and reduce threats to supply chain continuity and profitability.
- There are many structures to tackle supply chain risks. A very simple way would be to look at risk factors according to where they appear.
- To keep their supply chains running smoothly, manufacturers and distributors must closely manage supply chain partner relationships and company-specific operations.
- A business that proactively plans how to mitigate supply chain disruptions may have a competitive advantage and be better positioned to grow its customer base and revenues. The following can help minimise potential supply chain disruptions:

  – have a formal business continuity plan
  – know your partners (and their partners) well
  – build in contingencies
  – make product safety a priority
  – reduce risk through contracts and insurance.

- Like cyber risks, supply chain risks do not have borders. Effective third-party cyber risk management is essential to ensure that the use of external service and goods do not generate adverse events that could negatively impact the company's business performance.

- Reputational risk from supply chain failures is now a greater threat than that posed by supply chain inefficiencies to production because of its long-term impact on the organisation and a lack of adequate insurance covers to mitigate the risk.
- An organisation's reputation can be tarnished when the organisation does not take enough precautions to make sure that no member of its supply chain is in breach of CSR principles and ethics.
- Risk managers need to involve all necessary stakeholders, including strategy, and obtain the wide range of information needed to properly get assess a risk while keeping things simple when reporting to the C-suite and the board.
- Engaging with the whole business on SCRM is essential; otherwise, risk management runs the risk of falling through the gap.
- Risk committees are very important when tackling complex threats such as those in the supply chain. They can give very clear and precise information to the board after taking a more in-depth look at the issues.
- Understanding your third-party network ecosystem can help you identify vulnerabilities to your own production and product development and anticipate which third-party risks could have the greatest impact on your day-to-day operations and strategic priorities.

Chapter 9

# Project Management

## Introduction

This section introduces some basic project management concepts to integrate the management of risk into the project and business context. This section also suggests how organisations can integrate project management into the ERM process.

## Learning Outcomes

By the end of this topic, you should be able to:

- describe the concept of project management
- outline a project management framework
- identify and document potential sources of risk within project stages
- describe and apply tools/techniques and strategies (including plans and reports) that are useful to assessing, treating and monitoring risk in projects
- describe how you may be able to integrate the risk work undertaken within the project management function into the overall ERM process.

***Case Study (Background) – Cityshore Development and Construction***

Cityshore's executive and general managers are meeting as part of the company's ongoing risk identification, planning and management process.

**Risk Measurement and Monitoring, 203–253**

**Published under exclusive licence by Emerald Publishing Limited**
**doi:10.1108/978-1-83662-310-620251021**

**Ted:**

Hi everyone. I'd like to allocate the first 15 minutes of the agenda to Arthur James from risk management. He'll lead a quick brainstorm on the key risk issues that seem to be coming up either as a potential impact from general organisational activity or from different areas of projects in their current stages.

**Arthur:**

Thanks, Ted. We've identified the Villas project, consisting of the combined villa multi-storey apartment and retail outlet project down on the local Melbourne shoreline, as a risk hotspot for immediate attention.

Could I open the floor to some thoughts and ideas?

**Ted:**

Before we begin, I'd like to remind everyone that this business has grown rapidly with considerable operations revenue growth in the past two financial years. We've made some strides in the development area of our core businesses by taking on the financing of projects like the Villas project but we're not going to fully realise profit from this project until the next financial year onwards — so that's at least one risk context we need to keep in mind.

**Bob:**

As the construction manager, I'm concerned about construction cost control on this project.

**Ed:**

Fair point, Bob. The design phase went over budget as well. We also haven't received final council approval for some of the plans.

**Ratanya:**

I would like to add that we're highly leveraged on this project. Interest rates may rise, and any rise is going to influence profits.

**Cindy:**

From a marketing perspective, there's a worrying softening in off-the-plan sales. We're likely to see delays in sales, some forfeiting of current deposits and reduced sales.

**Peter:**

From the HR perspective, a couple of very senior people are leaving the Villas project, one to retirement and the other to resignation, and we have yet to replace them.

Also, the cost of fit-out, such as appliances, is another issue. We have suggested sourcing these fit-out items from China but a selling point of the Villas project was name-brand appliances from Europe.

**Cindy:**

The marketing department fears the reputation of the project would suffer if cheaper appliances are installed.

**Ted:**

Cityshore's 'green' credentials are at risk, too. We've failed to implement our sustainable policies fully on two recent projects. I think we need to re-assert our reputation by making sure we follow through on existing policy, and by marketing the Villas projects as a premium site using green-friendly materials and solar power.

**Bob:**

Maybe you're right, Ted, but that would blow out construction costs on this project, and they're already too high.

**Arthur:**

This is a pretty substantial list of risk issues. I think the best next step is for Tim, as project manager, to redraft the existing risk management plan for the Villas project. If we can have the draft plan ready for the next managers' meeting in two weeks' time, we can all work on finalising it.

**Tim:**

Of course. I may need to consult each of you according to your different areas. I'll also need to identify and separate out direct project risks from other risks resulting from and impacting on the organisation.

***Case study (issues)***

Consider the following issues as you proceed through this section.

- What are the organisational risks impacting on the Villas project?
- How might the identified risks affect Cityshore as an organisation?
- How might Cityshore assess the potential impact/consequences of the risks identified in this project?
- What strategies could Cityshore use to manage the risks identified so far in the project?

---

Answers to self-help questions are provided at the end of each section.

## Project Management

Risk in project management can be as relevant to one part of a project as it is to the entire project since each part of a project is, by itself, a project.

### *Definition*

The term project management is frequently used to define a process that includes:

> [...] managing resources to achieve a unique task within a set framework of performance.

### *Delivering Change*

Operational managers often use project management processes to deliver important changes so the organisation needs to manage the associated risks.

### *The Business Framework*

A project begins with a business requirement and endeavours to conclude with a business improvement. Consequently, all projects exist within a business framework. Project risk/opportunity is therefore integral to business risk.

**EXAMPLE**

**Charity**

A charity may licence its name for a fundraising project but, in the process, run the risk of reputational damage through aggressive or inappropriate fundraising methods. The following table distinguishes between the output and outcome of the fundraising.

**Outputs and Outcomes of Fundraising**

| Outputs | Outcomes |
|---|---|
| **Acquiring funds** | A decrease in the charity's:<br>• goodwill status<br>• future capacity to raise funds for its work |

### *Critical Components of a Project*

A project's level of quality is defined by the three main elements listed in the following diagram. As such, there is a whole subset of risks for each project governing its ability to deliver on time, with minimal cost and maximum quality.

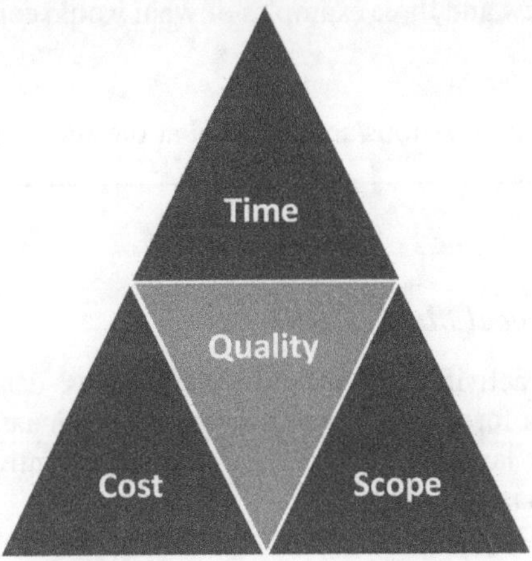


**Critical Components of a Project**

These three elements closely interrelate: to effectively manage one component requires an understanding of its relationship to each of the others. One can express this relationship simply, in the sense that a change in one component will most likely produce a change in one or both of the others.

While there is always an element of optimisation within any project management task, the pressures to achieve maximum scope, minimum cost and faster delivery can lead to conflict.

**EXAMPLE**

**Cost Risks**

Cost risk is the risk that a project will cost more than what was budgeted. For example, cost risk can arise from a failure to lock in costs with contactors or material suppliers.

As you may have experienced in your working life, projects often fail or fail to deliver on certain promises. Therefore, there is an important role for risk management in reducing this risk of failure.

**Self-Help Question 9.1**

Provide an overview and three examples of what would constitute a project.

Answers to self-help questions are provided at the end of each section.

### *Project and Operational Management*

Projects are unique activities for which a team forms, delivers outcomes and disbands (or reforms for a new project). By their continually changing nature, delivery and the risk landscape for projects are significantly different from the continuous processes in operations.

The following table summarises the difference between project and operational management.

**Difference Between Project and Operational Management**

| Project Management | Operational Management |
|---|---|
| A process which generally delivers a *unique* outcome | A process which generally uses *repetitive* processes to deliver a continuous stream of product with *similar* specifications |

### *The Project Life Cycle*

One of the key differences between project and operational management is the evolution of the project (and therefore its risk profile) through stages, as the project owner progressively commits funding to the delivery.

Project management is a staged process that moves a project from an idea through an endorsed product requirement to a design or plan for delivery followed by delivery or implementation to a commissioning or handover to the project owner or user.

This subsection describes the most common four-stage (or phase) project process as a model for identifying, tracking and managing project risk. The following table summarises these stages.

**The Four Stages of the Project Process**

| Stage | Description |
|---|---|
| **1. Initiation** | Define project expectations |
| **2. Planning** | Finalise specification and delivery plan |
| **3. Implementation** | Create the product |
| **4. Handover** | Put the product to work for the owner |

**Note:** There are many different project management methodologies, but those stages listed in the previous table are the most common.

This section progressively considers identifying and treating risk during each stage of the project life cycle, to provide you with an insight into the project management process both for the:

- deliverable stage (as a project in its own right)
- overall project.

Whatever method your organisation uses to manage its projects, the important thing is for you to be satisfied with the integrity of the risk management component and how this integrates with the overall ERM process.

This subsection describes project management by examining:

- meanings inherent in its concepts and terms
- core project objectives
- the project manager's role and principal tasks
- how to define a project across its scope, cost and time elements
- how risk management is integrated within project management.

### *Concepts*

Considering the concepts of project and management individually can assist those new to the area in understanding the project management concept. To integrate project risk management into this understanding requires organisations to draw on standards and guides, both familiar and new.

*Project*

The term project is associated with a unique set of objectives; for example:

- constructing a building
- developing a software package
- setting up an industrial plant
- undertaking organisational change.

The outcomes of a project must be achieved within a predetermined:

- scope
- cost budget (both operating and capital)
- time frame.

As previously highlighted, a project is a once-only or unique task usually carried out by a project team. This contrasts with the repetitive tasks undertaken by a line or production manager.

***The Project Manager***

The project manager usually manages a project from conception to completion and hands over outcomes to the line manager. This role and process is distinct from that of, say, a marketing manager, designer or financier, who may each have a role during one stage of a project only.

*Management*

Management is essentially associated with functions such as:

- leading a team
- determining team objectives
- controlling team communication with a client or sponsor
- comparing achievements against set objectives
- having the authority to change what a team is doing
- resolving conflict.

*Project + management*

Project management combines the essential attributes of both the *project* and *management* concepts. Project *risk* management is also inherent in all the previously listed management functions.

Project management can be a part or full-time, internal or outsourced task for an individual. Alternatively, project management may require a team of project management personnel for major projects.

## Project Risk Management and Standards

The concepts, processes and tools for risk management within ISO 31000:2018 provide a starting point for understanding how to identify, assess and manage risks in a project. Another guide that might be useful is the *PMBOK® Guide: A guide to the project management body of knowledge* (2017) from the Project Management Institute (PMI).

### *PMBOK®*

The *PMBOK® Guide* is structured around the following nine functions:

1. Integration management
2. Scope management
3. Time management
4. Cost management
5. Quality management
6. Human resources management
7. Communications management
8. Risk management
9. Procurement management.

**Note:** While the *PMBOK®* was developed to guide best practice standards for project management, it also deals with project risk management and follows similar risk management processes and definitions to those in ISO 31000.

### *Managing Opportunities and Threats*

As previously explored, organisations should manage positive risk or opportunities within the same framework as negative risk or threats. This is an ongoing issue in project management, because positive risk is rarely defined in the same framework as negative, often resulting in lost opportunities to improve project outcomes. Please keep this issue in mind as you progress through this section.

Objectives driving any project

The starting point for managing any project should be a clear definition of the project objectives and priorities in terms of scope, time and cost. While these may change at various stages throughout the project life cycle, defining these factors serves as a baseline against which to measure and judge achievement and variations.

#### *Primary or Core Project Objectives*

The core objectives driving any project/project manager are to:

- achieve the organisation's goals (project scope)
- keep the cost within budget (the price the organisation is prepared to pay: project cost)
- handover at the expected date (within the requested time: project time).

The following table describes each of these elements in further detail.

**The Three Core Project Elements**

| Element | Description |
|---|---|
| **Scope** | The scope of a project:<br>• is the desired outcome as set by the aims and objectives of the project sponsor?<br>• identifies project needs and outcomes<br>• is expressed in terms of function and performance.<br>• provides a narrative description of work to be accomplished, including:<br>– objectives<br>– brief description<br>– specifications<br>– summary. |
| **Cost** | A summary or cost plan of financial constraints including:<br>• project and ongoing revenue/operating costs<br>• budget allocation. |
| **Time** | A milestone schedule defining:<br>• key progress dates for the project team<br>• tasks. |

**Note:** There are also other elements (or functions/objectives) but they are subsets of the previous three core objectives.

Firstly, the project manager must control these core functions within the client or sponsor's business environment-defined boundaries, including:

- risk
- quality
- procurement.

As part of the process, the project manager also coordinates and manages:

- human resources
- communications
- the integration of all project elements.

**EXAMPLE**

**Delivering a Project in Faster Time**

It is possible to deliver a project in a faster timeframe but quality and cost may suffer. This is because quality checking at each stage takes time and speeding up a project may involve the payment of penalty rates such as overtime or public holidays.

## Establish the Context

The standard risk management approach requires understanding the contexts within which the risk is managed, whether they be:

- strategic
- organisational
- management.

A project manager preparing a risk management plan must undertake the same process of establishing the project risk context, as this determines the:

- sources of risk
- appropriate approach (and therefore treatment) to managing the risk.

Integrating the impact of risk to the project that arises from an organisation's strategic policy and goal/strategy is therefore the first step.

### *Defining the Project*

Organisations first define a project by developing and documenting the three core project elements or functions:

- project scope
- project cost
- project schedule (time).

**EXAMPLE**

**Public Transport Project**

Key stakeholders need to decide on the following objectives in a public transport project:

- number of passengers
- speed
- time per journey
- reliability
- safety
- maintainability.

### *A Work Breakdown Structure*

For a project manager to be successful in achieving the set project objectives, (including the risk objectives), it can be useful to 'scope' the project tasks using a work breakdown structure (WBS) or work plan. A WBS is now the accepted technique or tool for integrating scope, cost/resource and time requirements according to the allocation of individual and organisational responsibilities.

The WBS also provides a framework for:

- identifying risk (for example, what could go wrong for each step)
- associating this with each project part's:
  - scope
  - cost
  - time
  - quality
  - procurement functions.

### *Risk Management*

Organisations can manage risk through changes to the scope, cost, time, communications, procurement, quality and human resources equation.

**EXAMPLE**

**Contract Change**

Changing from an open-order to a fixed-price contract can change cost risk.

The following figure illustrates how some of the previously described project elements and management functions can be defined and integrated.

### *Accountability*

With regards to accountability, organisations need to:

- assign and document risk management accountability in risk registers
- decentralise responsibility for risks
- ensure the project risk manager is responsible for coordinating the risk management process.

### *The Project Team*

The project team needs to measure and monitor the project milestones to ensure the organisation will meet its objectives. Critical to measurement and monitoring are:

- the oversight of the risk management process
- reliable risk management reporting.

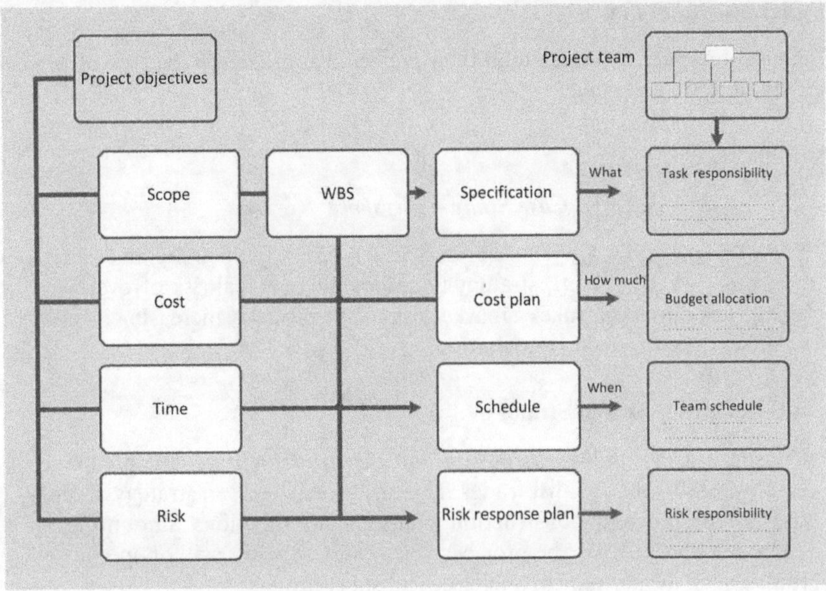


**Integrated Project Management**

*Project Initiation*

The project manager needs to engage the project team to set the project context and articulate the objectives and elements of the project.

*Planning*

The project team needs to specify and document how it will deliver the project to meet project cost, time and scope objectives. This phase involves analysing project risks and developing risk registers, processes and accountabilities.

*Implementation*

The project team needs to engage stakeholders, key personnel and the organisation more broadly when responsibility for managing risk resides outside of the project team.

***Other Factors to Consider***

Organisations also need to consider the following items in understanding the context:

- organisational policy
- stakeholder attitudes
- stakeholder risk appetite/tolerance
- the project risk management plan.

### *Organisational Policy*

Organisations need to understand their preferred approach to the type of project activity they are assessing.

***Case Study – Cityshore***

In its Villas project, Cityshore prefers to sell property off-the-plan as a risk minimisation (treatment) strategy to reduce the financial risk of overleveraging. The purchaser takes a market risk of the property increasing in value to offset their up-front contribution.

**A Strategically Driven Strategy**

Cityshore also employs its design and construction staff, but no longer employs staff for specialist trades. This strategically driven strategy accepts risk for design and construction management functions amounting to approximately 20% of the project's worth; but offloads risk for specialised trades, such as mechanical and electrical subcontracts.

Cityshore also intends to outsource human resources (particularly injury services) to be able to:

- offload other risks
- concentrate on its field of expertise.

These actions illustrate examples of risk sharing, transference or acceptance based on the business's policy decisions.

Tim Allsop and other managers working on the draft risk management plan for the Villas project need to integrate these more universal risk management policies into the identification, assessment and treatment of risks arising from the individual project.

### *Stakeholder Attitudes*

A critical part of establishing the risk context is identifying and analysing the project stakeholders':

- values
- expectations
- tolerances of and attitudes towards risk.

In addition, you need to explore how these factors may influence project outcomes.

Stakeholder attitudes to risk may significantly influence the policy objectives or success of any phase of a project. Consequently, the project manager needs to determine stakeholder attitude to risk as, itself, a risk to the project requiring management. For example, what is the stakeholder's tolerance to not being able to meet time, cost or quality objectives?

Differing stakeholder tolerances may also affect how a project manager should respond as risks change. Therefore, strategies to manage stakeholder attitudes to risk in a project inevitably differ between stakeholders depending on the kind of role they might have in that project.

---

**Tip – Stakeholder Involvement**

Closely involving stakeholders reduces the risk of miscommunication regarding the required outcomes, particularly as projects mature.

---

**Self-Help Question 9.2**

Consider some of the following stakeholders you might find engaged in a development and construction project.

Describe their attitudes to risk in qualitative terms, as well as their desired target rate of return, before committing to the project.

| Stakeholder | Attitude to Risk | Target Rate of Return |
|---|---|---|
| Venture capital funds manager | | |
| Banker | | |
| Project developer | | |

---

Answers to self-help questions are provided at the end of each section.

**Activity | Stakeholders in your workplace**

Reflect on two recent projects in your organisation. Identify the key stakeholders and their sensitivity to the three elements of cost, quality and time.

- Did the projects deliver what stakeholders expected?
- If not, what risks did the organisation fail to manage which resulted in this outcome?
- Could the organisation have managed these risks more effectively?
- Were the lessons incorporated in the organisation's project management and risk management processes?

---

**Self-Help Question 9.3**

List three strategies you could utilise for gaining input from and assessing stakeholder attitudes to (or tolerances of) risk.

---

Answers to self-help questions are provided at the end of each section.

---

### *The Project Risk Management Plan*

The project risk management plan, prepared as part of the project's first or initiation stage, sets out the context and strategy for managing risk in a project. Some organisations may not approve the project unless stakeholders conduct and include a comprehensive analysis of the project's risks in the project submission. The project scope document can include the risk management plan. Alternatively, the organisation can develop the project scope document as a separate document (depending on the size of the project).

The project scope documents what is and isn't included in the project. According to the Tasmanian State Government (2005) the project scope should cover:

- the process for identification, analysis, evaluation and treatment of risks, both initially and throughout the life of the project, including estimated costing
- the process for transferring approved risk costing into the project budget
- the process for transferring risk mitigation activities into the project work breakdown structure
- how often the risk register will be reviewed, the process for review and who will be involved
- how risk status will be reported and to whom
- who will be responsible for which aspects of risk management
- a snapshot [for example, risk register] of the major risks, current gradings, planned mitigation strategies and costings, and who will be responsible for implementing any mitigation strategies.

If they are not involved in preparing the plan, it is important that the risk manager reviews the plan carefully to ensure it:

- is well prepared
- provides appropriate linkages into the ERM process (such as capturing the material risks identified for central reporting).

**Activity | Project risk management plans**

Research templates/examples of project risk management plans online. Consider, what 'inputs' such plans require.

In addition, research templates/examples of project risk management plans within your organisation. Answer the following questions:

- How do they relate to the examples you researched online?
- What are the relative strengths and weaknesses?
- Is there any integration with your ERM process? For example, consider measurement, reporting and accountability.

## Risk Assessment

To be able to identify and manage risk, the project risk management stages need to align with the previously identified four project stages:

- initiation
- planning
- implementation
- handover.

When applying the ISO 31000:2018 risk management process, each step relates to the stage of the project.

**Note:** It is not possible to fully identify, analyse and manage project risk until the relevant stages of the project are underway and the required information is available.

### *The Project Risk Assessment Framework*

The following table provides a suggested framework for identifying, assessing and managing project risk. Organisations should perform this initial assessment at the project approval stage to ensure there are no risks which would render the project unviable.

**Note:** Risk assessment at this stage is usually fairly high level.

**Project Risk Assessment Framework**

| Project stage | Main activities | Risk management activities |
|---|---|---|
| Initiation | • Define the product/project requirement<br>• Establish feasibility<br>• The client approves the project | After defining the risk context and preparing the risk management plan (which identifies risk tolerances), the organisation needs to:<br>• identify and assess attitudes and strategies<br>• list major categories<br>• start a risk register |
| Planning | Finalise specification and delivery plan | • Analyse risk<br>• Prepare a risk treatment plan<br>• Integrate the risk treatment plan with other project plans, including quality assurance |
| Implementation | • Create product/project<br>• Manage all aspects of the project delivery<br>• Apply project controls | • Manage risk<br>• Implement control/ treatment as risk events arise<br>• Regularly reassess risk as the project plan changes and the organisation identifies new factors |
| Handover | Product/project is put to work for the owner | • Define operator risk<br>• Commence the operational risk management plan |

Typically, the most significant tools/documents required in working with this kind of framework are the:

- work breakdown structure (WBS) or work plan
- project risk management plan
- project risk register
- project risk treatment plan (or project risk response plan).

*The WBS or Work Plan*

The WBS is an almost essential tool for assessing project risk because it identifies every task and activity, allowing for more precise identification and management.

*A Breakdown of Tasks*

Beginning with the total project, the WBS technique successively deconstructs tasks into smaller subdivisions that organisations can independently assign and manage. This breakdown can work progressively through the project stages as the level of detail increases.

*A Critical Project Risk Assessment Tool*

The WBS also identifies interdependencies where some tasks cannot be started until others have been completed. For example, the WBS can show that a small change in the project will have ramifications for the amount of work and, therefore, the budget.

*Purpose*

By breaking the project down, the organisation can exercise greater visibility and control over each of the project components.

In its simplest expression, a WBS is an outline of the work to create, manage and shut down a project. It outlines the scope of, and provides the framework for, the project.

Using the WBS, the project manager can:

- plan the budget
- code costs
- outline tasks
- define responsibilities
- analyse resources
- plan the project schedule.

*Achieving a Detailed WBS*

Organisations can best achieve a detailed WBS through using all project team members and, for example, a brainstorming technique to identify the tasks required.

*Various Formats*

A WBS can take various forms. Some project managers use the project budget as their WBS and others will use a software package such as Microsoft® Project.

*Risk Classification*

The number of risks organisations can identify using the WBS can be difficult to control if there is no classification system. During the process of discovery, the organisation will inevitably classify risks into those:

- worth taking note of (and therefore treating)
- to which exposure poses no significant threat.

The measurement criteria set up for likelihood, consequence and overall risk in the ERM system should form the basis for this exercise.

By working with the WBS technique, organisations can first classify risks according to the activity, task or functional area of project management in which the risk has first been identified or sourced.

*Case Study – Cityshore*

Cityshore decides to address one of the identified risks to their Villas Project by developing a series of open-day events to promote and market the project as a premium site using green-friendly materials and solar power.

Cindy Leiden in marketing oversees managing this project.

**Risk classification – Areas or activities**

Using the WBS technique within such a project, Cindy might classify risks by the following areas or activities:

- funding and sponsors
- location
- human resources
- suppliers.

**Risk classification – Processes or activities**

Risks in this kind of project might also be categorised in terms of processes or activities, such as:

- outsourcing (procurement)
- communication
- management
- logistics.

**Risk classification – Consequences**

Alternatively, risks could be categorised according to their consequences. One way of identifying triggers (actions or lack of actions that indicate a potential problem) for a project such as staging an event (or series of events) is to examine an event incident and list its possible causes.

**EXAMPLE**

**Crowd Management**

Poor crowd management could result from several factors such as:

- poorly positioned barricades
- incorrect signage
- errors in promotional literature.

***Risk classification — Cityshore Villas Project***

Cindy decides to categorise the risks for the Cityshore Villas Project open-day events in the following way:

- marketing and promotion
- human resources
- stakeholder communication
- on-site
- catering
- entertainment
- subcontractors
- legal
- occupational/workplace health and safety
- finance.

> **Activity | WBS examples**
>
> Locate examples of different approaches to a WBS on the internet by using the full term or its acronym.

*Project Risk Register*

The project risk register is the basis for the project risk management plan. In small projects, the plan may only consist of the risk register. A project risk register is likely to include:

- a description of each risk and how it affects the project
- an assessment of likelihood and consequence, and overall risk
- a description of mitigation strategies, which can include preventative (to reduce the likelihood) and contingency actions (to reduce the impact)
- who is allocated responsibility
- pricing of each mitigation strategy (in larger projects).

***A Subset of the ERM Register***

Essentially, the project risk register has the same format and information needs as the ERM register (of which it is a subset). For this reason, consistency between the ERM register and the project risk register is preferred.

The project risk register can be a separate register, but if the organisation accepts a more integrated approach it can set up the project register as a different category in the ERM register. This serves the purpose of allocating all the risks for the project to that category.

In this way, project risk is seamlessly integrated, yet can be separately reported for project management purposes. Reports of enterprise-wide risks then include project risks without the need for any further intervention or consolidation.

**Activity | Project risk register examples**

Research examples of project risk registers or templates online.

In addition, research templates/examples of project risk registers within your organisation. Answer the following questions:

- How does your organisation's project risk register relate to the examples you researched online?
- What are the relative strengths and weaknesses?
- Is there any integration with your organisation's ERM process? Consider measurement, reporting and accountability (for example).

### *Risk Treatment Plan*

Organisations identify and analyse risk and prepare a treatment plan in the second or planning stage of a project. This forms part of the project's delivery specification to be handed to the project's third stage implementation team. Unlike ERM, a project is not business as usual (BAU) and the risk treatment plan usually provides for developing all the required controls (because there are no pre-existing controls). At this stage, prior to developing the risk treatment plan, inherent risk is equivalent to residual risk.

---

**Self-Help Question 9.4**

Imagine you are one of the managers involved in the Cityshore case study. Describe two foreseeable organisational and project risks you would ensure you included in the draft risk management plan for Cityshore's Villas project.

**Note:** Keep in mind that organisational and project risks can sometimes be similar; for example, an interest rate rise can affect both:

- a project's profit through sales
- the company's performance through borrowing costs.

---

Answers to self-help questions are provided at the end of each section.

---

## Identify Risks – Stage 1: Project Initiation

This section has suggested that in the project initiation stage, the organisation defines the project to:

- establish its feasibility
- gain implementation approval (for example, from a project owner, a company client or a government department).

The organisation prepares the risk management plan in this stage, which:

- outlines the risk context
- identifies risk tolerances and attitudes of stakeholders
- identifies sources of risk
- integrates these into a risk register.

### *Sources of Project Risk*

The sources of project risk, and the categories within which they fall, arise from how a project is initially scoped and defined and include:

- overall risk sources
- specific risk issues
- other risks.

The following table outlines these three types of sources of risk.

**Sources of Risk**

| Risk Sources | Examples |
|---|---|
| Overall risk source | • cost<br>• time for delivery<br>• regulatory<br>• marketing<br>• environmental<br>• contractor failure |
| Specific risk issues | • a delay in delivering key components |
| Other risk issues | • design compliance<br>• lack of skilled personnel<br>• failure to meet delivery dates<br>• defaults |

**EXAMPLE**

**Time Delay**

At times, risk sources and categories may have the same name and a source of risk may often give rise to risk in several categories.

Time delay could cause cost increases as well as a purchaser's default.

Alternatively, time delay could lead to the opportunity (positive risk) for an increase in prices in a rising market.

*Identification*

You can use a range of tools and techniques to identify sources of risk; for example:

- brainstorming
- fault diagrams
- cause and effect.

The most useful approach is usually a short workshop with staff who are experienced in the project type.

***Registering Identified Risk***

The following table provides an example of a spreadsheet approach to registering identified project risk issues or vulnerabilities.

**Part of Project Risk Issues/Vulnerabilities Register for a Construction Project**

| **Vulnerabilities** | **Planning** | | **Implementation (construction)** | | **Handover** | |
|---|---|---|---|---|---|---|
| | Action | Sign-off | Action | Sign-off | Action | Sign-off |
| 1. Cost | Plan and report on design | Project manager (PM) | | PM | | PM |
| 2. Delivery time | Analyse and propose resources | PM | | Construction manager (CM) | | PM |
| 3. Design | | Design manager (DM) | | CM | | PM |

(*Continued*)

| **Vulnerabilities** | **Planning** | | **Implementation (construction)** | **Handover** |
|---|---|---|---|---|
| – Site/building | Design review | DM | CM | CM |
| – Buildability | Design | DM | Equipment manager | PM/ Equipment manager |
| – Equipment | Design | DM | Equipment manager | Manager |
| – Cabling | Follow-up | DM | | PM/ Equipment manager |
| – Approvals | | PM/DM | | Manager |

The previous table:

- assigns potential risk issues to team members to track
- associates each potential risk issue to a project stage.

In some models of risk identification, a preliminary likelihood and consequence matrix accompany this table; however, this may be counterproductive in the early stages of a project.

The risk issues register should be as extensive as possible in capturing material project risk because it will act as a dynamic reminder throughout the life of the project.

Organisations should develop the project risk register after the risk issues register.

---

**Self-Help Question 9.5**

List the sources of risk and some specific examples of risk Cityshore's risk management plan should consider.

---

Answers to self-help questions are provided at the end of each section.

---

**Activity | Identify project risk**

1. Select a current project in your organisation.
2. Without consulting the risk analysis prepared for the project, list the top 10 risks you think the organisation should have considered in the execution phase.
3. Compare your list with the risk register prepared for the project and comment on any omissions from your list or the risk register.
4. Consider whether the organisation:
   - adequately leveraged a risk-based approach for the project
   - properly maintained and monitored the risk register.
5. If not, what would you recommend generating more effective risk management processes within your organisation's projects?

## Analyse risk – Stage 2: Project planning

The project planning stage finalises the project's:

- specification
- delivery plan
- budget
- schedule.

The organisation analyses risk and prepares a risk treatment plan, which it integrates with other project plans.

### *Risk Analysis*

You may already be familiar with the risk analysis process and terms such as:

- likelihood and probability
- impact and consequence
- risk level.

This subsection briefly applies this risk analysis process to the project environment.

Although not all stakeholders are involved in a detailed quantitative analysis of risk likelihood (such as statistical analysis or failure rates), organisations should nevertheless be able to:

- distinguish between simple and more complex uses
- recognise when real expertise for complex analysis is required.

**EXAMPLE**

**Building Evacuation**

When there is a risk of having to evacuate a building, a risk management plan may call for a peer or expert review of risk in areas requiring legislative compliance.

*Simple Analysis*

***Personnel Risk***

A simple case in which an organisation can readily use statistical analysis without needing to employ additional expertise is analysing the risk of losing key staff. The organisation can undertake this analysis by using a variety of data sets, including:

- mortality and morbidity risk levels in the project team/company
- sickness levels
- resignation rates.

The organisation may also find a significant exposure to risk of loss of key staff.

Personnel risk is not usually a safety issue, as the team works under its own occupational/workplace health and safety systems; however, sickness and death rates and resignation rates all contribute.

On a major project with high performance individuals, the following situations may occur:

- deaths from natural causes
- resignation rates of one for every 500 working days.

Sickness rates are factored into sick leave entitlements of five days per person per year. A project manager can therefore calculate 'failure' rates for personnel to reasonable levels of accuracy using some actuarial data.

Although the project manager could delve into this level of detail for this type of risk, they typically would avoid such an analysis—it is enough to know the risk exists and there are risk management strategies in place.

*Complex analysis*

***The Risk Matrix***

If the risk is at a high or business threatening level, a risk matrix is usually the starting point for complex analysis (followed by detailed expert analysis).

Organisations can extend a semi-quantitative risk matrix approach by using formulae to calculate relative risks of events, which they usually accomplish with a high degree of subjective analysis and comment.

***Improving the Risk Treatment***

To improve the risk treatment, organisations may often use other tools like:

- scenario analysis (what happens if x?)
- benchmarking against common industry standards and/or practices (for what dollar cost should the organisation allow?)

***Probabilistic Analysis Tools***

Probabilistic analysis tools using decision trees and historical failure rate analysis to calculate event likelihood based on failure rate frequency are rarely used in project risk analysis.

In high-risk scenarios (such as oil platform and petrochemical plant design), however, a risk management committee would normally retain appropriate specialists.

*Analysing Likelihood and Impact in Projects*

For project work, organisations need to determine the type of analysis appropriate for the risk level so they can establish priorities in a risk treatment plan. Often, organisations can conduct a brief review based on qualitative risk analysis methods to determine if they need to undertake further analysis. This analysis may progress through quantitative analysis as appropriate.

As previously highlighted, the likelihood of a risk incident or event can be described in the terms described in the following table.

**Describing Risk Incidents/Events in the Terms of Likelihood of a Risk Incident or Event**

| Term | Description |
|---|---|
| **Qualitative** | use words to describe the likelihood such as:<br>• low<br>• medium<br>• high |
| **Semi-quantitative terms** | • use numbers subjectively applied to qualitative scales to describe the likelihood<br>• the number assigned need not have an accurate relationship to the magnitude of the likelihood<br>• the objective is to produce a more detailed prioritisation of risks than is achieved through qualitative methods; for example:<br>– rare = 0.1<br>– unlikely = 0.3<br>– moderate = 0.5<br>– likely = 0.7<br>– almost certain = 0.9 |

(*Continued*)

| Term | Description |
|---|---|
| **Quantitative** | for example:<br>• likelihood in terms of probability or frequency (such as 1 in 1000 cycles)<br>• if there are a thousand employee days in a project and a lost time injury of one day per thousand days, there will be one lost time injury per day. In project terms this means that for a thousand-day project, the lost time injuries are (1/1000) × 1000 × 1000 = 1000 lost time injuries) |

The following table summarises how organisations can describe impacts in qualitative or quantitative terms.

**Describing Risk Incidents/Events in the Terms of Impact of a Risk Incident or Event**

| Term | Example/s |
|---|---|
| **Qualitative** | • severe<br>• major<br>• medium<br>• minor |
| **Quantitative** | • % reduction in return<br>• € cost to the project (for example, a one-day delay due to wet weather will cost €20,000) |

### *Combining Likelihood and Impact/Consequence*

By combining likelihood and impact/consequence using a matrix or mathematical formulae (such as *frequency x severity*), organisations can establish the level of risk and the associated need for a treatment plan and priorities.

### *The ERM Context*

In a true ERM context, the measures organisations use to determine likelihood and consequence are the same as those at an ERM level. This is important because lowering the thresholds to a project level can result in over-managing risk in relation to the organisation's risk appetite.

Notwithstanding, project managers may still like to highlight risks significant in the project context, but insignificant at the organisational level. Organisations can highlight these risks with tools like a red flag in the project risk register to ensure they more carefully monitor those risks.

In concluding this subsection, keep in mind that organisations need to analyse potential sources of project risk according to the organisation's resilience and inherent ability to avoid catastrophic side effects.

---

**Self-Help Question 9.6**

For Cityshore, a minor problem on a big project may seriously affect the company if the project forms a significant part of the business.

- What would you consider to be one high level risk (which a manager may have already identified) of Cityshore's Villas project?
- What might be the consequences of this risk?

---

Answers to self-help questions are provided at the end of each section.

---

**Activity | Integrating ERM and project risk measurement**

- Consider the measures your organisation uses at the project and ERM level for a project it is currently undertaking.
- Is the organisation using consistent measurement tools?
- If not, how has the organisation addressed the issue of reporting project risk through the ERM system?

*Risk Analysis Recording/Reporting*

The following table provides an example of a typical report format for recording and reporting risk analyses, which usually covers 10 to 15 risk categories. The report aims to capture the identification and analysis of risks associated with a project in preparation for the next step in risk assessment; namely, risk treatment/ response planning.

**Example Risk Analysis Report Proforma**

| Categories | Likelihood | Impact | Level | Priority and Comment |
|---|---|---|---|---|
| 1. | | | | |
| 2. | | | | |
| 3. | | | | |

### *Case Study – Cityshore Analyses the Risk Consequences of Project Delays*

Cityshore's executive and general management team approves Tim Allsop's revised risk management plan for the Villas project. Ted Williams, however, is particularly concerned the current schedule and completion date for the project means:

- the project will not be ready for the peak selling season for villas/ apartments
- the commercial component (the ground-level retail outlets) scheduled for the November completion will miss the Christmas trading period.

**Ted:**

If this happens, you can be sure we'll have requests for rent relief and rent and purchase defaults, as well as real trouble in selling the remaining apartments.

With Arthur's help, the team asks Tim to develop a detailed risk treatment plan for managing the time risk and the cost of time delays in the Villas project (should these delays occur).

Cindy Leiden would like to take up any opportunity to accelerate the project so:

- the company can realise a higher price for the units
- commercial tenants are in place before the Christmas trading period.

**Cindy:**

There's a very high likelihood of sales softening by around 10%. This will mean that off-the-plan sales (where we've already taken a deposit of 10%) would be likely to show a default rate of one in five!

This figure is based on my analysis of past projects.

---

**Self-Help Question 9.7**

Consider Cindy's statement that off-the-plan sales would be likely to show a default rate of one in five along with the following further details.

In the Villas project:

- each unit (villa, apartment or retail outlet) has a selling price of € 500,000
- each cost € 400,000 to construct
- 80% of the project is debt-funded (Cityshore has borrowed 80% of costs) with interest on borrowings running at 10%.

→

→

Answer the following questions:

1. What do you believe Cityshore's management team would need to do first to estimate the risk this entails?
2. If sales soften by 10%, how would you rate the level of risk to:
   a. the company
   b. the project?
3. What might be the cost of a one-month delay to project completion?
4. List some of the questions you would need to answer before requesting additional funds to accelerate the project and guarantee an on-target completion.
5. What costs (other than interest) might arise if there was a four-month delay in first-stage project completion?

---

Answers to self-help questions are provided at the end of each section.

---

**Activity | Risk in 'normal' business profile projects**

Using the internet, research the problems the development and construction company Multiplex had with its Wembley Soccer Stadium project.

**The Telegraph**

Visit www.telegraph.co.uk and search for 'Multiplex losses head skywards with soaring Wembley woes'. Read the article.

- Consider some of the reasons why a large company like Multiplex could struggle with a project that is well within its normal business profile.
- What lessons from the Wembley project could Cityshore apply to the Villas project?

## Treat Risks

### *The Two Key Steps*

There are two steps to the risk treatment part of the risk management process:

- treatment/response planning
- integrating the risk treatment plan into other plans.

**Note:** The ISO 31000:2018 process does not require this second step but it is critical in project planning activities (such as procurement and quality planning). This is because project planning activities may set aside, overrule or contradict the project risk treatment plan.

Additionally, if the project is subject to formal project management, it is better to incorporate treatment actions into the project plan itself as it then comes under the direct control of the project manager.

### *Developing a Risk Treatment Plan*

Once the project risks have been identified and quantified, it is necessary to develop a risk treatment plan for each significant risk item in the project risk register.

Developing a risk treatment plan ensures the organisation sets out all categories of risk-appropriate and risk-opportunity responses and treatments, which it can monitor during the project delivery stage. Organisations achieve this step by designing responses for risks it identifies with risk response requirements. Risk responses should be recorded in the treatment plan.

Depending on the project size and complexity, the project manager may complete this step during consultation with senior project designers or through a workshop process combined with a quality and procurement review.

The following table provides a simple sample template for a risk treatment/response plan.

**Example Risk Treatment/Response Plan Report**

| Risk | Level | Accountability | Response Plan |
|---|---|---|---|
| 1. | | | |
| 2. | | | |
| 3. | | | |
| 4. | | | |

### *PERT and Gantt Charts*

When a team needs to complete a project, they soon realise that there are many styles of diagram that can be used for project management. Breaking work into sequences help split the project into manageable pieces, and project management diagrams are established ways of doing this.

Gantt charts are used during a project to help the team see the progress they have made. These charts are named after their designer, Henry Gantt.

PERT is an acronym for *programme evaluation and review technique*. A PERT chart is a critical path method (CPM) chart considered statistically. In project management, a critical path is the sequence of project activities that add up to the longest overall duration, whether that longest duration has float. This determines the shortest time possible to complete the project.

A PERT chart allows project managers to break a project into smaller tasks or sequences, estimate how much time is needed to complete each task, and keep the project to schedule. They are generally developed before a project commences as a planning exercise.

PERT charts are often considered more useful than Gantt charts as they are more complex and show more clearly the interconnectedness of tasks.

James R. Chapman describes PERT charts as follows.

PERT is an acronym for Program Evaluation and Review Technique. A PERT chart is a Critical Path Method (CPM) chart considered statistically. It can be useful in assessing schedule risk, and schedule risk usually turns into cost risk. ((I have never actually seen this used on a project.))

The essential nature of PERT analysis is to determine the expected time for each activity by using a weighted average of the most likely along with the best case and worst case time estimate that can reasonably be imagined. The normal approach to PERT is to weights (sic) the 'most likely' four times heavier than the extremes, then sum them all and divide by six. When the expected times have been determined for all activities on the critical path, these can be summed to determine the expected time for the entire project.

The standard deviation can be determined for each element in the network using the formula (b-a)/6. The standard deviation for the entire project will be the square root of the sum of the squares of the standard deviations of the individual elements. Having the standard deviation for the total project, one can then assess the probability of different schedule outcomes.

If the standard deviation for a total project is one month, you can consult a Standard Normal Distribution table to see that one standard deviation includes 84% of the population. Therefore, the probability that the project will complete no more than one month late is 84%. The probability that it will complete at least one month early is 1-84% or 16%. You can use the standard deviation for the total project to evaluate probabilities for different outcomes by converting a completion date to standard deviations from the expected time and then using the table to find the probability of occurrence.

While this is an interesting concept, it is only used in practice for projects with often repeated tasks and highly standardised methodologies. In all other projects, there are so many other unknowns, uncertainties, and instabilities that PERT analysis is insensitive to all the most relevant issues driving the schedule risk. In other words, it may be pointless to do statistical analysis if you already understand where your problems are.

**Activity | PERT and GANTT charts**

Read more about PERT and Gantt charts and the critical path method in the following articles:

- 'Critical Path Analysis and PERT Charts' from MindTools. www.mindtools.com/pages/article/critical-path-analysis.htm
- 'Advantages of PERT charts vs Gantt charts' from Lucidchart. www.lucidchart.com/blog/advantages-of-pert-charts-vs-gantt-charts
- 'Difference between Gantt chart vs PERT chart in tabular form', from AhirLabs

### *Integrating the Risk Treatment Plan into Other Plans*

Integrating the risk treatment plan into other plans is a step requiring the organisation to integrate quality and procurement plans with the risk treatment plan. The organisation may also need to integrate plans such as scope, cost and time.

Project designers and other project experts involved in the response planning steps need to ensure they review the following plans (for example):

- the quality plan for overlaps/gaps with the risk treatment plan
- the procurement plan for consistency with the risk treatment plan
- the risk treatment plan for actions in the quality and procurement plans.

---

**Self-Help Question 9.8**

Reflecting on the project scope, cost and time trade-off, consider how Cityshore might respond to/ treat the:

- potential risk of a delay in completion of the Villas project
- issues for potential response/treatment which this raises.

Note how these responses vary depending on the goal of stakeholders, specifically:

- Cityshore itself as a stakeholder
- Cityshore's banker.

---

Answers to self-help questions are provided at the end of each section.

---

## Monitor and Review – Stage 3: Project Implementation

In the project implementation stage, the organisation:

- creates the project
- manages all aspects of the project's delivery
- applies project controls.

The organisation monitors risk through project risk reports and implements agreed treatments as part of the project management process.

Because project timelines can often be tight, risks can rapidly change as new issues arise. For this reason, organisations need to carefully manage this phase.

### *Risk Monitoring and Controlling*

Organisations should include the risk treatment/response plan in the implementation plan for the project (which is in fact the first thing a project manager needs to check).

#### *Start-Up Workshops*

The organisation should also run a 'start-up' workshop on project risk treatment/response to ensure it understands and integrates the risk treatment/response plan into the implementation plan.

A start-up workshop at the project implementation stage should:

- take the project risk management process to the level of detailed checking
- set up an audit process as a way of monitoring, and therefore improving, the project performance on an ongoing basis.

**EXAMPLE**

**Selecting Contractors**

Organisations normally manage statutory compliance and injury risk through selecting contractors. The risk management and treatment plans should set out the process of selecting contractors, but the organisation still needs to investigate and confirm other critical issues (for example, is the contractor/designer qualified and insured?).

There have been many instances when organisations have planned (but never implemented) risk responses, which have resulted in plaintiffs suing project owners (for example, Cityshore in this module's case study), who may in fact be covered by a relevant policy.

***Case Study – City Shore Project Delay***

Cityshore may be able to improve its project delay situation by:

- building a time delay risk response (through acceleration incentives) into construction contracts (not leaving these to be negotiated later);
- monitoring community complaints (for example, through newsletters) that may result in hold-ups due to noise bans;
- integrating proactive risk mitigation responses (for example, including community projects in the project budget, such as repainting the town hall or sponsoring a local arts festival);
- scheduling and marketing open days and sausage sizzles (for example) on completion;
- scheduling risk reviews at key project points (such as design completion and implementation start) to investigate available opportunities to reduce risk/increase profit.

*Implementation Stage Checkpoints*

High-profit companies can use implementation stage checkpoints to leverage opportunities from the project environment.

**EXAMPLE**

**A Community Involvement Programme**

A community involvement programme will lead to sales to neighbours. Staff and worker involvement can lead to sales to staff through finance packages linked to fringe benefits (for example).

***Case Study – Cityshore Monitors Project Risks***

Cityshore's management team considers Tim Allsop's:

- draft risk treatment plan for the Villas project;
- proposed risk response to a possible delay in completion/accelerating the project.

**Risk responses**

The team notes that the risk treatment plan outlines the risk responses summarised in the following table.

| Risk | Response Plan |
|---|---|
| Bank will not finalise lending until seeing 60% of total cost commitment in sales | Target of 60% for off-the-plan sales |
| High cost of construction | Lower cost through the use of generic appliances and standard finishes |
| Delay in completion | Take on after-hours construction work to accelerate the contract |

**Neglected risks**

The team is concerned they have not dealt with the following risks in the risk response planning:

- reduced potential sales/defaults on purchases;
- potential community opposition to after-hours work leading to stop-work orders.

**Cindy's report**

The team asks Cindy Leiden (marketing) for a summary report on:

- how they can monitor these risk events;
- recommended actions before such risks jeopardise the project.

The team also requests Cindy to:

- allow for sales contingency funding measures to offset potential sales risks;
- make recommendations on integrating staged reporting.

---

**Self-Help Question 9.9**

Imagine you are Cindy Leiden. Create a brief bullet-point form report to the Cityshore management team detailing:

- actions to take on monitoring the risks of reduced potential sales/default on sales made
- the risk of potential community opposition to after-hours work leading to stop-work orders
- recommendations on sales contingency funding and staged reporting.

---

### *Tools for Project Risk Monitoring*

Two useful tools for monitoring and controlling risk in the project implementation stage are the:

- risk treatment report register
- risk monitoring and review audit record.

#### *Risk Treatment Report Register*

The following table provides a simple example risk treatment report register, which aims to:

- ensure the organisation implements the risk treatment/response plan in the project design and in contract specifications;
- enable a project manager to record and monitor the implementation of the risk and treatment plan.

**Example Project Risk Treatment Report Register**

| Risk | Level | Agreed Controls | Action Taken to Implement | Comment |
|---|---|---|---|---|
| 1. | | | | |
| 2. | | | | |
| 3. | | | | |
| 4. | | | | |

## Operational Risk Management – Stage 4: Project Handover

At the project handover stage, the project owner takes control of the project. In addition, the organisation defines its operational risks and commences an operational risk management plan.

### *Operational Risks*

During project handover, the organisation has largely eliminated the project risk because the project is physically complete. The project is not yet, however, producing benefits for stakeholders. Until the project handover stage is complete, many key risk issues can arise, depending on the nature of the project. Some examples of key risk issues include:

- the risk of the project outcome (whatever the product or system) not delivering the returns or profits expected;
- the risk of the project outcome not integrating well with the stakeholder's other operations and activities;

- the need for operational staff to be trained to achieve the envisaged project outcome;
- the need for changes to the product/outcome to improve its operational performance;
- the need to maintain the product/outcome;
- the risk of ongoing issues to be resolved (for example, industrial issues or issues with IT systems);
- the risk of an operational occupational/workplace health and safety system not being fully in place;
- the need for shut-down or sell-off (for example, replacing a product/system with a new one);
- the need to recruit new staff/make staff redundant to achieve profit targets;
- the need to insure for operational risk.

### *The Need to Insure for Operational Risk*

Depending on the project, the final operational risk issue in the previous list can become an important risk consideration for the project stakeholders at the start of the project handover stage.

#### *Handover*

At handover, a contractor or delivery team (for example) ceases to have responsibility for the project or product. Liability for the project's operation (except for any remaining warranty) shifts to the project owner. In terms of insurance for operational risk, organisations need to insure the asset (the project outcome) as an operating entity – not as a construction or work-in-progress.

This means all project owner's risk management procedures involving insurance need to be solidly in place. It also becomes critical that a project owner has asset management staff in place to cover all aspects of managing the ongoing/operational risk associated with a project outcome (for example, a product/system).

**EXAMPLE**

**Operational Loss or Damage Risk Insurance**

In terms of operational loss or damage risk insurance, consider the case of a contractor ceasing to cover the project for public liability since they have handed over the project. What would be the consequences of a purchaser on a site inspection being injured?

**EXAMPLE**

**Cost Risk Management**

When moving from the implementation to the handover (operational) stage, consider the options available to Cityshore if a construction manager on the Villas project negotiates discounts on equipment in return for long-term maintenance contracts from suppliers.

Cityshore may achieve reductions in construction costs, but may discover an increase in operating costs. There is a risk, for example, of potential purchasers of the project units having to pay higher body corporate and maintenance charges.

---

**Self-Help Question 9.10**

The Cityshore team meets to consider risk management through the handover stage of the Melbourne Villas project. The team now must list the operational risk items requiring management to ensure the company is not exposed to claims from purchasers or contractors (from this point onwards).

## The agenda

Outline the agenda for this meeting by listing the risk management items/tasks you would consider the company must address to ensure it is not exposed to claims from purchasers or contractors.

---

Answers to self-help questions are provided at the end of each section.

---

### *A Tool for Operational Risk Transfer*

One useful tool at the project handover stage is the operational risk transfer report/register. This tool identifies any open and therefore operational risks requiring transfer at the handover point. The tool ensures the organisation communicates the following to those managing the project outcome/asset (for example, the product or system):

- risks it identifies during the implementation stage;
- operational issues related to ongoing management.

**EXAMPLE**

**Industrial Equipment**

The following table provides a simple example of a tool for operational risk transfer for industrial equipment.

**Example Operational Risk Transfer Report/Register**

| Operational Risks | Comments/Hazards | Responsible Person |
|---|---|---|
| 1. | Critical procedures | |
| 2. | Start-up | |
| 3. | Shut-down | |
| 4. | Emergency procedure | |
| 5. | Access | |
| 6. | Maintenance | |
| 7. | Future decommissioning upgrade | |

**Activity | Develop a risk plan and analysis**

For a prospective project on which your organisation has yet to undertake any detailed risk work, liaise with the project sponsors and the project manager to develop:

- a project risk plan
- a project risk register
- the documents you develop should demonstrate integration points with your organisation's ERM system.

**Note:** Depending on the stage, some of the information you include will be judgemental rather than factual.

Determine whether your outputs meet the project sponsor's needs. Inquire as to if this type of analysis provides the project sponsor with greater confidence in the project.

## Summary

Please keep the following points from this topic in mind:

- Project management integrates the need to manage risk within projects and is a key management strategy.
- Project are usually managed with charts to reach both main objectives: on time, and on budget. The two main charts are PERT and Gantt.

- Project management follows a typical four-stage process, from initiation to handover.
- Placing these stages within a project risk management framework aligns with project risk identification, assessment and treatment, and finally operational risk identification and transfer.
- The most comprehensive guide to project management is the Project Management Institute's Guide to the Project Management Body of Knowledge (PMBOK®).
- The risk manager needs to understand that project management uses a separate set of standards – it is not appropriate or efficient to duplicate this work in the enterprise-wide risk management (ERM) system.
- The challenge for the risk manager is to ensure the project management and ERM systems integrate effectively.
- The following table provides some example ways to increase the effective integration of the project management and ERM system.

| Step | Description |
|---|---|
| **Identify** | • Ensure the organisation develops a project risk plan.<br>• Encourage the project team to use their own section of the ERM register for the project to seamlessly integrate the two processes.<br>• The risk manager should be satisfied that the organisation has undertaken a robust risk identification process (attending risk workshops for major projects is one ideal and effective way). |
| **Assess** | • Getting involved at an early stage helps ensure the organisation uses consistent measures and effectively communicates key risks.<br>• Has the organisation worked with the project manager to align the measurement systems so all are speaking the same language?<br>• Has the organisation documented the risks and the associated controls to an appropriate level of detail? |
| **Evaluate** | • Is the risk manager satisfied that the organisation's evaluation decisions are consistent with its risk appetite?<br>• Is there a process for tracking agreed actions (and their implementation) if the risk data is not in the ERM risk system? |
| **Monitor** | • Is the risk manager satisfied that project risk reporting is appropriate and that the organisation is reviewing documented controls periodically for their continued operation?<br>• Is the risk manager satisfied that the project management process is properly monitoring treatment plan implementation?<br>• If not, the organisation should incorporate the implementation of the treatment plan into the ERM monitoring process as an alternative |

## Answers to Self-Help Questions

### Self-help question 9.1

What constitutes a project can range from the traditional, such as building construction, product development and developing a new IT system, through to completing a design (in which the design is the deliverable) and issuing a new singer's album.

In recent times, the project process has become the dominant management process for IT infrastructure and system delivery.

### Self-help question 9.2

| Stakeholder | Attitude to Risk | Target Rate of Return |
|---|---|---|
| Venture capital funds manager | unlikely to be risk averse | • expects a high rate of failure in projects<br>• takes a portfolio view, where the average risk is reduced<br>• an individual project will have a high rate of return (perhaps 100%) but also a failure rate (perhaps 1 out of 10 projects) |
| Banker | will be risk averse | • expects a real rate of return of 5% with a low rate of failure (perhaps 1 in 100)<br>• may require guarantees outside the project and against company assets<br>• may limit project lending to the value of some underlying asset that can be sold if the borrower defaults<br>• forfeits the project when lending exceeds this limit<br>• may have caveats in the lending documentation which might include delivering a minimum number of pre-sales prior to starting construction |
| Project developer | | • may be prepared to lose all their project equity for a higher return on funds (sometimes called leverage)<br>• will risk a small amount of capital for a high return while guaranteeing the bank a lower return through a mortgage on the land |

→

→

Each stakeholder has a different risk appetite and the project risk management plan needs to integrate each accordingly.

---

**Self-help question 9.3**

Strategies for gaining input from and assessing stakeholder attitudes to or tolerance of risk include:

- interviews or discussions with individual stakeholders
- brainstorming, workshops or focus groups with groups of stakeholders to discuss how to address their interests, issues and concerns
- sending questionnaires or survey forms to stakeholders, designed to encourage sharing of views and participation in the process of identifying a project's risk exposures
- researching sources of information originating from stakeholders such as publicly available documents reflecting stakeholder points of view; for example:
  - regulator's written copies of rules
  - relevant government-produced statutes
  - local newspapers
  - key supplier advertising or news releases.

---

**Self-help question 9.4**

| Role | Organisational Risks | Project Risks |
|---|---|---|
| Construction manager | • the company cannot raise funds to support the project during the development application phase<br>• the over-budget design may mean the project is not viable and, if implemented, may cause a loss significant enough to damage the company | • cost overrun due to design over-budget may damage the project returns<br>• delays to approvals mean increased construction costs |

→

| Role | Organisational Risks | Project Risks |
|---|---|---|
| Finance manager | • interest rate rises causing loss of investor confidence and inability to raise funds<br>• cost of funds rising beyond a level that can be recovered in sales | • the Villas project with capitalised interest will suffer from a higher than normal cost of funds and banks may not approve the project<br>• mezzanine investors in the Villas project are at high risk and may withdraw their funds, causing the project to fail |
| Marketing manager | • changes to the project for cost reduction could damage the company's image in quality development and construction<br>• sales shortfalls and forfeitures will cause a loss of confidence in the company's other projects | • the project will not progress because it does not have sufficient presale<br>• at project handover, owners will not settle as the price is higher than equivalent units for sale elsewhere |
| Human resources manager | • the loss of key staff members will see the company without the expertise to hold and develop staff in the future<br>• key staff retiring or leaving can take projects and skills to competitors | • there will be inexperienced staff on the project, with risk of poor control<br>• the project could have cost rises because of confusion over the development scope |
| Procurement manager | • if the company fitted cheaper no-name brand appliances, the company could lose its image for quality<br>• the opportunity exists to cut costs through using generic and unknown brands as well as to build reputation for those brands, thus converting a negative into a positive | • the project could substantially cut its costs<br>• the warranty costs for replacements are unknown<br>• the construction would need to allow for increased supervision in the warranty period to ensure the purchaser does not give the project a 'bad name' |

| Role | Organisational Risks | Project Risks |
|---|---|---|
| Managing Director (responsible for environment and sustainable development) | • the company would be perceived to be not living up to its environmental credentials, with damage to reputation<br>• the company may lose its high-level environmental credit rating | • the cost of the project would blow out if the project was to adopt this manager's green recommendations<br>• a marketing edge may be developed by offering lower life cycle costs in the Villas project |

**Self-help question 9.5**

The following table identifies some possible risk sources and examples.

| Risk Sources | Examples |
|---|---|
| Market | • sales shortfall, owing to softening in the market.<br>• forfeiting of deposit, owing value less than deposit |
| Finance | • bank refusal to lend to the project or withdraw finance when the project is underway<br>• cost of investment/loan funds rising |
| Quality | • cost-cutting leading to lower cost, but poorer quality and lower sales and realisable pricing<br>• cheaper inclusions, leading to loss of quality image<br>• failure in building design resulting in material warranty issues or habitation threats<br>• sub-standard materials resulting in construction rework or building failure |
| Cost | • rising construction costs, owing to a lack of skilled tradespersons<br>• cheaper inclusions, but an opportunity for lower costs<br>• subcontractor costs not locked down<br>• land acquisition costs exceed expectations<br>• above forecasted wage increases<br>• appliance inflation due to devaluation of the Euro |
| Time | • council approval delaying project start and in turn completion<br>• selling agent defaulting on delivery (owing to time overrun) and sales are cancelled<br>• on-costs rise, as time-related costs increase<br>• strikes |

→

| Risk Sources | Examples |
|---|---|
| Personnel | • unavailable skilled managers<br>• poor control by inexperienced staff<br>• staff leave at critical points, leaving high costs to recover knowledge<br>• unreached union site agreement, raising industrial disputes<br>• workplace occupational/workplace health and safety breaches by contractors leaving Cityshore liable |
| Technical | • costs rise/fall due to unforeseen site conditions<br>• structural faults cause rework<br>• unsatisfactory engineering<br>• unappealing architecture to the market |

**Self-help question 9.6**

On Cityshore's Villa project, there is a high likelihood of villa/apartment prices falling.

The consequences could be defaults on completion for villa/apartment sales, coupled with a high probability of a reduced cash flow, which would mean a high level of risk for the company. Once registered as a high-risk level, however, the project risk management team can look at solutions to manage this risk to both the project and the company

**Self-help question 9.7**

The team needs to determine the level of risk, which it would derive from a risk matrix. The project and marketing manager would develop the risk matrix to cover the time delay and sales forfeiture.

If sales soften by 10%, the risk to both the company and the project is high (there is a high likelihood and a high impact). The risk of failure in the project is therefore high.

The risk to the company is also high because the project represents the essentials of work and sales in that period. The high level of risk warrants a specific action plan for risks both to the project and to the company.

The following table summarises costs to the project due to a one-month delay to project completion.

| Cost Factor | Cost | Interest Rate | Total Cost Per Month |
|---|---|---|---|
| Borrowings | € 80 million | 10% | € 0.67 million |
| Equity | € 20 million | 20% | € 0.33 million (minus earnings on funds received as deposits) |

→

→

Some critical questions might include:

- How much can the company save by early completion?
- What will early completion cost?
- What is the allowed contingency to cover unforeseen costs at the construction start stage?
- If the project fails, what is the likely selling cost to protect the company?

Costs, other than interest, for a four-month delay, could include:

- legal costs to enforce sale contracts
- site overheads for company personnel
- claims for losses on sale of stock
- rent-start deferrals, to allow for loss of peak trading season.

---

**Self-help question 9.8**

The company could:

- accelerate the project (reduce the time required for completion) but at a higher cost and a reduced quality of outcome;
- outsource project parts in which they have expertise, by procuring through fixed-price contracts (this means the company will unnecessarily transfer risks with an associated cost);
- increase the scope of the project by redesigning and constructing more or bigger units (villas, apartments or retail outlets) to attract a higher price; this will increase project time and cost, and change the 'quality profile', thereby risking any net benefit;
- outsource project parts to lowest price tenders from unknown contractors. This approach may lower costs but increase the risk of contractor default.

Cityshore's project risk response/treatment actions will also vary depending on stakeholder attitude (particularly to the cost of risk reduction).

For example, Cityshore's bank (covering 80% of the project cost) will be interested in risk reduction, even to the detriment of accelerating the project, because the bank will not benefit from any profit on the project. The bank is exposed, should the company not be able to live up to its guarantees.

On the other hand, as a stakeholder, the bank's own risk response may be to support acceleration, while seeking additional securities.

→

→

As a stakeholder with their own attitude to risk affecting their risk response activity, Cityshore might choose to:

- spend to accelerate
- ramp up marketing
- discount units to gain additional sales
- offer rent-free periods to commercial tenants to gain key 'anchor' tenants.

Since the Cityshore company and project staff are also stakeholders, and given the risk of staff retiring or resigning during the project, Cityshore might:

- offer staff incentives to stay on;
- recruit new staff;
- transfer experienced staff to the project.

---

**Self-help question 9.9**

Actions for monitoring and controlling risk related to potential sales/ default on sales made, as well as risk of potential community opposition to after-hours work leading to stop-work orders include:

- planning for discounting to selected purchasers, so pricing is not undermined and to achieve sales targets of 60%;
- allowing for sales promotional activities and giveaways;
- developing a risk response to manage community opposition to noise and dust;
- undertaking frequent monitoring;
- providing monthly reporting sales graph for units;
- providing the opportunity for purchasers to start payments early (with discount incentives) to reduce Cityshore's borrowing costs;
- undertaking monthly monitoring of construction progress, with follow-up action to recover any delays.

Recommendations on sales contingency funding and staged reporting include:

- budgeting a build allowance for unforeseen needs for different project stages as follows:
- pre-development consent: 20%
- after construction tender awarded: 5% (including sales incentives of 2%)
- post-handover, after sales and additional marketing discounts: 2%.

---

→

→

**Self-help question 9.10**

An agenda for the handover meeting would cover risk management items such as:

- the insurance position regarding land and buildings, as well as the transfer to owner or body corporate;
- outstanding defects and the construction programme for rectification;
- tenancy access management and the security plan;
- warranties and maintenance contracts for essential services;
- ongoing operational risk management plans for structural/mechanical/hydraulic/security/ electrical systems;
- final payments and the return of deposits held against risk events;
- operational cost reports and verification of life cycle costing, with opportunities for cost reduction;
- promotional activities to enhance sales because of publicity at handover;
- community liaison plans to support sales.

Chapter 10

# Mergers and Acquisitions

## Introduction

Mergers and acquisitions (M&A) have become a common tool for doing business in a complex and constantly evolving world. It is a tool commonly considered in expansion strategies for companies acting in the global market, but should not be left aside when small and medium-sized companies try to get traction in difficult markets. Therefore, M&A participate in external corporate expansion, facilitating a strategy for corporate restructuring and control. M&A offer opportunities but bring threats different from those linked internal expansion decisions and cannot be decided purely on investment appraisal techniques. Whereas M&A can accelerate growth and innovation for firms, it constitutes also a vital mechanism for capital markets as it tends to improve management efficiency, thus maximising companies' profits and public welfare.

In developed economies, corporate M&A have become frequent and it is commonly accepted that if large mergers have huge wealth redistribution impacts they also raise concerns regarding corporate governance and takeover codes and ethics. This activity is a useful addition to the corporate strategy toolbox; organisations implement M&A to achieve various goals, but they also act as a mechanism for financial market discipline. Takeovers are varied and several aspects should be analysed including motives, financing and payment methods, wealth creation, and distribution between bidders' and target shareholders and the impact of takeovers on the competitors of predator and target companies.

Studies on takeover activity since the beginning of the century suggest that acquisition is an increasingly important corporate strategy for changing business environments, and has implications for future industrial restructuring and the emergence of a new competitive landscape, with new risks to be tackled, both opportunities and threats. M&A has become also

**Risk Measurement and Monitoring, 255–264**

**Published under exclusive licence by Emerald Publishing Limited**
**doi:10.1108/978-1-83662-310-620251024**

a strategic path for a firm, enabling further strengthening of core competence while embracing innovation and change.

Indeed, in the last 20 years, megamergers have brought about structural changes in some industries, and attracted international attention, like the automobile industry, the world of finance, and the chemistry and pharmaceutical industries, to name but a few.

An array of motivations for M&A are developed in the literature, mostly drawn directly from finance theory but with some inconsistencies, and too often leaving aside the human and societal consequences. As a matter of fact, distressed firms happen to be predators and the market reaction to these is not always predictable. Several financing options are associated with takeover activity and are generally specific to the acquiring firm. Given their impact, and the buzz they create in social media, M&A will continue to be an interesting but challenging strategy in the search for expanding corporate influence and profitability.

Accordingly, for organisations involved in ERM development and implementation, M&A should become a field of choice for risk management professionals, be they part of a predator's team or a target's.

Andy West from McKinsey says it best:

> *Managing the strategy to the concept – to the deal, to the actual value – is a lot of work, and the governance around it is typically very poorly articulated. It bounces between the board, managers of different business units, executive management, corporate development, strategy, and obviously all the back-office and corporate functions and operating functions that need to enable it. It is not easy. It's hard for others to emulate a mind-set for shedding assets. Companies that can crack the code can be quite successful.*

## Learning Outcomes

By the end of this chapter, you should be able to:

- define M&A and associated transactions;
- describe the role of M&A as an expansion strategy;
- identify the major risks involved in M&A and describe their ramifications;
- distinguish between the aims of general due diligence and cyber due diligence in M&A.

## Definitions

M&A are a tool of corporate finances, management and strategy aiming at purchasing and/or joining companies. A company that another organisation considers for a merger or acquisition can be referred to as the target, whereas the potential buyer is sometimes called the 'predator'.

Although the terms 'merger' and 'acquisition' are often used interchangeably, in reality, they embrace somewhat different situations:

- In a merger, two or more organisations combine forces to create a new business, often with a new name. In a merger, the partners involved are usually of similar size and stature, therefore it is often labelled a 'merger of equals'. Both companies' surrender their stocks and new company stock is issued instead.
- A recent situation illustrates the concept: both Daimler-Benz and Chrysler ceased to exist when the two firms merged, and a new company, Daimler Chrysler, was created.
- A purchase deal will also be called a merger when both boards of directors agree that joining forces is in the best interest of both companies.
- In an acquisition, one business purchases another, generally smaller, company, which may be either incorporated into the parent organisation or kept as a subsidiary in a conglomerate. From a legal point of view, the target company ceases to exist and the buyer absorbs the business; the buyer's stock continues to be traded, while the target company's stock ceases to trade.
- Therefore, M&A is a generic term used to reflect the consolidation of companies or assets through various types of financial transactions, including mergers, acquisitions, consolidations, tender offers, purchase of assets and management acquisitions.
- The term M&A is also used to refer to the departments in financial institutions, such as banks, insurers, and brokers, who deal in such activity.

**Activity | Definitions**

There is a variety of transactions that are available for companies considering entering a merger or acquisition deal.

Read definitions for the following terms at Investopedia: www.investopedia.com/terms/m/mergersandacquisitions.asp

- merger
- purchase merger
- consolidation merger
- acquisition
- tender offer
- acquisition of assets
- management acquisition
- horizontal merger
- vertical merger
- congeneric mergers
- market-extension merger
- product-extension merger.

**Activity | Project managing mergers and acquisitions**

Read how managing M&A with project management techniques can help to avoid the major pitfalls associated with these deals in the blog post entitled 'Mergers and acquisitions project failure' at Toby Elwin's website.

https://tobyelwin.com/mergers-acquisitions-project-failure

Toby Elwin concludes his blog post by highlighting the necessity of considering the human capital risk inherent in M&A deals. However, it is also important to consider the financial aspects of M&A. The global economic climate of low interest rates, excess capital requirements and fierce competition has made it difficult for many companies to grow organically. At the same time, historically low interest rates have made it easier to finance deals and generate superior returns with excess capital. As a result, businesses have been looking to allocate their existing capital more efficiently, with M&A being one way to do this. As George P. Schultz, former Treasury Secretary of the USA, says, 'With traditional investments failing to achieve required returns, businesses are looking to M&A as a means to expand'.

There has been a surge in M&A activity since 2015 that can be attributed to companies searching for diversification into new product and service categories, markets, and distribution channels. This can enhance business growth while strengthening partner networks (customer, supplier, and distributor).

**Activity | Planning for M&A: How to avoid hidden risks**

Read the Aon article 'Planning for M&A: How to avoid hidden risks' to discover the key factors Aon believes leaders should address to ensure that a proposed M&A deal can meet an organisation's long-term goals.

https://theonebrief.com/planning-for-m-and-a-how-to-avoid-hidden-risks

## Major Risks

Mergers are generally entered into or acquisitions acquired with one or more of the following objectives (this list combines acquiring and target company objectives):

- increasing market share and plant size
- geographic expansion
- diversifying product and services
- gaining market power
- enjoying benefits of economies of scale
- finding a solution to owner retirement
  or
- getting over corporate financial difficulties.

During the M&A process, both companies face substantial risk. Recent history has shown that it may happen that the company seeking to acquire another ends up being acquired itself; at the same time, acquisition schemes may end up as mergers.

There is an array of specific risks that leaderships of both companies must address when considering M&A:

### *Differences in Culture*

Corporate culture clashes have been observed in many M&A projects and they represent one of the most common reasons for the failure of the projects. Employees are the core strength of any organisation and if there is no fusion between the employees concerned, the resulting organisation is destined to fail. Therefore, it is essential to check the compatibility of the two cultures before entering the project.

One illustration of company culture clashes resulting in poor integration is the Daimler Benz-Chrysler merger where German efficiency clashed with American union work rules.

### *Employee Layoff and/or Resignation*

Both organisations may lose many staff during a merger. This may result in loss of competencies not easy to acquire and that may reinforce competition. Furthermore, the acquiring company may be unable to assess the value of the target's staff, which may lead to firing the wrong people when trying to reap the benefits of economies of scale regarding Human Resources.

### *Inefficient Communication and Lack of Transparency*

The acquiring company should clearly communicate the terms of the deal to the target firm. Leadership should be fully aware of the communication gaps and share all details pertaining to each firm's market share, consumer base, product/service details and personnel. Transparency will ensure that no discrepancies arise after the merger, which could lead to widespread discontent in both firms. Having a deep knowledge and understanding of the similitude and differences in each firm's partners' behaviours, both customers and suppliers, will enable them to develop appropriate strategies so that no partner is unhappy with the merger.

Furthermore, the vocabulary used in M&A projects is still somewhat fuzzy. So, it is essential that within each leadership and during their discussion, all involved in the project are clear as to the meaning of each word used and its implication in the context on the proposed contract. This is even more essential in the case of multilingual deals; even if the legal and regulatory context and the idiom of reference are clearly stated, this does not suffice to ensure that all involved share the same understanding and vision.

### *Miscalculations in the Valuation of Assets*

It is essential that both partners have reached a complete agreement before merging organisations or acquiring assets. Many complex calculations that are valuable for both parties can rest on different approaches. For example, even if both agree to use Discounted Cash Flow (DCF) there remain many variables on which both partners must come to an agreement. Manipulation of calculation or error in calculation can lead both to heavy losses of the combined entity and disruptive disputes between partners.

### Reckless Enthusiasm

M&A are initiated in strategic planning sessions, when company management decides to acquire another company, to be acquired or to merge. The next step is hiring an investment banker or attorney specialising in M&A work. The entire process is long, time-consuming and stressful, especially when no evident candidate is identified at the onset of the process. Most M&A specialists have identified project fatigue as a very dangerous trait in such projects; it may result in a company management to decide on a candidate just to get the task over with. Reckless enthusiasm generated by project fatigue proves a major cause of failures in mergers or acquisitions.

There is much debate in the M&A industry on whether organisations should conduct due diligence or merge with a company that seems appropriate and deal with the consequences later. M&A professionals advise a broad-based approach involving examination of all parts of a candidate company, with planned risk management at multiple levels.

### Return on Investment (ROI)

As in any investment project, assessing the expected ROI is a key variable in the decision process. A wrong acquisition/sale can cause significant harm to a company's profitability. For instance, following its acquisition of NCR, AT&T accumulated losses totalling $2 billion; after five years, AT&T sold its stake in NCR. A similar situation played out with Time Warner and AOL.

### Corporate Integration

Beyond the issue of culture mentioned here above, another main cause of failure in M&A projects is poor integration of the companies due to other causes. Such a case may be when a company acquires another for the specific innovating technology it developed and then in the confusion of integrating the two companies mistakenly closes the department that created the targeted technology asset. Another example of common integration failure is the loss of important customers who liked doing business with the old company, not the new one. The solution is detailed planning and testing of decisions, with a centralised integration management team comprising leaders of both companies that monitors every element of the project.

### Legal Risks

Companies need to comply with many laws and regulations during M&A. Failure to do so can lead to legal actions by governing bodies. They should also comply with laws and regulations relating to the termination of employees which may differ hugely depending on the jurisdictions involved. Prior understanding of the legal context and of the litigation process is vital. Both partners must gain a solid knowledge of each other's legal involvement as it can impact the profitability of the merger or acquisition. Caution must dictate every move throughout the process as, no matter how careful the due diligence effort, many M&A experience legal surprises, such as expiring patents, patent infringement, cancelled licences, unreported fraud and shareholder class action suits. Good M&A attorneys can help mitigate these surprises, as can appropriately managing the risks throughout the process.

M&A pose great scope for growth of companies through expansion and diversification. The company can mitigate the risks associated with it by prudent planning and compliance management. Costs of merging can be overwhelming but suitable measures can help reduce it. For instance, using compliance management software can prove to be cost-effective as well as efficient.

## Cyber Risks

> *A close examination of a company's exposure to cyber risk during the merger, acquisition or investment process is no longer optional. In fact, not doing so – or failing to structure transactions in a way that adequately manages existing and potential cyber threats – invites significant financial and legal challenges further down the line.*
>
> *Brian Finch, Partner and Global Security Practice Co-Chair, Pillsbury Winthrop Shaw Pittman LLP*

The complexity brought about by cyber issues requires predator organisations to perform specific cyber due diligence. This a step that uncovers an array of cyber-related strategic deal issues, hidden costs and operational risks before a target company is invested in. Cyber due diligence offers new insights to detect potential pitfalls, thus curbing risk to investor capital while providing a competitive way to increase returns.

Cyber risk today is so pervasive that all businesses have a cyber history. You may think that all you need to know is whether an organisation has suffered a data breach, but there are many other questions about cyber health that should be asked. For example, does the target organisation have a suitable digital system or do they need an expensive upgrade, or are there single points-of-failure in their digital ecosystem?

As Ian McCaw has uncovered, many predator organisations don't consider that cyber risks warrant investigation in the pre-deal period and wait until they have acquired their target to investigate. This could be due to a lack of appreciation of the extent of cyber risks or a mistaken belief that IT due diligence includes cyber due diligence. Furthermore, if they experience reckless enthusiasm, having already emotionally bought into the target business, they may prefer not to know. However, this is short-sighted, as cyber M&A risks can have wide-ranging and often unexpected ramifications.

**Activity | Top five cyber risks**

Ian McCaw, Head of Cyber M&A, Aon's M&A and Transaction Solutions EMEA, has identified his five top cyber risks in M&A. Read these risks in his article, 'Top five cyber risks in mergers and acquisitions' from Aon.

Ian then goes on to give five actions to help in addressing and managing cyber risk. Read to the end of the article to learn more.

www.aon.com/unitedkingdom/insights/top-5-cyber-risks-in-mergers-and-acquisitions.jsp

**Activity | Managing transaction risk**

Read 'Mitigating risk in M&A transactions' from Crain's Cleveland Business to discover some strategies designed to protect buyers and sellers during M&A.

www.crainscleveland.com/article/20180116/custom1718/148816/mitigating-risk-ma-transactions

Buyers should implement a due diligence process that includes a study of the target's historical risk issues. Among others, due diligence must identify liabilities that the buyer is expected to assume and quantify those liabilities for total loss costs. Furthermore, the process must discover all collateral requirements tied to those liabilities and assess what risk reduction tools could be put in place.

Once a company decides to go ahead with a bid, due diligence should encompass ERM, or holistic risk management, including:

- scenario analysis, to determine whether the two companies are aligned operationally and strategically
- crisis management and business continuity plan assessment
- insurance claims scenarios testing
- a business model risk assessment.

Assessing risks – threats as well as opportunities – can reveal the true value of a deal in a way that reviewing only the financials cannot.

**Activity | The need for an exit strategy**

To understand why an exit strategy is an essential aspect of risk management, read the following article from Rodriques Law:

https://rodriqueslaw.com/blog/how-mitigate-risk-effective-exit-strategy

**Activity | Practical issues**

Several practical issues, including the need to identify risks at prior due diligence, structuring contracts appropriately, managing risks after the acquisition, are outlined in 'Practical aspects of risk management in M&A transactions'.

Read this piece and consider how you will incorporate these elements into your risk management practice.

www.korpusprava.com/en/publications/analytics/practical-aspects-of-risk-management-in-m&a- transactions.html

**Activity | Using data**

Read 'Mergers and acquisitions today: Higher risks require new methods' from Forbes and consider the writer's position that the communication tools a company uses can highlight its capacity for change.

www.forbes.com/sites/ericadhawan/2016/10/05/mergers-acquisitions-today-higher-risks-require-new- methods/#4a750e27e9d

**Activity | Pitfalls of M&A**

Read 'M&A: Three easily mitigated but commonly overlooked pitfalls' to explore three of the most common errors people make in M&A transactions.

www.alliottgroup.net/practice-management-resources-for-owner-managed-firms/ma-pitfalls-lexcounsel

## Summary

Please keep the following points from this chapter in mind:

- M&A are a tool of corporate finances, management, and strategy aiming at purchasing and/or joining companies.
- Although the terms 'merger' and 'acquisition' are often used interchangeably they embrace somewhat different situations. However, M&A is a generic term used to reflect the consolidation of companies or assets through various types of financial transactions, including mergers, acquisitions, consolidations, tender offers, purchase of assets, and management acquisitions.
- There is a variety of transactions that are available for companies considering entering a merger or acquisition deal, including vertical mergers, tender offers, and congeneric mergers.
- 'With traditional investments failing to achieve required returns, businesses are looking to M&A as a means to expand'.

- There has been a surge in M&A activity since 2015 that can be attributed to companies searching for diversification into new product and service categories, markets and distribution channels. This can enhance business growth while strengthening partner networks (customer, supplier and distributor).
- During the M&A process, both companies face substantial risk. Recent history has shown that it may happen that the company seeking to acquire another ends up being acquired itself; at the same time, acquisition schemes may end up as mergers.
- Risks in M&A include culture clashes, poor communication, miscalculation and legal actions.
- Cyber risk in M&A is an area of growing importance and severity and should be investigated during pre-deal due diligence.
- Assessing risks – threats as well as opportunities – can reveal the true value of a deal in a way that reviewing only the financials cannot.

Chapter 11

# Cyber Security and Managing Cyber Risks

## Introduction

The leaders of large organisations are convinced of the very real existence of cyber risk. In the most data-culture advanced organisation, cyber security is now approached with an enterprise-wide perspective that involves all staff.

These organisations set in motion a team that typically includes the chief information security officer (CISO), the chief information officer (CIO), and the chief risk officer (CRO), with strong support relays within each business unit.

'Cyber security and the risk function' (2018) describes why it is important to involve all areas of the business:

> *A true partnership between these teams is the optimal approach, having emerged from a recognition that no single leader or team can gain the complete perspective needed to be effective in the cyber-domain. No one group within a company could manage the number and types of internal and external threats, the complex technological landscape, and the many actions needed to address vulnerabilities associated with people and technology. They rather need to work together.*

When referring to the three lines of defence, the first line, at the information level, can better grasp how cyber risk fits into ERM programmes and thus better equip them to meet the emerging cyber risk challenges when interventions are under way. The second line, the risk management function, has a deeper understanding of the capabilities and limits of the information-data department.

**Risk Measurement and Monitoring, 265–277**

**Published under exclusive licence by Emerald Publishing Limited**
**doi:10.1108/978-1-83662-310-620251026**

The 10 cases reported in this section are a limited sample of the most publicised cyber-attacks of the decade and should convince those that still doubt the potential severity of the cyber threat. Paul Proctor of the Gartner Group predicts that 'by 2020, 60 percent of digital businesses will suffer major service failures due to the inability of the IT security teams to manage digital risk' in new technology and use cases.

## Learning Outcomes

By the end of this chapter, you should be able to:

- define cyber risk;
- describe the importance of proper cyber protection and the magnitude of cyber risk;
- promote the need to take an integrated approach to managing cyber risk;
- define 'insider threat';
- identify the role of culture in an organisation's cyber protection arsenal;
- describe how social engineering works;
- recognise the risks associated with siloing;
- identify and evaluate measures that can be taken to protect against cyber risk, including the role of insurance.

## Cyber Risk Management – Definition

Cyber risk management is the combination of personnel, policies, processes, and technologies that enable an organisation to cost-effectively achieve and maintain an acceptable level of cyber-loss exposure and seize the opportunities offered by the cyber-space, thus enabling it to achieve its goals and enhance its resilience.

Upon closer examination, this definition provides some inroads:

- *Cost effectively:* The responsibility of risk management is not simply to help organisations manage risk, but to manage it in a cost-effective fashion, thus providing the organisation with a competitive advantage.
- *Achieving and maintaining:* This means that not only must a risk objective reflect the level at a given point in time (risk appetite/tolerance) but that it must be adapted to changing circumstances (context). Furthermore, it must be defined in quantifiable terms (risk criteria) so that it can be monitored and reviewed over time.
- *An acceptable level of loss exposure:* Managing cyber risk requires that one or more quantitative risk-based objectives exist in coordination with all other risks and there is an increasing correlation between all risks through their common dependence on an integrated information system.
- *Seize opportunities:* More than all other risk areas, cyber security should not impair the organisation in its path through the fourth industrial revolution (the technological revolution) to maintain its relevance as an efficient actor in its field.

### *Ten Most Publicised Recent Cyber Attacks*

Many organisations still see hacking as looking for loopholes in computer software that gives the attacker access to sensitive information. However, complex systems' major vulnerabilities tend to be human behaviour and habits (referred to as insider threat, explored further below). Hostile individuals, also called social engineers, rely on human gullibility and errors to bypass technological security measures.

Below are 10 of the most publicised social engineering attacks in the current decade, as selected by Infosec (2018).

### *2011: RSA SecurID*

In 2011, RSA fell victim to a phishing attack that compromised the security of their systems and cost the company $66 million.

RSA's SecurID tokens were designed to protect users by utilising two-factor authentication (2FA), intended to prevent attackers from breaching systems using a stolen password alone. However, in this instance, the 2FA technology was not secure.

The attack against RSA consisted of two different phishing emails that claimed to describe the recruitment plan of another organisation and had an attached Microsoft Excel document. If an employee opened the Excel document, a system vulnerability was exploited and a backdoor was installed, giving the attackers access to the system. While it is unknown what exactly was stolen, RSA believed the security of its SecurID tokens was jeopardised and had to spend millions to correct the problem.

### *2013: Associated Press Twitter*

The 2013 hack of the Associated Press Twitter account began as a spear-phishing email to Associated Press employees that appeared to come from other Associated Press employees. Employees who followed the link given in the email were sent to a phishing site where they entered login information for the Associated Press Twitter account.

Once the attackers had access to the account, they tweeted that the White House had been bombed and President Obama injured. The tweet was only live for three minutes before people began to realise that it was fake but it was long enough for the DOW to drop 150 points (the equivalent of about $136 billion).

While the DOW soon returned to close to its former level, this attack highlighted how cyber-crime could have a serious effect on country's economy.

### *2013: Bit9 Certificate Theft*

In 2013, Bit9 suffered a watering hole attack. Infotec defines a watering hole attack as one where:

> hackers infect websites that their target is likely to visit and wait until their malware successfully infects a target computer. For example, an attacker targeting developers may attempt to infect websites like Stack Overflow, which programmers frequently visit to ask or answer programming-related questions.

In this attack, the hackers stole the code signing certificates used by Bit9, which enabled them to create malware that appeared to be legitimate software from Bit9. This meant they could continue the attack by targeting other organisations that use Bit9 software.

### *2013: Target Point of Sale*

The Target point of sale attack demonstrated the importance of having reliable and secure third-party providers.

Target had given access to its network, including its payment network, to one of its vendors. This vendor then suffered a phishing attack that installed malware on their machines, which then enabled the attacker to steal the vendor's log in details to the Target network.

The attackers then logged in to the Target network and installed malware that extracted credit and debit card information from every card used at the infected machines. This attack resulted in the theft of 40 million customers' credit and debit card information.

### *2013: United States Department of Labour Watering Hole*

In 2013, the United States Department of Labour suffered a watering hole attack (like Bit9). In this attack, the hackers infected webpages related to toxic nuclear substances regulated by the Department of Energy with the intention of targeting Department of Labour and Department of Energy employees with a background in nuclear sciences and likely a security clearance.

It is unknown how many employees were infected, what was stolen or who the hackers were.

### *2014: Sony Pictures Hack*

In 2014, North Korea hacked Sony Pictures networks in response to Sony's movie, *The Interview,* a comedy about two men intending to assassinate Kim Jong-Un. Sony Pictures employees were sent a phishing email that directed them to verify their Apple credentials on a page controlled by the hackers.

The hackers then accessed the LinkedIn profiles of employees to guess their Sony login credentials and found that at least one executive used the same password for their Apple and Sony accounts. This gave the attackers access to the Sony networks, through which they stole a claimed 100 terabytes of sensitive company and employee information.

### *2014: Yahoo Hack*

The Yahoo hack of 2014 stole data from 500 million users, including usernames, phone numbers, cryptographic values, and recovery emails.

This was another email spear-phishing attack that targeted Yahoo employees with some level of clearance. One employee accessed the email, enabling the hackers to download the Yahoo user database. They used the stolen recovery email addresses to identify further targets then used the linked cryptographic values to create fake Yahoo cookies, which enabled them to access users' accounts without passwords. Over 6,500 Yahoo users were compromised in this manner.

### *2015: Ubiquiti Networks BEC Attack*

Ubiquiti Networks suffered a business email compromise (BEC) attack in 2015 that cost the company approximately $46.7 million dollars. Infotec defines a BEC attack as,

> a special form of spear-phishing email in which an attacker masquerades as someone high in the organisation's hierarchy, such as the CEO. The attacker then targets an employee with the power to perform certain functions, like transferring money or accessing HR records.

In this instance, the attackers targeted employees in the finance department by sending an email, supposedly from an executive's account, that request that money be sent to certain accounts. As a result, $46.7 million dollars were transferred into hacker-controlled accounts.

Ubiquiti recovered $8.1 million and expected to recover another $6.8 million (though at the time of writing it was not clear whether this was achieved), meaning the total loss is at $31.8 million.

### *2016: Democratic National Convention Emails*

During the 2016 United States presidential election, over 150,000 emails containing sensitive campaign information were stolen from twelve of Clinton's staff members and leaked.

This hack was again the result of a phishing email. In this scenario, the email appeared to be from Google and asked recipients to reset their password by clicking on a link, which also appeared to be from Google. The employees had to enter their Google credentials, which then gave the hackers access to the related email accounts.

### *2016: United States Department of Justice*

In 2016, the personal details of 20,000 FBI and 9,000 Department of Homeland Security were leaked following a social engineering attack on the United States Department of Justice (DOJ). It is unknown whether the hacker.

The hacker managed to gain access to the email account of a DOJ employee then the DOJ intranet, which gave him access to three computers on the DOJ network as well as databases containing military emails and credit card information. The hacker obtained the required intranet access code by pretending to be a new employee.

Apart from the leaked personal details, it is unknown what else the hacker had access to and could have stolen.

**Activity | UK firms 'severely unprepared' for cyber attacks**

Read the article 'UK firms "severely unprepared" for cyber attacks' from *Insurance Times* (2017) and consider how cyber risk is viewed by the business sector despite the numerous cyber-attacks that have occurred in recent years.

Why do you think cyber risk is still so underestimated?

www.insurancetimes.co.uk/uk-firms-severely-unprepared-for-cyber-attacks/1422258.article

**Activity | Cyber and data loss top priority for senior managers**

Read the article 'Cyber and data loss overtake regulatory concerns as top priority facing senior managers' from *Strategic Risk Europe*. Consider the conclusions of this article then decide what your top concern is out of the following risks (taken from the top five risks to businesses from 2011 to 2018 in the Allen & Overy LLP and Willis Towers Watson 'Directors' liability' report)?

| | |
|---|---|
| • Cyber attack<br>• Data loss/breach<br>• Regulatory and other investigations<br>• Health and safety legislation<br>• Criminal and regulatory fines and penalties<br>• Concerns in the post-Brexit landscape<br>• Anti-corruption legislation | • Risk of being sued abroad<br>• Multiplicity of sanctions regimes and of affected countries<br>• Securities/shareholder claims<br>• Employment practices claims (harassment, age and sex discrimination |

Do you think cyber concerns will continue to increase given the introduction of the General Data Protection Regulation (GDPR)?

www.strategic-risk-europe.com/cyber-and-data-loss-overtake-regulatory-concerns-as-top-priority-facing-senior-managers/1428922.article

**Activity | The Snapchat thief**

Listen to episode #130 'The Snapchat thief', from Reply all, to hear about 'SIM swapping' and how hackers can thwart 2FA.

https://gimletmedia.com/shows/reply-all/v4he6k

### *Helping the Board Understand Cyber Risk and Exposure*

In the current context, one of the key questions for risk management professionals to ponder what they can do to help the board get a handle on cyber-security issues. This was one of the main questions discussed at a recent technology event run by Airmic. Some of their conclusions are outlined below.

Camilla Kampmann, a non-executive director on the board of AIG Europe, recommended identifying the data and applications that are essential to your organisation (your 'crown jewels') and prioritising these when considering cyber risk solutions. She also recommended making a list of old legacy systems that are no longer used as the old technology is easier to breach.

Eleni Petros of Marsh suggested that all boards ensure that at least one member has cyber risk expertise to ensure that key areas of liability can be properly identified and addressed.

Dr Jamie Saunders, a strategic security consultant and visiting professor at UCL, highlighted the importance of businesses understanding the risk environment in which they operate and of crisis management plans.

**Activity | How do you help the board get to grips with cyber risk and exposure?**

Read the article 'How do you help the board get to grips with cyber risk and exposure?' from Airmic and consider the panel's conclusions in relation to your own organisation.

www.airmic.com/news/guest-stories/how-do-you-help-board-get-grips-cyber-risk-and-exposure

### *Cyber Risk Management*

For several decades, risk and cyber specialists have insisted on the need to manage the risks of the cyber-enterprise rather than focusing on the cyber risks themselves. With the fourth industrial revolution already underway and the pervasive presence of data and information on the life of all organisations, the ERM, global, and integrated approach to managing risks offers a framework in which cyber issues find their place naturally. It remains for leaders to understand that cyber risks are so pervasive that their management cannot be delegated to a CIO or a CISO alone and require that all staff and partners are on board.

**Activity | The three pillars approach**

The three pillars approach described by Brett Tucker is a useful method designed to assist organisations to decide what risk management framework to use and to determine whether investing in risk management is financially warranted.

This approach mirrors to some extent the pillars in the Basel III recommendations for banks (Minimum capital requirements, Supervisory review process and Market discipline).

For a summary table of the Basel III pillars, see www.bis.org/bcbs/basel3/b3summarytable.pdf.

Read Tucker's approach in 'The 3 pillars of enterprise cyber risk management' on the Software Engineering Institute blog.

https://insights.sei.cmu.edu/insider-threat/2017/11/the-3-pillars-of-enterprise-cyber-risk-management.html

**Activity | Ransomware attacks rising but human error a cause for concern**

Read the article 'Ransomware attacks rising but human error a cause for concern' from Insurance Business Australia to learn more about one of the major cyber risks facing companies today.

www.insurancebusinessmag.com/au/news/breaking-news/ransomware-attacks-rising-but-human-error-a-cause-for-concern-75415.aspx

### *Insider Threat*

The McKinsey & Company article, 'Insider threat: The human element of cyberrisk', describes insider threat as 'the cyberrisk posed to an organisation due to the behaviour of its employees', including contractors and vendors. As it is a behavioural risk, monitoring technologies are often ineffective as they are reactive (they can't respond until after the employee has acted) and can provide false or inaccurate results. The authors consider that while these technologies do have a role to play, they are most effective when combined with micro segmentation, culture change and prediction. They define these concepts as follows:

- *Microsegmentation* allows the organisation to home in on the 'hot spots' of risk and take a targeted rather than blanket approach to threat monitoring and mitigation.
- *Culture change* makes malicious, co-opted, or negligent risk events less likely, and puts the company in a preventive rather than reactive posture.
- *Prediction* allows an organisation to identify and disrupt insider activities much earlier in the threat life cycle.

Culture change is then further explored.

> While many programmes focus on catching and responding to negative behaviours, it's also vitally important to directly and assertively address the cultural issues that drive negligence and

malicious behaviour. To combat negligence and co-opting, companies often conduct rudimentary cyber security trainings, as well as phishing testing. Too often these efforts focus only on behaviour – educating employees on proper cyber-procedures – and miss the attitudes-and-beliefs part of the equation.

Targeted interventions (such as periodic communications on cyber-impact) help employees see and feel the importance of 'cyber-hygiene', and purposeful reinforcement from senior executives is critical to achieving workforce buy-in. Best-in-class organisations rigorously measure both behaviours and attitudes and develop comprehensive change plans to beat cyber-negligence, complete with targets and clear owners within the organisation.

Culture can be a compounding problem or a compounding solution. When an organisation's data mission is detached from business strategy and core operations, it should come as no surprise that the results of analytics initiatives may fail to meet expectations. But when excitement about data analytics infuses the entire organisation, it becomes a source of energy and momentum. The technology, after all, is amazing. Imagine how far it can go with a culture to match.

### *Social Engineering*

As evidenced by numerous cases of cyber security breaches in the current decade, the weakest link in any cyber security programme is the human component of the complex system.

Hackers are increasingly using an array of 'social engineering' scams designed to fool people into giving up personal and/or organisational information voluntarily.

Social engineering defined in the context of cyber security refers to the psychological manipulation of people so they act in a manner desired by the perpetrator or divulge confidential information. (Be aware that social engineering within the scope of social sciences has a different meaning and does not include the disclosure of confidential information.)

So how does an organisation protect itself from human malicious acts?

The reality is that hacking is still effective and is becoming increasingly more lucrative. As such, hackers have learned which of their tools and techniques work to breach organisations' defences.

Many organisations are still relying on technology-based cyber security, which focuses on identifying and protecting the weaknesses in an organisation's cyber defences that result from programming flaws or misconfigurations. However, social engineers target the weaknesses caused by human error. Humans are creatures of habit and often fail to follow security protocols. Social engineers take advantage this as it is usually easier than bypassing technology-based barricades.

**Activity | How the social engineering threat works**

Read the content under 'How the social engineering threat works' in 'Hacking humans: The social engineering threat', which informed the above paragraphs, for more details on social engineering as a cyber-attack technique, including how effective it is and how to protect yourself and your organisation.

www.swordshield.com/blog/hacking-humans-social-engineering

Many experts have been investigating social engineering and have come to some common conclusions including that staff and partners constitute the first line of defence and that human beings are very complex and inserted in a complex web of social relations. The key to long-term resilience is creating a culture of cyber risk awareness and recognising the value of information. This means that any 'awareness programme' that would be grafted on a laisser-faire culture would be vain, and that it is unnecessary if the culture is robust.

One key is to get everyone to do their own job securely in all its aspects by including cyber security as a key element of the overall security. This requires that all functions involved in the process – risk management, HSE, and information – coordinate their efforts. In too many instances, they tend to operate in silos, and in silos jealous of their own responsibilities.

### *Cyber Insurance Tips for Small Organisations*

Buying specific cyber insurance covers is an important issue for most risk management professionals. While having cyber insurance coverage is a good defensive move to help protect organisations against cyber-attacks, it is never enough to confront all the disturbances that may ensue.

As previously publicised cyber-attacks teach us, it is not enough to defend an organisation with cyber insurance and rely only on the insurance compensation when the threat materialises. It is essential that all organisations develop a strong offensive strategy to ensure cyber security.

When it comes to small business, their leadership needs also to be vigilant and take proactive steps to help protect their company's data. Their survival depends on developing a strong offensive strategy to ensure cyber security.

Even if they are entangled in daily operations, they must keep in mind that a cyber-attack may be just around the corner and they could develop and implement a cyber-strategy by following these five steps:

1. Invest in cyber protection:
   Purchase anti-virus and anti-phishing email software, data encryption, and off-site backups for your data and website.

2. Create a cyber response plan.
   Be ready in case the worst happens. Make sure you add concrete steps about what to do in the event of a cyber-attack to your business continuity plan – and make sure that each employee understands their role.
3. Develop procedures for cyber protection.
   Create secure, concrete procedures for disposing of paper records, computers, and other storage devices. Keep records no longer than absolutely needed (but beware of regulations in some sectors).
4. Control access to data and sensitive material.
   Limit access to sensitive information and provide authorised users with individual passwords renewed regularly. Make sure employees know not to share passwords or use their personal email for sensitive information. When employees leave, immediately terminate their access.
5. Train employees.
   All your employees should know how to spot suspicious activity, both online and otherwise. Develop a data security culture and encourage reporting so that potential security breaches get discovered sooner.

**Activity | Cyber insurance**

Read more about purchasing cyber insurance in these articles:

- 'Focus on cyber threats', in 'FERMA European risk manager report', FERMA, 2018. www.ferma.eu/app/uploads/2019/02/ferma-european-risk-manager-report-2018_final_19-12.pdf
- 'At the junction of corporate governance and cyber security', ECIIA and FERMA, October 2018. www.eciia.eu/wp-content/uploads/2019/02/FERMA-Perspectives-Cyber-risk-governance-09.10.2018_0.pdf
- 'Preparing for cyber insurance', FERMA, October 2018. www.ferma.eu/app/uploads/2019/02/preparing-for-cyber-insurance-web-04-10-2018.pdf
- 'Small business insurance and cyber-attacks: Are you covered?', Liberty Mutual Insurance. https://protectmybusiness.libertymutual.com/article/small-business-insurance-cyber-attacks-covered/

## Risk Managers and the Use of Technology

Although the use of technology to perform risk management missions may seem outside of the present chapter, it is important to mention it here as it both generates additional cyber vulnerabilities that must be considered and provides new opportunities to develop more quantitative modelling for future risks (threats as well as opportunities). It also assists risk management professionals in becoming more cyber savvy.

**Activity | How technology helps with risk management**

In 'How can technology enable risk management and mitigation? What steps should I be taking to use technology as a risk manager?' from Strategic Risk Knowledge, Chris Corless, Enterprise Risk & Audit Leader – Transformation & Continuous Improvement – Global Execution at KPMG, describes three ways in which technology is improving risk management.

www.strategicrisk-asiapacific.com/the-knowledge/how-can-technology-enable-risk-management-and-mitigation-what-steps-should-i-be-taking-to-use-technology-as-a-risk-manager/1427431.article

### *Risk Managers and Cyber Strategy*

The digital/data transformation, the fourth industrial revolution, is changing every aspect of the business landscape at an exponential pace, bringing the full force of innovation and disruption to all sectors and markets. While it offers vast opportunities, it brings also major challenges. Directors and officers in all organisations are faced with difficult strategic decisions. Insurers too are being transformed by digital advances. As they position themselves to respond to an ever-evolving context, several trends and strategic challenges that apply to all businesses in this new and digitally advanced environment have emerged such as:

- customer demand and customisation
- digital routes versus traditional distribution
- dematerialisation (moving from paper to digital).

Risk managers have a crucial role to play in supporting senior executives in making these strategic decisions. Take the simple example of creating and launching a new digital insurance product; this involves regulatory compliance, licencing rules, data protection, risk to reputation, etc.

Risk managers need to ensure that they are protecting both the consumer and their company from three main challenges:

- *Coping with interconnected risks:* Today's risks are more complex; in this new digital environment, risks are more interconnected and the speed at which these risks evolve is increasing. How can risk managers show these interconnected webs to their managers?
- *Taking their part in the decision-making process:* Risk managers must bring to the table new competencies and talent to improve the information on which decisions are made and implemented.
- *Ensuring that risk appetite/tolerance is defined and allocated to operational units:* This results in such questions as what can be absorbed and what should be transferred (including the purchase of insurance covers).

Therefore, it is essential that risk managers are part of their company's digital transformation decision-making process so that they can add value to all strategic decisions rather than just being a disruption stopper and are able to promote enterprise risk management for the cyber-dependent organisation. It will be efficient only if a strong co-operation between all staff results in a cyber-security aware culture as the human element is often the weakest link in the complex system and subject to malicious acts stemming from social engineering.

## Summary

Please keep the following points from this chapter in mind:

- Cyber risk management is the combination of personnel, policies, processes, and technologies that enable an organisation to cost-effectively achieve and maintain an acceptable level of cyber-loss exposure and seize the opportunities offered by the cyberspace, thus enabling it to achieve its goals and enhance its resilience.
- Complex systems' major vulnerabilities tend to be human behaviour and habits. Hostile individuals, also called social engineers, rely on human gullibility and errors to bypass technological security measures.
- Social engineering defined in the context of cyber security refers to the psychological manipulation of people so they act in a manner desired by the perpetrator or divulge confidential information.
- One of the key questions for risk management professionals to ponder what they can do to help the board get a handle on cyber-security issues.
- It remains for leaders to understand that cyber risks are so pervasive that their management cannot be delegated to a CIO or a CISO alone and require that all staff and partners are on board.
- Insider threat is 'the cyberrisk posed to an organisation due to the behaviour of its employees'.
- The key to long-term resilience is creating a culture of cyber risk awareness and recognising the value of information.
- Cyber insurance coverage is a good defensive move to help protect organisations against cyber-attacks but it is never enough to confront all the disturbances that may ensue.
- Technology both generates additional cyber vulnerabilities that must be considered and provides new opportunities to develop more quantitative modelling for future risks.
- Risk managers have a crucial role to play in supporting senior executives in making these strategic decisions.

Chapter 12

# Managing Terrorism Risks

## Introduction

Risks, from economic, natural, industrial or human sources, offer organisations both threats and opportunities that shape the physical, natural and human environments in which they operate. Most stakeholders demand healthy and safe products and services, and expect that the technologies that are meant to serve them cannot harm their vital interests; furthermore, they trust regulatory agencies to reduce risks to levels deemed tolerable by most citizens.

However, they fail to grasp that the scientific foundation for understanding and controlling risks is still far from being established. The main factor behind this open situation is the complex nature of risk that calls for a multidisciplinary approach. Risk means something different in the natural, engineering, psychological, social and cultural disciplines. Therefore, risk management professionals must compare and confront the main disciplinary approaches to understanding and analysing risk to use the insights from these approaches in a more coherent and consistent fashion.

Terrorism can dramatically influence the world, as evidenced by the far-reaching and prolonged effects of the attacks in New York on 11 September 2001 and the following uninterrupted chain of terror attacks worldwide. Indeed, although modern-day terrorist attacks started much earlier – for example, what happened in France in 1995, let alone the terrorist attacks in Northern Ireland and in the Basque Country in Spain – the terrorist attacks of 11 September 2001 on the World Trade Center in New York triggered the development of an entirely new field for risk management that some have called terrorism-risk management. Since then, industry and the academic risk analysis communities have all invested heavily in the development of tools and approaches that can assist decision-makers in effectively

**Risk Measurement and Monitoring, 279–284**

**doi:10.1108/978-1-83662-310-620251028**

allocating limited resources across the vast array of potential investments that could mitigate risks from terrorism and other threats to the homeland in all countries, especially, but not exclusively developed countries and their interests or citizens worldwide.

Decision-makers, both private and public, demand models, analyses and decision support that are useful for this task and based on state-of-the-art techniques. Since terrorism risk analysis is new, no single method is likely to meet this challenge. Therefore, any risk and/or security professional must explore an array of approaches for terrorism risk analysis, both in already tested and new unchartered territories. It is particularly important to understand the recent discussions on the applicability of probabilistic and decision analytic approaches to terrorism, and more specifically to bio and cyber-terrorism risks.

Intelligent adversary modelling has become increasingly important for risk analysis, and numerous approaches for incorporating intelligent adversaries in risk analysis models have been suggested. However, these approaches are based on a range of often-implicit assumptions about the desirable properties of intelligent adversary models. Specialists propose a set of four basic necessary conditions for intelligent adversary models; these are:

1. behavioural accuracy to the degree possible
2. computational tractability to support decision-making
3. explicit consideration of uncertainty
4. ability to gain confidence in the model.

These suggested necessary conditions set the stage for a serious discussion on the goals and assumptions underlying intelligent adversary modelling in risk analysis, keeping in mind that terrorism risk cannot be mitigated without a holistic approach involving all the private and public actors of safety/security.

The situation may be summarised by the EU position:

> *Terrorism threatens our security, the values of our democratic societies and the rights and freedoms of European citizens. Fighting terrorism is a top priority for the EU and its member states as well as its international partners.*

## Learning Outcomes

By the end of this chapter, you should:

- have a working understanding of terrorism and its relevance to risk management;
- be able to identify current trends in terrorism;
- have some understanding of how to manage terrorism risk.

## A Definition of Terrorism

Like for many issues concerning risk, defining the issue is key to grasping it and setting the course for effective risk management. Providing a clear definition of terrorism impacts diagnostic, communication and response to this issue and so has consequences for society and politics. However, a suitable universal definition remains elusive because different bodies, organisations, and government agencies have different definitions to suit their own role, purpose, or bias.

**Activity | Defining terrorism**

Read the section '*Defining terrorism*' from Bruce Hoffman's book, Inside terrorism, available online at http://movies2.nytimes.com/books/first/h/hoffman-terrorism.html.

Consider the current dictionary definitions and how the definition of terrorism as a political concept is useful to risk management professionals.

Hoffman concludes that:

> *By distinguishing terrorists from other types of criminals and terrorism from other forms of crime, we come to appreciate that terrorism is*
>
> - *ineluctably political in aims and motives;*
> - *violent – or, equally important, threatens violence;*
> - *designed to have far-reaching psychological repercussions beyond the immediate victim or target;*
> - *conducted by an organisation with an identifiable chain of command or conspiratorial cell structure (whose members wear no uniform or identifying insignia); and*
> - *perpetrated by a subnational group or non-state entity.*
>
> *We may therefore now attempt to define terrorism as the deliberate creation and exploitation of fear through violence or the threat of violence in the pursuit of political change. All terrorist acts involve violence or the threat of violence. Terrorism is specifically designed to have far-reaching psychological effects beyond the immediate victim(s) or object of the terrorist attack. It is meant to instil fear within, and thereby intimidate, a wider `target audience' that might include a rival ethnic or religious group, an entire country, a national government or political party, or public opinion in general. Terrorism is designed to create power where there is none or to consolidate power where there is very little. Through the publicity generated by their violence, terrorists seek to obtain the leverage, influence and power they otherwise lack to effect political change on either a local or an international scale.*

The effects of terrorism are enhanced by the possibilities offered by social media, which provides multiple platforms on which these acts can be discussed, shared, and promoted.

## Brief History of Terrorism

Terrorism has been used throughout history to intimidate and discourage opposition from enemies and subordinates. From ancient Greece to the French Revolution, the Sicarii to Nazi Germany, the Spanish Inquisition to the Ku Klux Klan, history is littered with examples of groups using violence, threats, psychological cruelty and anarchy to achieve their aims.

There are multiple types of terrorist activity, with one theory identifying three main types:

- revolutionary, in which terrorists seek to overthrow a political system (as used by the Italian Red Brigades and the Baader-Meinhof Gang);
- sub revolutionary, in which terrorists seek to modify an existing regime (as used by the ANC in attempting to end apartheid in South Africa);
- establishment, or state-sponsored, in which governments use terrorist techniques against citizens, governmental factions or foreign governments (as used during the Cold War). This type of terrorism can be hard to identify as state support is generally covert.

Tactics have changed over the years as technology advances enable different opportunities for attacks. Suicide bombing has increased in prominence since the 1980s, and air travel has enabled hijacking tactics that led to attacks such as the one that took place on September 11 on the twin towers, which remains the deadliest terror attack to date.

**Activity | History of terrorism**

For more information on the history of terrorism, read the Encyclopaedia Britannica entry on the topic. www.britannica.com/topic/terrorism/Types-of-terrorism.

**Activity | Understanding terrorism**

Read about the psychology of terrorism, the way cultural values feed into it and the potential to deradicalise terrorist detainees in 'Understanding terrorism' from *Monitor on psychology* by the American Psychological Association.

www.apa.org/monitor/2009/11/terrorism

## Current Trends in Terrorism Threats

Since the beginning of the 21st century, the terrorist threat has continued to increase and specialists have forged a new word to describe the September 11 attacks in the USA: hyper-terrorism.

Hyper-terrorism is not only the consequence of ideology, but also technological and organisational evolutions that impart the individuals with increasing power. Massive destruction capacity is now available to non-governmental groups or even to determined individuals. Hyper-terrorism is one version of the transfer of power from states to what is not the state. Hyper-terrorism is illustrated by a synergy between the capacity to kill many people and the choice of targets worldwide

Insurers, state programmes, and private sector offers are aware of these evolutions. Although the elements of terrorism insurance will be treated in a different section to illustrate the major country programmes as government are leading the way in most developed countries, it is nevertheless important to consider the insurers' position.

**Activity | The changing face of terrorism risk**

Read about insurance options for terrorism risk in 'The changing face of terrorism risk' from Strategic Risk Asia Pacific.

www.strategicrisk-asiapacific.com/latest-updates/the-changing-face-of-terrorism-risk/1427565.article

## Managing Terrorism Risk

Managing terrorism risk can seem like an impossible task for many organisations. Terrorism can be unpredictable and it is laden with fear and incomprehension.

However, Nathan C. Gould, Director and Chief of Technology, Advanced Engineering, ABS Group, believes terrorism risk can be managed in much the same way as any other risk. To assist risk management professionals and organisations to prepare for this risk, he has come up with a three-phase terrorism risk management programme that he describes in his article, 'Managing terrorism risk' for IRMI.

His three steps are:

1. Identify the threat and assess the initial site
2. Conduct a detailed risk assessment
3. Manage the risk.

From this basic outline, it should be immediately clear to any risk management professional that terrorism risk can be approached like any other risk, and that the key is to identify the physical possibilities and to prioritise assets.

To read more on how to manage this risk, read Gould's article: www.irmi.com/articles/expert-commentary/managing-terrorism-risk.

## Cyberterrorism and Security Measures

This development could have been included in the previous chapter on cybersecurity but the terrorism risk requires specific approaches that are prevalent over the 'cyber' side of the issue. However, there is no practical generally accepted definition 'cyberterrorism', as the one we find is 'the politically motivated use of computers and information technology to cause severe disruption or widespread fear in society'.

Even the FBI definition is not really operational: 'premeditated, politically motivated attack against information, computer systems, computer programs, and data which results in violence against non-combatant targets by subnational groups or clandestine agents'.

**Activity | Cyberterrorism**

How do we deal with cyberterrorism if we can't define what it is?

Seymour Goodman, author of Science and technology to counter terrorism, suggests we consider these two questions:

- What would terrorists want to do in cyberspace?
- How do we try to deal with such activities?

Read his thoughts on these questions, his recommendations for dealing with cyberterrorists and his three stages of defence in his book, available online at: www.nap.edu/read/11848/chapter/6#44.

## Summary

Please keep the following points from this chapter in mind:

- A suitable universal definition for terrorism remains elusive because different bodies, organisations, and government agencies have different definitions to suit their own role, purpose, or bias.
- The effects of terrorism are enhanced by the possibilities offered by social media, which provides multiple platforms on which these acts can be discussed, shared, and promoted.
- Terrorism has been used throughout history to intimidate and discourage opposition from enemies and subordinates but tactics have changed over the years as technology advances enable different opportunities for attacks.
- It is hard to deal with a threat if we cannot define it, which is one of the issues involved with 'cyberterrorism'.

Chapter 13

# Reputation

## Introduction

This section provides you with an overview of reputation risk and its causes. It also explores whether reputation risks result in catastrophic consequences.

Reputation is the main asset of any organisation and managing reputation is therefore one of the major tasks of executives and board members. Future uncertainties may be both threats and opportunities depending on how decisions are made and stakeholders involved in an information consultation process to develop their trust in the future of the organisation and their understanding of its contribution to the sustainable development of the society so that the organisation establishes and reinforces its 'social licence to operate'.

## Learning Outcomes

By the end of this chapter, you should be able to:

- describe the concepts of reputation and reputation risk;
- identify potential sources of risk relating to reputation;
- describe the role of directors and management in managing risk to reputation;
- describe and apply tools/techniques and strategies useful to identifying and managing reputation risk;
- identify strategies for managing a reputation risk event.

**Risk Measurement and Monitoring, 285–316**

**Published under exclusive licence by Emerald Publishing Limited**
**doi:10.1108/978-1-83662-310-620251030**

**Cityshore Development and Construction**

Sir Charles Bilton, Cityshore's chairperson, expresses concern to Ted Williams about Cityshore maintaining their reputation, especially as they plan to become a public company.

**Sir Charles:**

*I know that you and your executive management team have been working hard on the risk management framework, but I don't really see how we're integrating and managing reputation risk.*

*I was talking with a colleague the other day who is the chair of one of the local banks, and you know how important reputation risk is for them. He mentioned a consultant, Jay Clarke, who's an expert in reputation risk, and is well known in the development and construction industry. What I'd like is for you to get Jay to our next meeting to give us a briefing on how we should be dealing with reputation risk at Cityshore.*

Ted agrees to contact Jay and to invite him to address the next board meeting.

***Case Study Issues***

Keep the following questions in mind as you progress through this section.

1. How should Cityshore define reputation risk?
2. When, where and how might reputation risks arise for Cityshore?
3. Who should be responsible for managing reputation risk in the company?
4. How can Cityshore recognise reputation risk issues and their potential consequences?
5. How would Cityshore manage its reputation risks?
6. What should Cityshore do if a reputation risk event manifests?

## What Is Reputation?

The question is worth asking as there is still some confusion between brand and reputation. Here we reserve the word reputation to cover all aspects of the stakeholders' perception of an organisation whereas the name 'brand' applies more to a specific product or service. Therefore, a company's reputation may incorporate several brands and be influenced by them. It is therefore of interest to the 'reputation scholar' to study brand building and maintaining. A recent study shed an interesting light on a five stages process stressing for brands attributes similar to those described here for reputation:

Differentiation: how to stand out from competition?

Positioning: Why do consumers and employees need this new product in their lives?

According to the Compact Oxford English Dictionary, reputation is 'the beliefs or opinions that are generally held about someone or something'. Depending on the field studied, reputation may have different meanings (Gaultier-Gaillard and Louisot, 2006) but always constitutes an intangible asset. The main question should then be to determine what makes a good reputation. The theory is simple: an organisation enjoys a good reputation when it consistently meets or exceeds the expectations of its stakeholders. A bad reputation occurs when the organisation's words or deeds fall short of stakeholder expectations. This concept is expressed in the following reputation equation:

**Reputation = experience – expectations**

Oonagh Mary Harpur

*Stakeholder expectations are shaped by their beliefs about what a business is and what it does. These beliefs are influenced by what the business says about itself and by what others say about it. Stakeholders then measure their actual experience of how the business acts against their expectations.*

*A good reputation is achieved when there is congruence between a business's purpose, its goals and values (what it professes to be), its conduct and actions (what it does it practice) and the experience and expectations of its stakeholders.*

Maintaining a good reputation therefore requires continuing identification and management of emerging gaps.

As the key to a good reputation is meeting stakeholder expectations, it is vital to establish who your most significant stakeholders are, what expectations they have of you and how they currently perceive you. Only then can you pinpoint any gaps and start to correct them. You might start by listing and then prioritising your business's stakeholders – both internal (employers) and external (shareholders, investors, suppliers, customers, regulators, analysts, insurers, regulators, government etc). The relative importance of stakeholders will vary between sectors. For example, in heavily regulated sectors such as financial services the regulator is likely to be a key stakeholder. It also is vital to consider a sufficiently broad range of stakeholders to ensure that no major interest group is neglected, as the sole omission may prove to be the source of an unidentified killer risk.

Their expectations depend on the sum of their perceptions and their representations. As reputational risk is a social construct, their expectations on reputational risk are also a social construct.

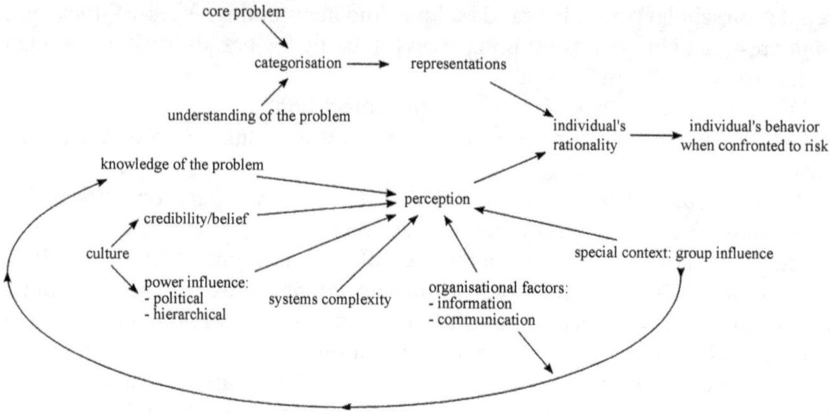


*Source*: 'Managing Reputational Risk – From theory to practice' by Sophie Gaultier Gaillard, Jean-Paul Louisot and Jenny Rayner in Joachim Klewes and Robert Wreschniok's Reputation capital: Building and maintaining trust in the 21st century.

## Risk to Reputation

An organisation's reputation is a highly valuable intangible asset and as such requires protection. An organisation with a positive reputation may attract better people, more customers, more loyalty and higher share prices, and can often charge more for products. Reputation is a key element of market value, and the main drivers are summarised in the following schemes.

*Source*: 'Managing Reputational Risk – From theory to practice' by Sophie Gaultier Gaillard, Jean-Paul Louisot and Jenny Rayner in Joachim Klewes and Robert Wreschniok's Reputation capital: Building and maintaining trust in the 21st century.

Despite its importance, reputation and ways to manage it are heard to define and measure and are therefore not clearly defined in risk management standards. As a result, many organisations don't adequately manage their reputation risk. This can be problematic as the actions of a small number of individuals can easily damage this reputation. The following examples provide some context for the ways in which reputation risks affect/have affected:

- government organisations
- Target
- Toyota
- Aon.

***Case Study – Government Organisations***

Maintaining a government's reputation is a particular challenge because the parliamentary opposition (with media assistance) often attempts to discredit the government. The opposition can often discredit the governmental organisation indirectly by attacking the departments and statutory bodies for which the government is responsible. What may seem too many to be small errors in process or judgement become a major public relations challenge.

***Case Study – Target***

In 2013, Target US was the victim of a cyber attack that compromised the personal data of up to 40 million customers. The hackers stole data – including names, addresses, card numbers, and PINs – from credit and debit cards used by shoppers between 27 November and 18 December. It was later discovered that Target had been informed of the breach on 30 November but failed to act. The three-week delay was the cause of the volume of data leaked, and ultimately led to negligence lawsuits.

Besides needing to pay out up to US \$202 million (€ 169 million) to reissue cards and to cover investigative fees, lawsuits and probes, including US \$18.5 million (€ 15.5 million) to settle claims from 48 US states and districts, Target's profits fell 46% in the quarter and share prices fell 11% – these results were lower than expected. Additionally, the delay in responding incident tarnished Target's reputation for providing a top-rate shopping experience and led its Buzz score (a measurement of brand popularity) to drop 45 points by the third day after the breach was announced.

### *Case Study – Toyota*

As explored in this book volume, in 2009, Toyota had trouble with sticking accelerator pedals which resulted in uncontrolled acceleration. It had numerous complaints across the world and was slow to recognise the issue and address it with a vehicle recall. The issue was caused by one of two unrelated issues (a slipping floor mat and a flaw in the pedal design). By the time the company began recalling vehicles there was a major public uproar regarding the safety of Toyota cars. The recall involved millions of vehicles worldwide.

#### The backlash

The problem for Toyota was that the issue existed and they were perceived by the public as attempting to hide it. Because it was a safety issue, the backlash by the media and the motoring public was substantial and significantly damaged the reputation of the company – a reputation which until this time was the envy of the industry – one of providing well-built, reliable cars.

#### Lessons learned

The lesson learned was that, when it comes to safety, there is an expectation that the company should react quickly and consistently worldwide – the response was initially different in various world markets.

#### Associated costs

The ultimate cost to the company was significant and was added to the cost of the recall, which would have had to occur in any event. The CEO was forced to resign over the issue and it is certain that the company lost customers, some of whom will never return to the brand.

### *Case Study – AON Survey*

In AON's 2017 'Global risk management survey', *Damage to reputation/ brand* was identified as the number one risk for 36.4% of the industries surveyed, and a top five risks for 45.5%.

The report also identified the interconnected risks that either lead to or result from damage to reputation/brand.

| Risks That Lead to Damage to Reputation/Brand | Risks That Result from Damage to Reputation/Brand |
|---|---|
| Cyber crime | Cyber crime |
| Business interruption | Share price volatility |
| Injury to workers | Increasing competition |
| Unethical behaviour | Unethical behaviour |
| Product recall | Product recall |
| Social media | Merger/acquisition |

The interactive report is available at www.aon.com/2017-global-risk-management-survey. The full report can be downloaded upon request.

***Reputation and Stakeholders' Opinion***

> While reputation is 'intangible', damage to an institution's reputation (and the resulting loss of consumer trust and confidence) can have very tangible consequences – a stock price decline, a run on the bank, a rating downgrade, an evaporation of available credit, regulatory investigations, shareholder litigation etc.

Reputation may impact:

- Stockholders' decisions to hold onto their shares
- Customers' desire to buy products and services
- Suppliers' desire to establish partnerships
- Competitors' eagerness to enter the market
- Media coverage
- Pressure groups/NGO activity
- Control and regulatory authority attitudes
- Cost of capital
- Recruitment of high potential individuals
- Motivation of current workforce
- Inclination of stakeholders to grant the benefit of the doubt when a crisis emerges.

What makes risks to reputation particularly difficult to evaluate is the random nature of a strike. Often, an issue deemed minor by a business can cause severe reputational damage, whereas an apparently major issue can pass without comment. Geography can also play a part. A minor event at a distant manufacturing site in a developing country may attract little or no media or stakeholder interest, whereas that same event in the business's heartland can provoke a reputational storm.

An assessment of reputational impact also needs to consider the resilience of corporate reputation.

This will depend on the amount of 'reputational capital' built with stakeholders and the nature and extent of the issue or risk. Was this a predictable and preventable incident, such as anti-competitive activity, bribery condoned by senior management or an accident resulting from blatant disregard for human safety? If so, stakeholders are unlikely to be forgiving. Or was it an unforeseeable occurrence which could not have been avoided, such as 9/11 or natural disaster where stakeholders will be sympathetic?

Even after such catastrophic events stakeholders expect businesses to learn and adapt. So, post 9/11 and Hurricane Katrina, investors, regulators, and customers now require businesses to have risk management systems and business continuity plans in place to counter the effect of such risks.

Another challenge in assessing impacts on reputation is that the initial impact of a risk crystallising may be relatively small, perhaps a fine resulting from a minor breach or regulations. However, this may chip away insidiously at stakeholder trust. A series of minor bad news stories can have a cumulative effect whereby a 'tipping point' is reached, after which stakeholders suddenly lose confidence, the business's share price plummets and current and all past misdemeanours are raked over in the ensuing media frenzy making it very difficult to recover.

Oil and gas company BP enjoyed a formidable reputation with investors and other stakeholders under the leadership of its much-admired former CEO Lord John Browne. Its hard-won reputation allowed it to withstand a number of crises in the early 2000s. However, the death of 15 workers and injury of 500 others when overfilled storage tanks exploded at BP's Texas City refinery in the US resulted in a massive loss of confidence in the company, a top-management shake-out and a new strategic approach.

Understanding precisely how stakeholders perceive your business at any point in time can help you judge whether you are approaching your reputational tipping point, where just one more bad news story could push you over the brink, and to evaluate the reputational impact and respond accordingly.

It may be possible to place a monetary value on reputational risk e.g. via loss of future contracts/income; cost of loss of licence to operate; impact on Net Present Value (NPV); impact on share price; impact on brand value. However, these cannot be applied to all reputational risks. Many businesses therefore use a qualitative approach to initially assess reputational impact (see Exhibit 6 below which uses a four-level scale), alongside financial and other relevant impact criteria. Both the short-term and longer-term impacts of a risk on the business's reputation should be considered, including the effect on stakeholder behaviour and hence on the future value of the business.

Therefore, stakeholders' confidence, including public opinion, plays a critical part in the loss of reputation and, therefore, in defining the concept of risk to reputation.

Consider the following case study.

### *Case Study – Brent Spar*

In 1991, Shell Oil concluded that its North Sea oil platform, Brent Spar, reached the end of its useful life. After researching different options for its disposal, based on each option's engineering complexity, the safety of the workforce and the likely environmental impact, the company reached an agreement with the UK Government to tow the platform to the North Atlantic and sink it in deep water.

#### Lack of scientific research publicity

At the time of the announcement, Shell did not publicise the results of its extensive scientific research into the least environmentally damaging options for disposal and, therefore, the basis for its decision.

#### Greenpeace's response

Activists from the environmental organisation Greenpeace occupied the Brent Spar to protest the sinking decision. Shell's reaction to the protest, and the forced evacuation of the protesters from the platform in full view of much of the world's media, gave Greenpeace the foundation for a successful campaign to influence the public against the company's approved option.

The public ignored the subsequent release of the company's scientific reasoning behind their decision, and perceived it as an excuse or a cover-up, rather than proof of a rational decision.

#### Effects of continuing public support

The continuing public support for the Greenpeace view, which included a boycott of the company's petroleum products throughout Europe, resulted in Shell revising its decision and towing the platform to a deep-water harbour in Norway in June 1995. In January 1998, the company announced that the platform would be dismantled in Norway and recycled as the foundation for a new ferry terminal.

#### Associated costs

The revised scrapping plan cost Shell some A$40 million more than its original sinking option and, as most commentators subsequently agreed, was carried out at a far greater risk to both the environment and to the workers employed on the dismantling (some analysts say six times more dangerous).

#### Greenpeace versus shell

Dirk Maxeiner, a leading environmental journalist at the time of the incident (Maxeiner, 2003), commented that in 1995:

> [...] Greenpeace had the credibility and Shell only had the truth, so the oil company didn't have the slightest chance against Greenpeace.

***Case Study – Cityshore Defines Reputation Risk***

Jay Clarke explains to the Cityshore team that reputation risk can be defined as:

> […] the current and prospective impact on earnings and capital arising from negative public opinion.

A good reputation is built up over a period, but can be destroyed in a single day by negative public opinion because of events over which the average director or manager feels they have little or no control.

Jay continues to explain the importance of reputation risk and that ownership should be the concern of all employees, right up to board level.

**Jay:**

*Risk to reputation is not really a separate class of risk like, for example, market, credit or operational risk. Reputation risk generally arises as a consequence of an adverse risk event occurring within the business.*

*Most major reputation risk events are the result of a single problem, often a human mistake, being compounded by a string of other mishaps, none of which by itself would have resulted in the adverse event.*

The next step for Cityshore is to implement a process for handling reputation risk.

**Activity | Effect of stakeholder trust and confidence on corporate reputation**

Read the article, 'Does a data breach really affect your firm's reputation?' from CSO Online.

1. Consider the author's argument that a reputational breach does not affect profitability in the long term.
2. Can you list any organisations for which this was not true, i.e. that suffered or collapsed due to damage to their reputations?
3. Can you list any organisations, other than those listed in the article, that have survived and prospered after damage done to their reputation?
4. Consider the reports mentioned, like the Forbes report, 'Fallout: The reputational impact of IT risk', that have found that reputational risk has a significant effect on organisations.
5. What factors, e.g. industry or age, might alter the way reputational damage affects an organisation?
6. Which argument do you agree with more?

www.csoonline.com/article/3019283/data-breach/does-a-data-breach-really-affect-your-firm-s-reputation.html

## Identifying Reputation Risk

### *Sources of Reputation Risk*

Risk to reputation can arise both from internal practices and external practices (things that a third party can do to an organisation).

**Self-Help Question 13.1**

- Identify one area of an organisation's activities that can give rise to reputation risk.
- Provide examples of such reputation risks.

| Area | Example |
|---|---|
| | |
| | |

Answers to self-help questions are provided at the end of each section.

*Case Study – Johnson & Johnson*

**Public tampering**

In 1982, an unknown member of the public tampered with Johnson & Johnson's Tylenol product, which resulted in the death of seven innocent consumers.

**Effects**

This could have had a major effect on the reputation of Johnson & Johnson. It certainly had a significant financial impact, as the company had to recall/replace 31 million bottles of the drug and its market share fell 30%. The company eventually ended up spending more than US$100 million on the recall and later relaunch of the product.

**Effective management**

Fortunately, the company's effective management of the issue resulted in an improved reputation rather than the disastrous loss that the incident could have triggered.

As soon as the link was uncovered, the company chairman ordered that all bottles be recalled from the market. This was a landmark action, as at the time very little was recalled. The action gave the public the impression that Johnson & Johnson cared more for public safety than it did for profits, and the company came to be seen as the eighth victim of the poisonings, rather than a perpetrator.

Despite the initial drop, within five months of the poisonings Johnson & Johnson's market share had reached up to 70% of its earlier position. Additionally, consumer confidence increased, and the company emerged from the crisis with a stronger reputation than before.

Johnson & Johnson's management of the event was so effective it is still used as a crisis management case study and referred to as the gold standard.

### *Tools for Identifying Reputation Risk Triggers*

There are a variety of tools organisations can use for identifying reputation risk triggers. Some of these include:

- risk measures
- current risk registers
- brainstorming
- interviewing
- research.

The following table outlines each of these tools.

**Tools Organisations Can Use for Identifying Reputation Risk Triggers**

| Tool | Description |
|---|---|
| Risk measures | • Risk measures, including reputation risk in consequence measurement tables, are an effective way of ensuring organisations consider the impacts of reputation risk<br>• Risk measures are important, because reputation risk can be the result of many risks that organisations tent to forget |
| Current risk registers | • If risk management practices are already embedded in an organisation, the organisation should review its risk registers and ensure it has also identified the reputation consequences of all identified risks |

(*Continued*)

(*Continued*)

| Tool | Description |
|---|---|
| Brainstorming | • Brainstorming is an effective tool for identifying issues which can have an impact on public opinion and, hence, on an organisation's reputation<br>• The brainstorming team or teams should comprise people from various levels, disciplines or business units within the organisation<br>• Brainstorming can combine a variety of experiences, knowledge, cultures, and backgrounds to converge on an issue<br>• Since public opinion is based on an individual's perception (not necessarily on facts), the variety of input is an excellent way of identifying issues that one group of participants (for example, the executives of the organisation) may not perceive |
| Interviewing | • Organisations can interview their key constituents or stakeholders, including managers and appropriate staff to uncover issues which did affect, (or could have influenced, the organisation's reputation) |
| Research | • Those responsible for identifying potential reputation risk in an organisation should research the internet (for example), as well as back copies of newspapers, for instances of reputation risk events that have previously impacted similar organisations/third parties |

**Self-Help Question 13.2**

Under the categories listed in the following table, list some potential risk events of Cityshore's activities that could have a major adverse impact on the company's reputation.

| **Potential Reputation Risk Events for Cityshore** |
|---|
| **Products and services** |
| |
| **Environment** |
| |
| **Financial** |
| |
| Governance and control |
| |

Answers to self-help questions are provided at the end of each section.

**Activity | Identifying potential risk events**

Reputation risk applies not only to large publicly quoted companies, but to all organisations (and individuals); for example:

- public and private
- large and small
- incorporated or unincorporated
- profit making or philanthropic.

**A charitable organisation**

Consider a charitable organisation with which you are familiar. Use the categories of products and services, environment, and governance and control practices to list potential risk events (sources of risks) under each category that could result in a major loss of reputation for that organisation.

**Your organisation**

Consider your organisation. Use the categories of products and services, environment, and governance and control practices to list potential risk events (sources of risks) under each category that could result in a major loss of reputation for your organisation.

When complete, assess if your ERM system has adequately addressed these risks. If not, consider why.

*Consequences of Reputation Risk Events*

***Potential Impact***

Risk to reputation may impact how the public perceives an organisation's:

- product (its brand); or
- activities and products (its 'franchise').

In addition, risk to reputation can:

- be limited to certain geographic (or market segments); or
- impact all markets and locations (nationally and internationally) in which the organisation conducts its business.

The more the adverse public opinion affects the organisation's activities/products (or markets), the greater the financial consequences.

### *Case Study – Potential Impacts*

**Johnson and Johnson**

The impact of Johnson and Johnson's crisis was limited to one market (North America) and one product (Tylenol). If the crisis had been less effectively managed, the impact could easily have transferred to all markets and all products.

**Toyota**

In the case of Toyota, the impact of the faulty accelerator pedal was worldwide. In addition, the power of modern communications exponentially exacerbated the problem.

The use of the internet and other new technologies (such as SMS messaging) can mean:

- cheap and rapid distribution of adverse commentary on an organisation's problems;
- ease and speed in arranging protests or boycotts against the organisation.

This increases the probability of localised issues rapidly becoming attacks on all the organisation's products and markets.

### *Evaluating Potential Consequences*

As in any typical risk management process, once organisations identify issues that could give rise to adverse public opinion, they should evaluate their consequences. This consists of identifying the constituencies or stakeholders a risk event would affect as well as how it would affect them. The organisation also needs to have some understanding of the likelihood of the risk events arising.

This information needs to be related to the potential impact on the organisation by way of, for example:

- increased costs
- reduced sales
- decreases in contributions or government grants
- stakeholder loss of trust, resulting in the organisation's failure.

#### ***Shareholder Distrust***

If an organisation loses the trust of its shareholders in business, it will find difficulty in raising capital at cost-effective rates. This applies to debt capital as well as to equity capital. The share price if the company is publicly listed will also suffer.

**Self-Help Question 13.3**

Identify three stakeholders who may lose faith in an organisation after a risk event, which would therefore affect its reputation.

Answers to self-help questions are provided at the end of each section.

### *Effect on Acquisitions*

The capacity of large companies for acquisitions, especially acquisitions using equity, will consequently be reduced. A smaller company may find that not only is it no longer in a position to make acquisitions, it may very well find itself vulnerable to an unwanted takeover bid.

**EXAMPLE**

**NAB**

Shareholder distrust resulted in a 'market penalty' for the National Australia Bank (NAB) for a long period after the specific reputation risk event. The company's shares continued to trade at a discount to the other major banks.

### *Government*

In the case of a not-for-profit organisation, constituents no longer support the organisation or its endeavours if they lose trust. Government organisations, for example, lose both the confidence of their ministers and budget backing. Governments themselves also lose the confidence of the voting public.

**EXAMPLE**

**Cross City Tunnel**

In an interview about the motorists' boycott of the Sydney Cross City Tunnel, built and operated by a private consortium, New South Wales Premier, Morris Iemma, stated the circumstances had negatively affected the Government's reputation. He commented that the Government had become the target of motorists' fury.

Cityshore may achieve reductions in construction costs, but may discover an increase in operating costs. There is a risk, for example, of potential purchasers of the project units having to pay higher body corporate and maintenance charges.

*Customer Distrust*

Loss of customer trust could have even more major impacts than those caused by shareholder distrust. Without the support of its customers, no organisation can continue in the long-term.

In the case of a government organisation, the definition of customers may be broader and include:

- regulated individuals and entities
- grant recipients
- users of services facilitated by a department such as transport, and health and education.

**EXAMPLE**

**Victorian Public Transport**

Consider the impact of the performance of the Victorian public transport system. It is causing considerable damage to current and prior governments, even though it is said to be the result of under-investment over a period of many years. Many argue that the system is good but public expectations are higher than its inherent delivery capability.

*Employee Distrust*

Employee distrust covers both distrust of and by employees. In all organisations suffering a major reputation loss, the impact on employees originates from two directions.

The first is the impact on the culture of the organisation. If employees believe the organisation has transgressed some rule or has not acted ethically (for example) there will be a major negative impact upon their morale and effectiveness. This in turn will affect the way employees carry out their duties, to the detriment of customer service.

The second is the long-term impact on the ability of the organisation to attract and retain quality staff. This will affect the future growth and profitability of the organisation.

These consequences will probably be even more noticeable in organisations using voluntary staff.

**EXAMPLE**

**NAB**

In the NAB case, the board's distrust of the Chief Executive Officer (CEO) and senior management resulted in a complete replacement of much of the senior management team. Things eventually went even further, resulting in a major turnover in the board itself.

*Supplier and Other Constituencies Distrust*

In any organisation suffering an adverse reputational impact, difficulties will arise with suppliers and other third parties. Joint venture partners could seek to distance themselves from dealings with the organisation. Some organisations (especially smaller businesses) may find that terms of trade are suddenly tightened or that some suppliers will not wish to supply them at all.

Any organisation subject to third-party regulation or scrutiny or reliant on government grants and subsidies can expect reputation losses to impact upon their relations with those parties. For example, if an organisation develops a reputation for poor control, it can expect much closer scrutiny by a regulator.

**EXAMPLE**

**NAB**

APRA carried out an extensive review of NAB's risk management and compliance processes, and imposed a variety of additional requirements on the bank. Addressing these requirements imposed substantial additional costs on the NAB for compliance and audits, not only in the period immediately following the fraud, but on an ongoing basis.

---

**Self-Help Question 13.4**

1. Review the risk events you identified in Self-Help Question 13.2 in this section.
2. List the reputation risk consequences for Cityshore against each.
3. Consider how each consequence is likely to affect a product or activity of the company (its brand), or Cityshore as a whole (its franchise). Will this effect be felt only locally, or across all Cityshore activities?
4. Note if the risk event will impact Cityshore's brand or franchise (or both) and the extent of the impact (for example, locally, nationally or internationally) against the consequences you have listed.

| Potential Reputation Risk Events for Cityshore | Potential Consequences | Potential Impact |
|---|---|---|
| **Products and services** | | |
| | | |
| | | |
| | | |

→

→

| Potential Reputation Risk Events for Cityshore | Potential Consequences | Potential Impact |
|---|---|---|
| | | |
| | | |
| | | |
| | | |
| | | |
| **Environment** | | |
| | | |
| **Financial** | | |
| | | |
| | | |
| **Environmental** | | |
| | | |
| **Governance and control** | | |
| | | |
| Answers to self-help questions are provided at the end of each section. | | |

**Activity | Consequences of risk events**

Imagine you are a governor or a council member for a not-for-profit organisation. Identify some of the activities your organisation carries out that might result in a risk event that impacts that organisation's reputation. Decide how this impact would manifest itself (the consequences).

Alternatively, carry out the activity as if you were on the board of governors of an old, established, fee-paying primary/elementary school.

***Case Study – Cityshore Identifies Responsibilities and Accountabilities***

The Cityshore team reviews the reputation risks they need to manage. The team still needs to decide appropriate responsibilities and accountabilities. Jay approaches the directors with the following information.

**Jay:**

*Just like strategic risk, the directors of a company, the board of governors or the council of an unincorporated or non-profit organisation set the agenda for reputation risk management.*

*Your management is still responsible for identifying and managing the risk, but you as the board must ensure that you monitor management's activities. You must stay engaged with all your stakeholders and continuously monitor the public's perception and opinion of your organisation.*

*Reputation risk management is always the collective responsibility of all directors (or their equivalent), but also of management and staff. Essentially, every part of the organisation needs to drive reputation risk management.*

## Managing Risk to Reputation

It is critical that all organisations use effective practices to manage reputation risks on an ongoing basis. Boards and executive management are responsible and accountable for developing and implementing effective risk management practices appropriate to the reputation risks organisations face. Since reputation risk arises from activities or operations, the organisation should fully integrate these practices with the normal operational risk processes.

Several tools, techniques, and strategies can help an organisation manage the reputation risks it has identified, including:

- ensuring that reputation risk is a discrete risk category;
- considering potential reputation impacts when assessing risk;
- designing risk mitigation strategies, such as escalation procedures and crisis management plans (CMPs);
- training staff on the existence and functions of policies, procedures and CMPs;
- undertaking some crisis 'scenario' planning and role playing.

### *Developing Policies and Procedures*

All organisations should have effective policies that establish the framework for managing reputation risk. These policies:

- may be stand-alone policies and procedures addressing reputation risk issues only; or
- can be integrated with other organisational policies and procedures to address the reputation risk elements of the issue being addressed.

**Self-Help Question 13.5**

List three areas/issues organisational policies and procedures should cover to assist the organisation in managing its reputation risks.

Answers to self-help questions are provided at the end of each section.

### *Designing Risk Mitigates*

The aims of reputation risk mitigation are to:

- reduce the likelihood of an adverse incident;
- quickly identify and react to the occurrence of an event, minimising the consequences and the effect on the organisation.

Management needs to consider individual organisational reputation risk triggers and consequences in designing specific mitigates.

Remember, reputation risk is an area in which 'an ounce of prevention is worth a pound of cure'.

#### *Escalation Procedures*

All organisations should implement an escalation procedure (what should happen if and when a reputation risk event escalates in its impact). This ensures the organisation applies an appropriate level of management on a timely basis to all possible crisis events.

#### *Crisis Management Plan*

Similarly, all organisations with a governing council or with more than one executive must have a CMP in place. The organisation must train the relevant staff and executives in using and implementing this plan to ensure a prompt and structured risk response. In fact, poor crisis management is one of the main causes of reputational damage.

The CMP should be a generic document and is an integral part of business continuity management. See this book volume for further details.

### *Training and Education*

An essential element in the management of reputation risk is educating and training all directors, management and staff in the organisation's reputation risk policies, including:

- ethics
- codes of conduct

- conflict of interest
- legislative and regulatory requirements
- the interface with, and communication to, the organisation's stakeholders.

Organisations should perform refresher training in these areas on an appropriate periodical basis. Other tactics include scenario planning, as described in this book volume.

---

**Self-Help Question 13.6**

Consider some of the issues organisations may need to manage in a crisis. List three crisis management positions and their associated responsibilities.

---

Answers to self-help questions are provided at the end of each section.

---

**Activity | Crisis management**

- Consider the reputation risks you identified earlier for your organisation.
- Analyse your organisation's CMP (if available) to consider if is sufficient enough to ensure the organisation can manage your identified top five reputation risks.
- What were the elements of the plan which you consider:
  - would assist in the management of such a situation?
  - need to be improved?
- What would you do to improve the CMP?

### *Monitoring Policies and Procedures*

The final phase of any risk management process is to implement steps and procedures to monitor the reputation risk management process on an ongoing basis. This monitoring ensures the risk management process' continuing effectiveness in a changing risk environment.

The following table distinguishes between monitoring at the micro and macro level.

**Monitoring at the Micro and Macro Level**

| The Micro Level | The Macro Level |
|---|---|
| • identifying and monitoring the predictive indicators<br>• predictive indicators are early warning signs that events which could result in reputation risk are occurring<br>• for example, an increasing number of complaints about services, other company activities or product returns | • the processes could include management reporting and internal and external audits<br>• the organisation should also implement a process to report risk events, or near misses), to the board in terms of how the identified risks may, or did, impact on the organisation's reputation |

Monitoring is only effective if boards and management receive the results of the monitoring, and take actions to ensure compliance at all times with previously agreed risk mitigates.

## If an Event Occurs Causing Damage to Reputation

If a reputation risk event or a crisis occurs, the organisation's response determines if the company's reputation is:

- destroyed, with all the resulting consequences
- remains intact
- enhanced (as in the case of Johnson and Johnson).

**EXAMPLE**

**Johnson & Johnson**

Johnson and Johnson's charter begins with the following:

> We believe that our first responsibility is to satisfy the doctors, nurses, patients, mothers and all those who use our products and services.

When the company had to make a decision during its Tylenol crisis, it only considered solutions that primarily satisfied consumer safety and welfare.

### *Effective Management*

There is one main lesson in researching and analysing past events and crises that could have led to major reputation loss. An organisation needs to ensure it is managing:

- the risk in a risk event
- the public perception of the event.

This management means:

- maintaining transparency in dealing with the media, customers, and the public
- resolving issues with more regard for the public good than advantage to the organisation.

### *Trial by Media*

The organisation specifically needs to ensure it is not subject to 'trial by media', which today can cover several communication channels including:

- email campaigns
- short messaging service (SMS) messaging
- Internet sites
- traditional print, radio and television media.

As Judy Larkin (2003, p. 6) points out in *Strategic Reputation Risk Management:*

> [...] where organisations have failed to communicate effectively in the immediate aftermath of a crisis, research indicates that the consequences of adverse public perception, media scrutiny and pressure from tougher regulation means that the degree of financial loss can be greater, longer and more difficult to recover from.

---

**Self-Help Question 13.7**

List three critical points you believe organisations need to keep in mind when managing a risk event or crisis.

---

Answers to self-help questions are provided at the end of each section.

---

**Australian airline: Qantas**

John Harvey-Jones (1988), commenting on aspects of leadership in an organisation some time ago, wrote that:

> [...] trust, once it begins to deteriorate, quite suddenly flips over and becomes a sort of galloping corrosion of suspicion which is very difficult to halt. Trust is tremendously difficult to build up and all too easy to destroy, so it is worth taking all sorts of actions, even if they appear to be finicky, to avoid losing it.

## Qantas' Safety Record

Public trust in Qantas's safety record and no accidents is the basis for its reputation. When a company aircraft ran off the runway in Bangkok, the airline's approach to managing the risk to its reputation was, in all communications, to refer to what happened as an 'incident' (rather than an 'accident' or mechanical failure).

The airline subsequently fixed the 'minor damage' at great cost and brought the aircraft back into service, emphasising the trivial nature of the event and the lack of danger to the flying public. Qantas consequently kept the trust of that public.

*One Last Step*

It is critical for an organisation to:

- ensure it manages a risk event or crisis to its true resolution;
- keep emergency measures in place no longer than necessary;
- separate completing the technical management from ending the crisis;
- separate the end of the crisis from the end of the problems to be solved.

**Activity | Using risk identification to enhance reputation**

Earlier in this section, you considered your organisation and listed potential risk events that could result in a major loss of reputation.

Review your response to the activity and consider how your organisation could use this information to enhance its reputation (for example, as Johnson and Johnson did in their Tylenol crisis).

## Summary

Please keep the following points from this chapter in mind:

- The responsibility for reputation risk rests with the organisation's board of directors, and cannot be delegated solely to the public relations department (for example).
- There can be many sources for reputation risk, and the danger to the organisation can be severe because of negative publicity and public opinion.
- Various means of managing reputation risk include developing a crisis risk management team and procedures for handling a risk event.
- Scenario planning is a useful tool in testing how well the organisation may respond to a risk event.
- If an organisation handles reputation risk events effectively, the result for the organisation can be a positive opinion on the part of the public.

---

**Answers to Self-Help Questions**

**Self-help question 13.1**

Three organisational activity areas that can give rise to reputation risk.

**Areas of an Organisation's Activities Giving Rise to Reputation Risk**

| Area | Example |
|---|---|
| The products and services provided by the organisation | • the risk that arises when a car manufacturer must recall a model because of safety defects (for example, the previous Toyota case study)<br>• although the problem may be limited to the one product, the loss of reputation may also have an impact on all the organisation's products |
| The environment in which the organisation operates | • a manufacturer may be sourcing its raw materials from a country seen to have an oppressive government. Although the company may have implemented excellent work conditions and practices for its employees in that country, the company's overall reputation is tainted by dealing with an undemocratic government |

→

→

| Area | Example |
|---|---|
| The governance and control practices of the organisation | • a lack of financial control practices was the basis for the NAB's reputation loss when it has a trading loss in its foreign exchange trading desk – the company's reaction to this issue was perceived to be poor<br>• it was mainly the perceived lack of ethical governance practices that resulted in the demise of Arthur Andersen, the international firm of accountants, in 2002. |

**Self-help question 13.2**

**Potential Reputation Risk Events for Cityshore**

**Products and services**

- Quality of build resulting in defects or public incident because of a collapse (for example)
- Not built in accordance with development approval conditions or client's instructions
- Not completed on time, or for cost plus contracts, within budget

**Environment**

- Health and safety
- Death or major injury to construction worker or member of public
- Overall bad safety record

**Financial**

- Cash flow problems caused by collapse of major contractor or client
- Major damage to natural environment because of construction work
- Destruction of, or damage to, heritage buildings included I construction site

**Governance and control**

Breach of Competition and Consumer Act:

- Communication of misleading information
- Price fixing against other suppliers

Keep in mind that sources of reputation risk or potential risk events can arise from many of a business's core activities and many more generic organisational risk contexts; for example:

→

→

- undertaking projects
- the environment
- managing IT security
- workplace safety
- outsourcing
- privacy regulation.

---

**Self-help question 13.3**

Stakeholders with whom a risk event may provoke distrust of an organisation, and therefore affect its reputation, can include:

- shareholders
- government
- customers
- employees
- suppliers.

---

**Self-help question 13.4**

| Potential Reputation Risk Events for Cityshore | Potential Consequences | Potential Impact |
|---|---|---|
| **Products and services** | | |
| • Quality of build resulting in defects or public incident because of a collapse (for example) | • Residential dwellings – customer distrust | • Brand; local |
| | • Commercial premises – customer distrust | • Brand; national |
| | • Showcase building – customer and third-party distrust | • Franchise; national |
| | • Public incident as result of collapse (for example) –customer, public and regulator distrust | • Franchise; national |

→

| Potential Reputation Risk Events for Cityshore | Potential Consequences | Potential Impact |
|---|---|---|
| • Not built in accordance with Development Approval conditions or client's instructions | • Residential dwellings – customer, public and regulator distrust<br>• Commercial premises – customer, public and regulator distrust | • Brand; local<br>• Franchise; local<br>• Brand; national<br>• Franchise; local |
| • Not completed on time, or for cost plus contracts, within budget | • Residential dwellings – customer distrust<br>• Commercial premises – customer distrust<br>• Showcase building – customer and third-party distrust | • Brand; local<br>• Brand; national<br>• Franchise; national |
| **Environment** | | |
| • Health and safety<br>• Death or major injury to construction worker or member of public | • Breach of occupational/ workplace health and safety legislation; closedown of site by regulators; possible action by unions—closure of site, possibly all union sites<br>• Employee distrust; customer distrust; regulator distrust | • Brand; local and national<br>• Franchise; local and national<br>• Depending on union involvement, publicity, and type of project |
| • Overall bad safety record | • Employee distrust; customer distrust | • Brand; local and national<br>• Franchise; local and national<br>• Depending on union involvement, publicity, and type of project |

→

| Potential Reputation Risk Events for Cityshore | Potential Consequences | Potential Impact |
|---|---|---|
| **Financial** | | |
| • Cash flow problems caused by collapse of major contractor or client | • Residential dwellings – customer distrust | • Brand; local |
| | • Commercial premises – customer distrust | • Brand; national |
| | • Showcase buildings – customer and third-party distrust | • Franchise; national |
| **Environmental** | | |
| • Major damage to natural environment because of construction work | • Public and regulator distrust | • Franchise; national |
| • Destruction of, or damage to, heritage buildings included I construction site | • Public and regulator distrust | • Franchise; national |
| **Governance and control** | | |
| **Breach of the Competition and Consumer Act:** | | |
| • Communication of misleading information | • Customer, public and regulator distrust | • Brand; local or national<br>• Franchise; local or national<br>• To clients depending on extent of breach and publicity (for example). |
| • Price fixing against other suppliers | • Supplier, public and regulator distrust | • Franchise; national<br>• Depending on extent of breach and publicity (for example). |

→

→

**Self-help question 13.5**

Policies and procedures covering the following issues can assist the organisation in managing its reputation risks:

- activity or product development
- transaction approval processes
- advertising
- conflict of interest
- contact with the media
- governance
- dealing with statutory authorities
- reporting.

**Self-help question 13.6**

**Ross Campbell (1999, pp. 43–51) in *Crisis Control: Preventing and Managing Corporate Crises* offers the following useful list of crisis management positions and responsibilities.**

| Crisis Management Position | Responsibility |
|---|---|
| Team leader | Team co-ordinator and leader of the response |
| Emergency and security co-ordinator | Provides the internal policy, response and interface with law enforcement, government agencies and emergency services |
| Human resources and family co-ordinator | Communication with the employees, community, and family; provision of welfare, rehabilitation and counselling services |
| Corporate affairs and media co-ordinator | Provides information for media and internal stakeholders; liaises with law enforcement and emergency services |
| Operations co-ordinator | Maintains continuity of operations and recovery |
| Command centre and call-out co-ordinator | • Calls out the CMT<br>• provides command centre or alternative |
| Administration co-ordinator | Co-ordinates legal, insurance and financial issues |
| Recovery co-ordinator | Identifies resources to manage business resumption |

→

→

**Self-help question 13.7**

Key points to remember when managing a risk event or crisis are:

- acknowledge your mistakes quickly;
- be transparent in your actions;
- open the communication lines with all your constituencies and stakeholders, and keep them open;
- be honest in all the steps you take.

All of this can assist an organisation in managing the trust the public has in its activities, services/products.

Chapter 14

# Emerging and Future Risks

## Introduction

Technology is disrupting and reinventing traditional business models at a rapid rate. It is affecting all countries, sectors and markets, and these changes, along with the increasing complexity of risk, are creating new challenges for companies, boards, and risk professionals. This everchanging landscape creates new fault lines that may develop in new uncertainties that provide both opportunities and threats.

Some of these fault lines require risk professionals to revisit the traditional risks in a new light but there are also new risks that need to be included in the risk radar of all companies. They are referred to as 'emerging risks'.

Definitions vary when it comes to emerging risks:

- An issue that is perceived to be potentially significant but which may not be fully understood or allowed for in insurance terms and conditions, pricing, reserving or capital setting. (Lloyd's)
- Those large-scale events or circumstances beyond one's direct capacity to control, that impact in ways difficult to imagine today. (PWC)
- Risks that do not currently exist. (S&P)

Therefore, there are two main approaches to emerging risks:

- Completely new risks that have never been seen before (e.g. appearance of AIDS virus in humans, development of the first atomic bomb);
- Previously known risks that are evolving in unexpected ways with unanticipated consequences. (e.g. U.S. home mortgage market, liability regimes/regulatory changes).

Risk Measurement and Monitoring, 317–333

Published under exclusive licence by Emerald Publishing Limited
doi:10.1108/978-1-83662-310-620251032

And in all cases emerging risks share the following characteristics:

- Their significance is uncertain or not well understood;
- Quantification is difficult due to lack of data and/or volatility;
- Consequences and implications can be ambiguous;
- Interactions and interconnectedness with each other and/or other risks can be complex;
- They have a systemic nature, outside of organisational control.

Some professionals have summarised the context by the acronym VUCA, for Volatility, Uncertainty, Complexity, and Ambiguity.

These emerging risks pose a specific challenge to risk management professionals when it comes to insurance transfers and the nature of the current business landscape favours those who have expertise, previous success and are flexible and adaptable in their approach.

However, to stay one step ahead of this constant evolution, insurers are becoming more proactive in supporting clients by forming stronger and more meaningful partnerships. They work closely with their key clients and stakeholders to better understand their challenges, so that new solutions can be developed that effectively mitigates risk for both parties.

According to the World Economic Forum's 'Global risks report 2019', the core global emerging risk categories include geopolitical, societal, economic, technological, and environmental risk which represent a vast array of risks, among which the following have been selected for further exploration in this block:

- Geopolitical risk
- Climate change
- Regulatory changes and GDPR
- Algorithms and artificial intelligence
- Intellectual property and intangible assets
- Bribery risk.

## Learning Outcomes

By the end of this chapter, you should be able to:
- define the emerging risks described;
- assess the risks.

## Geopolitical Risk

Geopolitical risk is the risk of financial, market, or personnel losses because of political decisions or disruptions. Also known as 'political risk' it has become a serious issue for many global players due to the social and political volatility experienced in many parts of the world. Although it might be seen as mostly bearing on global players, in fact many medium size organisations have international trade relations with partners in sensitive parts of the world.

***Geopolitical Risk – Definition***

Read definitions of geopolitical risk at:

- 'Political risk', Investing Answers. https://investinganswers.com/dictionary/p/political-risk.
- 'The top evolving risk concerns and challenges', AIG, 12 June 2018. www.aig.co.uk/insights/top-evolving-risk-concerns-and-challenges.

### *Managing Geopolitical Risk Amid Global Instability*

Political and credit risks in both developed and developing markets, including changes in trade policy by Western countries, will continue to challenge multinational businesses, according to most economists and experts worldwide.

Several events in the recent years reflect the rise of anti-establishment, nationalist, and populist forces in several major economies: the two major political earthquakes were the 2016 US presidential election and the UK's decision to leave the European Union. However, in developed economies, there is also a growing backlash against globalisation, as was evidenced by the elections in 2018 in Italy and some Eastern Europe countries. This reaction against globalisation has contributed to opposition to free trade and the offshoring of jobs to developing countries.

If developed economies were to move away from multilateral trade agreements and cross-border co-operation, developing economies could be destabilised and political unrest could result. The change in US trade policy already erratically initiated by the President Trump could also adversely affect all countries, especially those that depend on the US for many of their foreign exchanges. At this stage, one cannot rule out insolvencies taking place in the most vulnerable countries, particularly in Central and South America, despite the revamping of the North American Free Trade Agreement (NAFTA), an agreement between Canada, Mexico, and the United States to eliminate tariffs on goods traded between themselves.

Further to these elements, key uncertainties bearing on global businesses include:

- A shift towards a 'multi-polar' world: The more aggressive US foreign policy of the Trump administration has added a layer of risk at a time, when China, Russia, and major regional powers such as Turkey, Iran, India, and Japan are becoming more influential. This could lead to clashes between these countries, beyond the current (as of September 2019) round of negotiations between China and the USA.

- Election and succession risks: The elections that took place in China, France, Germany, Italy, and South Korea in 2017 saw political landscape changes that have not yet settled down. Additionally, the European Parliament election in May 2019 resulted in liberal, environmentalist, Eurosceptic and national populist parties gaining a significant number of seats. The opposing views of these parties will likely be disruptive. In addition, the UK remains a member of the EU despite the Brexit vote, and the ramifications of that decision are yet to unfold entirely.

**Activity | Managing geopolitical risk**

Listen to Marsh's webcast 'Managing geopolitical risk amid global instability' to hear more. www.marsh.com/us/insights/research/managing-geopolitical-risk-amid-global-instability.html.

Geopolitical risk is increasingly a concern to risk managers. In the 2019 Aon Global Risk Management Survey, 'accelerated rates of change in market factors', which encompasses geopolitical risk, was considered the number three risk facing organisations. In 2017, this risk was ranked at 38. This is a huge increase in significance.

Geographic Flashpoints Around the World

| Nation | Issues | Risk/threat |
|---|---|---|
| China | Territorial disputes in the South China Sea; protectionist cyber security laws; increasing restrictions on foreign companies | China may take a more aggressive approach to territorial disputes; its new cyber security law may introduce new restrictions on foreign businesses |
| Iran | Uncertainty about the Joint Comprehensive Plan of Action (Iranian nuclear accord); increasing political friction with the US over Iranian nuclear programme and missile testing | Possible disruption of national critical infrastructures; may introduce new sanctions on entities believed to engage in malicious cyberactivity |
| North Korea | Rising attacks against South Korean government, businesses and power companies; launch of ballistic missiles weakens relations with US and Asian nations | Possible cyberespionage and destructive attacks on businesses and governments; possible escalation of hostilities because of missile testing |

(*Continued*)

(*Continued*)

| Nation | Issues | Risk/threat |
|---|---|---|
| Russia | Tensions within region and with Western nations; critical infrastructure cyber security; US continuing federal investigation of Russia and US presidential election | US Secretary of State said in July 2017 that US and Russia need a common framework on how to deal with cyber threats 'in terms of how these tools are used to interfere with the internal affairs of countries, but also how these tools are used to threaten infrastructure, how these tools are used from a terrorism standpoint as well' |
| Syria | Civil war between government and rebels; ISIS stronghold | Instability may spread to other nations in the region; Islamist political movement may fragment and spread. US troops' total withdrawal will add an additional element of uncertainty |
| United States | Protectionist policies and deglobulisation; federal investigation of Russia and US presidential election; critical infrastructure cyber security; sanctions against other governments | In the interest of increasing cyber deterrence, the White House may object more to the behaviour of some other nations in cyberspace and may aim to impose costs |

### *Geopolitical Risk Interrelated and Fluid*

As the geopolitical landscape changes, so must the way in which we respond. Therefore, innovation is critical to help prevent and protect against business risk events. Innovation must go beyond enhancements to traditional insurance coverage. That means new ways of working, financing, protecting, and responding. State-sponsored cyber disruption is an area where governments can struggle to keep pace with the resources and technologies required to protect infrastructure from attack.

**Activity**

Read more on geopolitical risks in Willis Tower Watson's 'Insights: Managing geopolitical risk' report. www.willistowerswatson.com/-/media/WTW/Insights/2018/10/managing-geopolitical-risk-flyer.pdf.

### *Conclusion on Geopolitical Risk*

Presently, people, information, and capital move across borders at a speed, frequency, and volume that is unprecedented in human history. Ultimately, successful long-term investors will be those who look not only at near-term market indicators but also seek to better understand the escalating tussle between nation-states trying to maintain control over their domestic economies and the inexorable global forces wresting that control away.

But geopolitical risk extends beyond market and financial risk, therefore a shared understanding is key to protecting, preventing, and responding to them. Any representation of geopolitical risk will lead to a complex web of interrelated risks and themes. What's apparent is that the connections – the direct and indirect relationships between events and themes – are as important as the risks.

The view from most expert observers is that resilient and thus successful organisations will be those that are able to understand, assess and quantify the connected risks, to take advantage of opportunities while mitigating or managing the threats of these geopolitical relationships.

## Climate Change Risk

The reality of climate change is practically not disputed and the issue ultimately is how to respond rather than how to stop it, or slow it down enough that that the horizon of major disruption is four or five decades away rather than imminent.

**Activity | Climate change**

Read the following articles about climate change:

- 'What is climate change? The definition, causes and effects' from Wired. www.wired.co.uk/article/what-is-climate-change-definition-causes-effects.
- Shardul Agrawala, Maëlis Carraro, Nicholas Kingsmill, Elisa Lanzi, Michael Mullan, Guillaume Prudent-Richard 'Private sector engagement in adaptation to climate change', OECD Environment Working Papers No. 39.

  www.oecd-ilibrary.org/environment/private-sector-engagement-in-adaptation-to-climate-change-approaches-to-managing-climate-risks_5kg221jkf1g7-en.
- Geoff O'Brien, Phil O'Keefe, Joanne Rose, Ben Wisner, 'Climate change and disaster management', Wiley.

### *Developing a Climate Resilience Strategy*

*The following content has been contributed by Amar Rahman, Risk Engineering Global Practice Leader, Natural Hazards Resilience, Commercial Insurance, Zurich Insurance Company Ltd.*

Climate change is no longer an 'emerging risk'. It has become a reality, with concentrations of carbon dioxide in the atmosphere now in excess of 400 parts per million and growing evidence of a rise in the frequency and intensity of extreme weather events. But it is more than just the climate that is changing. Rapid urbanisation, ageing infrastructure, increased industrialisation, and intricately interconnected factors mean the cost of natural catastrophes is soaring.

Economic losses from natural catastrophes rose to $306 billion in 2017, largely driven by the Atlantic Hurricanes Harvey, Irma, and Maria. The 10-year moving average for such losses was $190 billion, almost double the level seen in the decade ending in 2000.

It is therefore crucial that organisations develop a climate resilience strategy and act on it. To do this, they must first determine the magnitude of the risks they face, i.e. assess the potential scenarios and corresponding financial impact. The second step is to develop mitigation strategies based on these scenarios.

**Step 1: Determine the magnitude of risk**

Catastrophe modelling software can give a solid understanding of the potential economic impact and relative likelihood of natural catastrophe risks. This type of analysis is only as good as the data that underpins it, so the data must be meticulously checked and verified. Special attention needs to be given to location (preferably latitude and longitude, rather than address) and age of the site.

For those regions and perils not covered by existing catastrophe models, a hazard assessment applying a deterministic scenario-based approach using global hazard maps may be used.

However, one of the problems inherent in tools such as catastrophe models and hazard maps is that they cannot keep pace with the changes in the climate and environment. The evolution of climate change is extremely difficult to model, due to the complexity of the mathematical models and the high degree of interconnection between the variables.

Sustainability programmes to address climate changes, such as green energy or carbon capture, add an additional layer of complexity when modelling climate risks. Historical data is limited in depth and more data is needed to determine the impact of all these changes on catastrophe models.

Another aspect to consider is that catastrophe models do not cover all perils and countries. Other tools, such as global peril-specific hazard maps, are necessary to assess these 'non-modelled' perils and regions. Such tools are not as sophisticated as cat modelling software, as they do not include all the parameters necessary to accurately represent the location-specific variations of a specific peril, which could dramatically change within a short distance, for example, effects of soil properties on earthquake shaking levels, or changes of topography within a short distance on flood depths.

But they are an essential tool for performing a preliminary analysis of multiple locations with a global footprint to identify the natural hazard exposure levels and, correspondingly, the critical regions and single locations. Experience and judgement, in terms of local topographic conditions, construction practices, or local protection mechanisms, play an important role in analysing the output of the conventional tools used for multi-location hazard identification and assessment.

Besides information pertaining to accumulated annual loss, 'exceedance' occurrence probability and other parameters used in the design of the insurance policy, these tools may also help identify high-risk single locations, as well as concentrations of locations that could potentially be affected by a single event.

Prioritisation of locations for the second step of the resilience strategy is based on the definition of 'critical' in the organisation. For example, this may be a location or region that meets one or more of the following criteria:

- high concentration of value at one location
- long replacement time for equipment or stock at a location
- the location is a significant contributor to the group value chain or revenue
- large concentration of occupants
- large area around the site that could be impacted environmentally
- multiple locations that could be affected by a single event.

This review and analysis pertain to operations or locations within the stakeholder's own responsibility. Ideally, suppliers and critical infrastructure would also be included in the analysis.

**Step 2: Develop a mitigation strategy involving insurance and resilience**

For those locations defined in the first step as at risk, a deterministic scenario-based loss estimate should be developed, based on detailed information regarding site vulnerabilities (physical and organisational).

Such an analysis, which would include an onsite assessment of the reliability and effectiveness of emergency response and business continuity plans, any peril-specific protection measures (seismic gas shut-off values, mobile flood protection elements, etc.), quality of structures, and so on, is an essential component of the resilience strategy. With this information in hand, a medium- to long-term resilience strategy can be developed in which budget for capital expenditure projects, as well as reallocation of existing budget towards resilience measures, can be defined.

This type of integrated approach involves not only insurance, which supports the site in restoring operations after the event, but also physical and organisational measures that reduce the impact and severity of an event on the locations.

### *The Role of Risk Managers on Climate Change Risk*

During the 2018 FERMA seminar, one of the round table's main topics was the risk management professional's role in the control of climate change. Risk managers brings to the table a host of knowledge and they can participate in the strengthening of the public–private partnership needed to find a solution; at least such is the opinion of the experts called on by FERMA.

The conclusions of the Groupe d'experts intergouvernemental sur l'évolution du climat (GIEC) were published as the Seminar was held and were in line with the United Nations' Intergovernmental Panel on Climate Change (IPCC) report that the present planet trajectory would end up with a 3°C increase rather than the 1.5°C agreed on in the COP 21 Paris Agreement. Furthermore, the report concludes that a 1.5°C increase, rather than 2°C, would reduce the sea level rise by 10 cm; in the same time, the risk of the Arctic Ocean being totally freed of ice in summer would lower from a decennial risk to a centennial risk. While coral reefs would lose 70–90% of their extension with 1.5°C, it would be 100% with 2°C.

As a reminder, the Paris Agreement was agreed to by 195 countries in December 2015 as a world answer to global warming and it states that, 'It is essential that the increase of the average temperature be contained under the ceiling of 2°C as compared to the preindustrial era, in fact it would be best to limit at 1.2°C'.

The most recent IPCC meeting took place in Korea and was preceded by a dire warning by the Organisation for Economic Co-operation and Development (OECD, also OCDE, the Organisation de coopération et de développement économiques) that most governments have fallen short of fulfilling their obligations as defined in the Paris Agreement. OECD stresses that it is high time that they remedy this and become 'serious' about avoiding a disaster.

> *Three years after the Paris Agreement was signed, a great majority of the governments have not engaged the actions needed to contain global warming. Whereas contrary to the commitments made, the emissions of CO2 are still rising, it has become crucial that governments engage resolutely the actions that will transform their existing economic models into low carbon emission models and stop all investments in high carbon intensity infrastructures.*

When a report by the OECD, the UN and the World Bank Group titled 'Financing climate futures: Rethinking infrastructure' was released, the specialists stressed that only nine of the signatories of the Paris Agreement had submitted their strategies for long-term carbon economies (2050 horizon).

In addition, OECD notes that governments still spend $500 billion to subsidise oil, coal and gas, not to mention that most of them have not found ways to disengage from fossil energies tax dependency. Moreover, these governments have not learned to use public spending as a lever to 'decarbonise' their economies through investment in low emission infrastructures and enhance innovation.

The Secretary-General of the OECD, Angel Gurría, fears that despite all the promises made in Paris and although they have all the necessary tools at their disposal, governments through their inertia are responsible for the world losing the global warming battle. He stresses again the imperative for the world leaders to fully respect their commitments to keep the increase in temperature well under the 2°C mark. As one might expect, he hopes that the countries members of the OECD will lead this campaign and set an example for all the others.

As far as the experts gathered in Antwerp at the 2018 FERMA Seminar, they have joined the chorus and insisted on the need to redouble our efforts to contain and adapt to climate change. According to Ernst Rauch, in charge of climate and public-sector development with Munich Re, risk managers must indeed bring their expertise and knowledge to the discussion. And his message is clear and loud:

> *Efforts need to focus on mitigation and adaptation. But if I must favour one over the other, I would choose adaptation as I am afraid that we are already losing the battle for reduction. CO2 emissions have not decreased enough and as the emissions impact lag over a century, global warming will continue for generations well beyond the end of this century.*
>
> *It is pitiful to hide behind the lack of sufficient data. If all leaders in the world are serious when they call for resilience, it will require a strong public-private partnership, and the cornerstone of such cooperation will come from the risk management community thanks to competencies and knowledge they have amassed. However, this can be accomplished only it the risk managers are able to make them available to all at all levels in society.*

Manoelle Lepoutre, Executive Vice-President for sustainable development with Total Group, joins in the chorus stressing the need for partnership and cooperation if the global warming challenge is to be met. As a matter of fact, Total and their main competitors in the energy sector have already entered a partnership to share their substantial resources in an unprecedented manner and this is the only way ahead.

Total is a member of the Oil and Gas Industry Initiative (OGCI) that is a programme shared by CEO who volunteered to share the collective resources of the energy sector leaders to reduce the carbon footprint of the energy and transportation sectors and extend the value chain. In September 2018, OGCI announced an important step forward when it admitted three new members from the USA: Chevron, Exxon Mobil and Occidental Petroleum. Their combined share of the world production of oil and gas is 5%; thus, the OGCI now gathers nearly a third of the world production and its members supply 20% of primary energy consumption.

Mrs Lepoutre insisted on the importance of such partnerships if the global warming challenge is to be met.

> *It would be wrong to claim global warming as a private or a public problem, it is everyone's business! Without a public–private partnership, and trans-sectoral cooperation in key sectors like energy, no solution can be developed. We must be innovative and look for solutions other than those of the past. It is a long-haul project but the oil and gas industry has now a strong coalition that not only put $10 billion on the table but also wows to cooperate for innovation. Only ten years ago, such a rapprochement would have been unthinkable. But without such collaboration, no success would be reachable.*

Elena Visnar Malinovska oversees the unity adaptation to climate change at the European Commission and she joins her voice to Mrs Lepoutre's to stress the exceptional level of cooperation needed to meet the global warming challenge.

> *Climate change is a very serious issue and it is essential that public and private sectors be aligned. Furthermore, the window of opportunity is closing on us. Experts say we are now on a +3°C trajectory, and global warming could even reach the 4°C mark. During a recent meeting in Korea, a 2000 pages report was released that explains the impact of a change of only 0.5°C. It is the difference between the initial goal and the current results and the difference of impact level on the planet is huge.*

Ms Malinovska, like Mr Rauch before her, speaks to the necessity of combining adaptation and reduction to the extent that the impact of global warming is already significant and can only increase in the decade to come due to the delayed impact of the greenhouse effect. And she further states that:

> *It is clear that the issue is still solvable provided there is an unprecedented level of public–private cooperation with every citizen's support. We must still reduce emissions wherever possible as it is always the best solution; however, we have waited far too long to make an immediate difference. Global warming is here to stay as a top agenda issue for leaders in the foreseeable future; but it needs to be on the agenda as of today, tomorrow would be too late!*

If the costs of inaction are too high to risk incurring, the speakers at the FERMA Seminar were keen to stress the need to show the positive benefits of the investment of efforts to tackle the climate change issue. It is one of the key points made in the OECD report, 'Financing climate futures: Rethinking infrastructure', about financing climate futures.

OECD mentions progress on 'green' finance; an illustration of the progress is 'green' bonds issues: they have grown 1,000% in five years (2012–2017) and transparency on climate change issues has also improved. However, the OECD insists on the need for governments to change gears and adopt a much more ambitious agenda regarding financing a future with reduced carbon emissions.

The OECD report states:

> *OECD analysis demonstrates that shifting infrastructures investments to low carbon emission options to support the transition could boost the GNP by 5% by the year 2050. The forecast considers the reduction in damages resulting from extreme climate events. The cost of shifting from 'brown' infrastructures to 'green' infrastructures would be offset by savings on fuel. This being said too little has been done so far by governments to level the playing field between low and high emissions options.*

...

> *As things stand presently, power plants planned or under construction to generate energy will result in the doubling of emissions for energy generation. There are too little intensives to reduce and penalty to leave things as they are, in all sectors.*

However, the regulatory context may be changing, and it is notable that regulation authorities are concerned. As an example, in the UK, the Financial Conduct Authority (FCA) has published a report to feed the thinking process, 'Climate change and green finance' calling on banks and insurers to explain how they consider the climate risk.

**Activity | Reducing risk from a changing ocean**

Read 'Reducing risk from a changing ocean', Strategic Risk's interview of Chip Cunliffe, sustainable development director at XL Catlin, to learn about ocean risk, which sectors are most at risk and what risk managers need to consider.

www.strategic-risk-europe.com/reducing-risk-from-a-changing ocean/1427414.article?adredir=1 You will need to register to read this article. Registration is free.

## Regulatory Risk and GDPR

Even before the beginning of the previous century, in an 1890 Harvard Law Review article, the authors coined the phrase 'the right to be left alone' as a key tenet of privacy law. But this definition of privacy was conceived for the analogue world.

Today, we suffer unprecedented invasions into our privacy. Big data, cloud computing, predictive analytics, and the Internet of Things (IoT) have enabled organisations to collect and process vast amounts of information, which, when combined, can identify individuals. Earlier understandings of and concerns about privacy no longer seem to apply.

The amount of personal data stored by companies and governments has ballooned, and the value of that data has multiplied as more and more personal business is transacted on the internet. Identity theft has become far more prevalent. In addition to the disruption to businesses and the impact on customer loyalty that data breaches create, many jurisdictions are looking to bring their data protection legislation in line with the new, internet-based world – although unfortunately, not into alignment with each other.

However, there is a fundamental transformation underway. In the digital economy, information is the currency of exchange and information knows no boundaries. Harmonisation of regulations that fosters the free flow of information – while strengthening privacy and security rights – is an imperative for policy makers. Therefore, all organisations – even those outside Europe – should learn to cope with the GDPR before it becomes the law of the land under one of its avatars, like in California.

As the GDPR has been in force in the EU since 25 May 2018, and had been in the making for several years, one might debate if this is really an 'emerging risk'. However, it is true that compliance and regulations are always emerging as governments worldwide find new areas to regulate or make current regulations more constraining, and that may also include the proposals put forward by the IAIS (International Association of Insurance Supervisors) that impact not only the way insurance can be purchased but also the way captive insurers and reinsurers are managed.

Organisations that haven't prepared for the new requirements regarding data collection, storage and protection face a very real threat of bankruptcy/liquidation, as potential fines for noncompliance can reach in the millions of euros. In mid-2019, France fined Google €50 million for a breach of the data protection rules.

**Activity | Risk management and GDPR**

Read FERMA's 'Risk manager report 2018' and consider the following questions.

1. If you are a risk manager, are you also responsible for crisis management? If not, who is responsible?
2. How would you rate your personal relationships with the departments listed in the three lines of defence?
3. Who do you report to?

www.ferma.eu/app/uploads/2019/02/ferma-european-risk-manager-report-2018_final_19-12.pdf

**Activity | GDPR survival**

Read the following articles to learn more about GDPR and how to adhere to its guidelines.

- 'GDPR survival basics: 5 ways to help prepare' from RSA. www.rsa.com/content/dam/en/white-paper/gdpr-survival-basics.pdf.
- 'GDPR' from RSA. www.rsa.com/content/dam/en/e-book/how-gdpr-could-impact-your-business-organisation.pdf.
- 'GDPR: How to establish a strong defensible position' from ACL and Source Media. https://img1.wsimg.com/blobby/go/e086db95-5227-456c-a743-9254a88a6fed/downloads/1c86v3slh_744954.pdf.
- 'Managing third parties under GDPR' from MetricStream. https://assets.metricstream.com/pdf/insights/Insight_Managing_third_parties_under_GDPR.pdf.

**Activity | Effect on captives**

Read 'The implications of GDPR for captives' from Commercial Risk to learn how the GDP regulation will affect captives and what risk managers need to do.

www.commercialriskonline.com/implications-gdpr-captives/

### *Conclusions on Regulatory and GDPR Risk*

Modern governance software systems allow data managers to split regulatory obligations into requirements; map controls to these requirements to assess applicability and coverage; and determine compliance gaps. What's more, they can also help harmonise other data privacy principles from established frameworks (ISACA, NIST, ISO, COBIT) with a many-to-one mapping to single controls. Confidence that controls are effective is fuelled by insight into the entire data population.

GDPR is dictating extraordinary change in data-protection practices, and it will undoubtedly spread beyond the EU. As organisations strive to create modern gold standards, lessons will be learned. The best opportunity to avoid harsh penalties and participate in influencing the gold standards is for organisations to create a defensible position.

Technology will help organisations work smarter while developing a quick-to-serve defensible framework. Intelligent, automated workflow solutions will remove the uncertainty and replace complexity in GDPR compliance.

## Algorithms and Artificial Intelligence

**Activity | Technological advances**

Read the following articles about technological advances and consider how the world has changed over the past decade and how it is expected to continue to change.

- 'What's now and next in analytics, AI, and automation' from McKinsey Global Institute. www.mckinsey.com/featured-insights/digital-disruption/whats-now-and-next-in-analytics-ai-and-automation.
- 'Artificial intelligence: The time to act is now' from McKinsey & Company. www.mckinsey.com/industries/advanced-electronics/our-insights/artificial-intelligence-the-time-to-act-is-now.
- 'Why AI is both a risk and a way to manage risk' from EY. www.ey.com/en_gl/assurance/why-ai-is-both-a-risk-and-a-way-to-manage-risk.
- 'AI and risk management – innovating with confidence' from Deloitte. www2.deloitte.com/content/dam/Deloitte/global/Documents/Financial-Services/deloitte-gx-ai-and-risk-management.pdf.

**Activity | How artificial intelligence creates value**

Read how AI can create value in 'How artificial intelligence can deliver real value to companies' from McKinsey & Company.

www.mckinsey.com/business-functions/mckinsey-analytics/our-insights/how-artificial-intelligence-can-deliver-real-value-to-companies

**Activity | Mathematical models, algorithms, and risk management**

Read how mathematical models and algorithms apply to risk management in Geary Sikich's article for CERM® Risk Insights, 'Mathematical models, algorithms, and risk management methodologies'.

https://insights.cermacademy.com/172/#more-10035

**Activity | Risk management in the digital era**

Read how risk management fits into the digital era in 'The future of risk management in the digital era' from McKinsey & Company.

www.mckinsey.com/business-functions/risk/our-insights/the-future-of-risk-management-in-the-digital-era

**Activity | Data**

Read about algorithmic risk in Deloitte's report, 'Managing algorithmic risks: Safeguarding the use of complex algorithms and machine learning'.

www2.deloitte.com/content/dam/Deloitte/us/Documents/risk/us-risk-algorithmic-machine-learning-risk- management.pdf

## Intellectual Property and Intangible Assets

Intellectual property is one of the most important intangible asset classes driving the modern global economy. Intellectual property includes patents, trademarks, copyrights, trade secrets, and know how; all which factor ever more prominently in many companies' success and other organisations' ability to succeed. The global expansion of intellectual property as an intangible asset class is reflected in a variety of statistics and makes it necessary for risk management professionals to take up the issue.

**Activity | Intellectual property risk**

Read Aon's recommendations for best practices in managing intellectual property risk in 'Intellectual property: Risk landscape'.

www.aon.com/getmedia/3bc3c273-9b6a-4ac1-99fe-ccc4a6fa0a39/Aon-Intellectual-Property-Risk-Landscape-2019.aspx

**Activity | Intangible risk**

Read about intangible risk in the following articles from Strategic Risk Europe.

- 'Intangible risk a tangible threat'.

  www.strategic-risk-europe.com/intangible-risk-a-tangible-threat/1428912.article?adredir=1

- 'How risks to intangible assets could harm profits and revenue'.

  www.strategic-risk-europe.com/how-risks-to-intangible-assets-could-harm-profits-and-revenue/1428953.article

- 'Expert view: Managing business interruption in the intangible economy'.

  www.strategic-risk-europe.com/expert-view-managing-business-interruption-in-the-intangible-economy/1428921.article

(You may need to register to view some of these; registration is free.)

## Bribery Risks

**Activity | Bribery risks**

Read about bribery from the following sources:

- 'Bribery Risk Guide' from IRM and Transparency International UK. www.theirm.org/media/2218767/IRM-TI-UK-Bribery-Guide-A5-V6-Low-Res-proof.pdf.
- 'SFO charges Unaoil Executives with corruption', from The Wall Street Journal. https://blogs.wsj.com/riskandcompliance/2017/11/16/sfo-charges-unaoil-executives-with-corruption.
- 'ISO 37001 Standard for anti-bribery management systems: What you need to know', from MetricStream.

## Summary

Please keep the following points from this chapter in mind:

- In all cases emerging risks share the following characteristics:
  - Their significance is uncertain or not well understood
  - Quantification is difficult due to lack of data and/or volatility
  - Consequences and implications can be ambiguous
  - Interactions and interconnectedness with each other and/or other risks can be complex
  - They have a systemic nature, outside of organisational control.
- The view from most expert observers is that resilient and thus successful organisations will be those that are able to understand, assess, and quantify risks.
- Technology will help organisations work smarter while developing a quick-to-serve defensible framework.
- All risks are interrelated and a silo approach will not lead to efficient management of risks. Both opportunities and threats must be evaluated considering the overall context and stakeholders' expectations to ensure organisational resilience and the vitality of a society where all can find ways to develop their talents and competencies and achieve self-fulfilment.

Chapter 15

# Emerging Issues in Risk Management

## Introduction

The world is being rapidly disrupted by ever-changing technology; technology that creates previously unimaginable opportunities and incredible threats. The current situation has generated new issues for risk management professionals.

Risks are changing therefore risk management needs to change too. It falls on risk managers to change the scope of risk management to remain relevant in this 'brave new world'; it is all about enhancing risk management to include decision-focus and intelligent risk-taking to create value. This generates both emerging risks and emerging issues that are not always easy to contrast, for instance, we have chosen to include the GDPR as a 'risk' and some might have chosen to include it as an 'issue'.

In summary, whereas the previous chapter focused on emerging risks, this one will attempt to review the resulting emerging issues.

## Learning Outcomes

By the end of this chapter, you should be able to:

- discuss issues resulting from organisational and contextual complexity and potential coping strategies;
- promote change management and describe ten related principles;
- define different types of bias and suggest ways to overcome them;
- describe the importance culture and talent management have for risk managers today;
- highlight the importance of leadership by top management and the integration of risk management.

**Risk Measurement and Monitoring, 335–353**

**Published under exclusive licence by Emerald Publishing Limited**
**doi:10.1108/978-1-83662-310-620251035**

## Coping with Organisational and Contextual Complexity

Whereas the context in which organisations operate is increasing in complexity and becoming less predictable, their leaders must distinguish what is complex in the internal and the external context.

As organisations grow larger and more intricate, an array of functions gets performed in them. For example, an aircraft manufacturer firm could have aircraft designers, outsourced parts to many suppliers and sub-contractors, a workforce that assembles the aircraft, people in a human resources division that look out for employees, administrative and finance employees that aim to make sustainable the operation, and sales force and intermediaries (financial) that negotiate the contracts with airlines and/or leasing companies, etc.

In such a complex social arrangement, where many groups of people contribute in varied ways, managers have become central as they coordinate thousands of disparate single contributions into a single product or service. Therefore, managers at all levels (strategic, tactic, and operational) aim for internal consistency while trying to make their organisations relevant for the external context too. Thus, managing requires some level of understanding of what is happening, a sense of direction; short of that, managers could easily lose their stakeholders' trust and confidence leading their firms into a state of competitive deficit; when it comes to the internal context, misreading the forces at play would prevent managers from combining those dispersed contributions.

**Activity | Complexity**

Read the introduction and conclusion, and the section titled 'Complexity' of 'Managerial learning challenges in a complex world' to learn about the challenges that managers face in today's economic climate.

www.emerald.com/insight/content/doi/10.1108/JWAM-04-2018-0009/full/html

**Activity | Reduce and redirect complexity**

View the complexity taxonomy in the article, 'Putting organisational complexity in its place'.

Also read the section title 'Bolster skills where needed' to find out how different people respond to change.

www.mckinsey.com/business-functions/organisation/our-insights/putting-organisational-complexity-in-its-place

### *The Complexity Learning Process*

However, to establish a robust diagnostic on complexity, managers need to learn to 'read complexity' within and without their organisation and always keep the complexity radar operational. The main constraint of the managerial learning process for complexity is arguably the conditions under which it is carried out. Managers need understanding to accomplish the combination of internal contributions and the external relevance of their organisations; neither of these two missions is easy. The reason is that both internal and external contexts are nested in complex systems, particularly of the adaptive type. The complexity of internal or external context is generated by many subsystems and components that interact in a non-simple way that can be explained only when using fuzzy logic (a system of logic in which a statement can be true, false, or any of a continuum of values in between).

The question arises of what artificial intelligence and business analytics may bring to the table.

> **Fuzzy logic – Definitions**
>
> Read some definitions of fuzzy logic at the Free Dictionary. www.thefreedictionary.com/fuzzy+logic.

### *Ways to Meet the Challenges of Complexity Learning*

The ability for organisations to operate in complex and fast-paced environment is a key competitive advantage. The role and responsibilities of management must adapt constantly to this context, in particular in the following fields:

- strategic planning and decision making
- direction setting
- information and communication technology (ICT)
- human resources and change management.

Therefore, managers must learn to be able to:

- understand and assess environmental pressures on management historically and contemporarily, and how responsive is the management to external changes;
- apply the latest knowledge about management in planning, organising, leading, and controlling in various environments;
- analyse in a constructive manner the management roles at various levels.

> **Activity | Limitations to human intervention**
>
> Read the introduction to this article, 'Think biologically: Messy management for a complex world', to learn how humans struggle to identify limits to human intervention in complex systems.
>
> https://bcghendersoninstitute.com/think-biologically-messy-management-for-a-complex-world-7be3f5b08b44

**Activity | Cracking the complexity code**

Read 'Cracking the complexity code' to learn more about how to deal with complexity in organisations. The article is available on ResearchGate if you register for an account.

Complexity is increasingly unavoidable in organisations, but the answer is not to simplify. Instead, executives should focus on building processes, skills and culture to embrace complexity on a multitude of levels – institutional, individual, strategic, tactical, and operational – to gain a competitive advantage. Companies that understand this will create more value than their rivals, become more resilient in a constantly evolving context, even in a time of rupture that can become opportunities when turned into 'creative ruptures'.

## Change Management

In a time when organisations are confronted with increasing complexity and volatility, change is not a choice but a survival requirement. The economic landscape is full of projects that were delivered on time and within budget and scope but that do not deliver the expected results.

The key to bridging the gap between requirements and results is to ensure that staff of all levels are engaged and effectively adopt and implement the changes being introduced. Therefore, change must be managed.

According to ProSci, in their 'An introduction to change management':

> Change management is a structured and intentional approach to support people through change. It prepares, equips, and supports individuals through the changes to their jobs. With a dedicated focus on mobilizing adoption and usage, change management supports holistic and successful change.

It is the discipline that guides how we prepare, equip, and support individuals to successfully adopt change to drive organisational success and outcomes.

Since the beginning of the century, the discipline of change management has developed. This is why leaders must be aware of why and how managing the people side of change improves results.

Today, organisations are constantly transforming, with new markets, labour pools and technologies disrupting the world of work as we knew it. Business models that were once the blueprint for success no longer work, and capital flows and investor demand are now unpredictable. As a result of these challenges, organisations have had to improve their change management skills and are now more *au fait* with the importance of organisational culture. Organisations are finding that change management needs to be conducted throughout an entire project to ensure best results.

**Activity | The 10 principles of change management**

Read '10 Principles of Change Management' from Strategy + Business for some tools and techniques to help businesses effectively manage change.
www.strategy-business.com/article/rr00006?gko=dab72

**Activity | Making the case for change management**

Read about how cost-benefit analyses of change management can help organisations understand the importance of change management in 'Cost-benefit analysis of change management'.
www.prosci.com/resources/articles/cost-benefit-analysis-change-management

## Decision Making Under Uncertainty

This title might be an oxymoron to the extent that any decision concerning future developments is always by essence enveloped in a fog of uncertainty.

**Activity | Decision making under uncertain and risky situations**

Read about making decisions in uncertain situations in the following two articles:
'Decision making under uncertain and risky situations': 'Abstract' and 'Conclusions'. You can download this pdf from ResearchGate: *www.researchgate.net/publication/228876125_Decision_Making_Under_Uncertain_and_Risky_Situations*
'Decision making under uncertainty and reinforcement learning': 'Introduction'. www.cse.chalmers.se/~chrdimi/downloads/book.pdf

Even the most prominent leaders can make abysmal decisions. They may result only from a lack of luck, or calendar mistakes. However, many research studies have identified cognitive and behavioural biases that can explain most of them. Of course, techniques have been developed to get rid of the biases in the decisions making process, but it proves difficult to apply when it is the leader's own prejudices that are at stake. Here below, there is a list of situations where action is required.

### *Significance of Prejudices*

Experience shows that prejudices interfering with the decision-making process can be categorised in four main ways: confirmation, status quo, availability or over-self-confidence, and complacency.

- *Confirmation prejudice* defines an unconscious trend to give more credit to information that confirms our beliefs, hypotheses, and recent experiences over those that challenge them. In other words, are leaders capturing what people want you to hear rather than an accurate picture of what is or could be having an impact on your organisation?
- *Status quo prejudice* defines a conscious trend to reject changes; that is, do people not want to make any changes to the risks or controls as it will take (cognitive) effort to consider alternatives?
- *Availability prejudice* defines a trend to limit the decision-making process to the information readily available; that is, will people only talk about risks that relate to what is at the forefront of their mind, either in terms of what they're working on or what's in the press at the time of your discussion?
- *Complacency prejudice* defines a natural trend among leaders to overestimate their own competencies and, in that illusion, that they will always be able to control the consequences of their decisions; that is, will the chain of command question their judgement and be able to amend decisions as the events unfold?

Combining these four prejudices can lead to catastrophic outcomes. Two illustrations come to mind:

- Kodak was so sure of its technical superiority that it did not imagine it could be replaced;
- Blockbuster rejected takeover offers by Netflix to soon regret it.

And these are only highly symbolic situations.

Could it be that the situation cannot be redressed? Luckily, efficient methods exist to rid the decision processes of the prejudices that taint them. Precisely, to clear the room of prejudices, the presence of a risk management professional at the decision table is one of the essential components. If only by asking at the appropriate moment the key question 'What would happen if?', the risk management professional clearly aims to discover other points of view, commanding further analysis.

**Activity | Overcoming bias**

Read 'Are you ready to decide' from McKinsey & Company to learn about a simple checklist that could help you overcome your biases before making important decisions.

www.mckinsey.com/business-functions/strategy-and-corporate-finance/our-insights/are-you-ready-to-decide

### *Ways to Fight Prejudices*

There are a number of techniques available to leadership to help to either counter or harness existing prejudices to shift behaviour, including the concept of 'nudging'.

In practical terms, this means that the brain can be 'nudged' or guided into making better decisions in line with its own interests or good behaviours. A nudge influences behaviour without inducement, threat or argument and still allows for freedom of choice. It is designed to help anchor the unconscious mind on the desired outcome without the need to engage the rational part of the brain that may sabotage the behaviour. It's about framing options to influence choices.

Risk managers need to learn about the behavioural risks to our organisations and how to ensure that we build in practices that will make us more resilient. Most importantly, they need to ensure that a variety of perspectives is available to their leadership – diverse ways of thinking will enable them to make better decisions.

Consider the case of executives or directors being confronted with further uncertainties, further risks, potential threats, and/or opportunities that might have been left aside in the absence of a systematic risk assessment process. This may prove an efficient means to address the overconfidence issue and may also encourage dissident opinions in the group to be voiced and listened to. If all goes well this will dwindle down and contribute to the establishment of a listening culture, away from a one-leader culture, provided the CEO is really open to it.

The projection into the future with different alternatives puts the decision and the future in perspective, allowing for both less favourable and more favourable outcomes, none of which were envisioned in the first instance. If the organisation's culture does not allow staff to be frank and candid, it might prove useful to hire a consultant to play the king's jester and dare say when the king is naked (so to speak). In all cases, the issue is to envision what could go significantly differently than anticipated and become aware of the early signs of things going in a different direction as those envisioned when the decision was made.

Another solution would involve setting up a *brainstorming session* to widen the range of hypotheses underlying a project. Some practitioners even suggest holding 'war games' to allow each to change side, and imagine the competitors' positions. However, these methods can prove time- and resources-consuming. But, at any rate, the CEO should be the one to decide that such a move is needed even though they may not be introspective enough to analyse their own prejudices that will bias their decision-making process at the crucial time when a strategic course must be taken, curbed or even reversed.

When middle management makes an ordinary 'honest' mistake, like for measuring or calculating key drivers, they can learn from their mistakes and make sure they are not repeated. But when prejudices combined with a totalitarian culture lead them to cover up and find sideways, then they will not have a chance to correct their ways and even bring them to their conscience, until someone and/or some process brings them to reassess the situation.

So then, is there a way to make sure that leaders can verify whether they fall victims of their own prejudices, or those of their immediate advisors? As they are unlikely to easily spot their own prejudices or those of their advisors with similar backgrounds, the first improvement is to make sure that the proposal was developed through a robust and objective development process, even before giving attention to the proposal itself. Two main questions can validate the process:

- *Did the process include different perspectives and points of view?* Clearly, this requires the gathering of a diverse group of individuals from inside and/or outside the organisation, making sure that all main stakeholders' networks are represented. Sometimes this means empowering panels and using social media to investigate the situation. The number of persons involved is a good indicator of how robust the process is as long as they are really a diverse group. This may indicate that the initial solutions were submitted to the test of contradiction rather than adopted through a wishy-washy consensus.
- *Were all possible negative outcomes taken into account?* That supposes that all elements and drivers in the internal and external context of the organisation are properly considered; this means to identify all issues at the organisation level, at the branch level, at the macro-economic level without forgetting social and cultural issues, and political trends. Have they all been integrated into the threats and opportunities analysis?

The issue of propaedeutic is essential here: are executives and middle managers sufficiently trained for the development of a fruitful intercultural dialogue based on mutual understanding and respect? The questions asked in the meetings and panels must be sufficiently open and be relevant to the decision to be made. This will allow us to transcribe all the answers and remarks in a matrix using a decision-support tool. The decision-makers should consider a dual strategy to generate new prospects and new visions of the risk. The use of the proposed process is totally aligned with a mature ERM programme as it assures that all uncertainties, and their root causes are properly identified and considered; supplied with this widely open information, the directors and executives are less likely to let themselves fall into the biased decision. It is the best 'insurance' against hazardous decision that could lead to disaster until such time that the board of directors reflect within their ranks enough social and cultural diversity.

**Activity | Decision theory and reinforcement learning**

Read about decision theory in 'Decision making under uncertainty and reinforcement learning'. www.cse.chalmers.se/~chrdimi/downloads/book.pdf.

While one of the main streams of thought is Bayesian decision theory, approximate dynamic programming and stochastic approximation are also useful.

In practice, any algorithm that is going to be used to make autonomous decision is going to have a societal impact. In such cases, the algorithm designer must guard against negative externalities, such as hurting disadvantaged groups, violating privacy, or environmental damage. However, as a lot of these issues are context-dependent, we urge the leader to consult recent work in economics, algorithmic fairness and differential privacy.

**Activity | Mathematical fuzzy logic in reasoning and decision making under uncertainty**

Read Hykel Hosni's PowerPoint presentation to learn about using mathematical fuzzy logic when making decisions in uncertain situations.
www2.cs.cas.cz/~cintula/slides/fmfl_hosni.pdf

**Activity | Fuzzy targets**

Learn how to use fuzzy targets when making decisions in uncertain situations by reading the Abstract and Concluding remarks in the following paper: 'Decision making under uncertainty with fuzzy targets', which is available for download at ResearchGate.
www.researchgate.net/publication/29682360_Decision_making_under_uncertainty_with_fuzzy_targets

**Activity | Strategy under uncertainty**

Read about a good strategy for decision making under uncertainty in 'Strategy under uncertainty' from *Harvard Business Review*.
https://hbr.org/1997/11/strategy-under-uncertainty

## Uncertainty, Prejudices, and Risk Management

There are several cognitive biases or prejudices that corrupt the decision-making process. Over-confidence or over-optimism is one of them. In many management meetings, plans that raise alarm bells are presented, and yet fears raised by participants are dismissed by executives. This is an illustration of over-confidence and cognitive bias. When people at the top may be over-confident, they are subconsciously thinking that they have landed their position because they are good. Therefore, they know how to manage risk in their company, and do not need to go through a committee process.

Over-confidence and over-optimism can quickly turn into groupthink, with a host of executives buying into the same story. The overconfidence gets bound up in groupthink, it is contagious and a group of people can get together, and they all start to think the same way, which is dangerous.

Confirmation bias is another issue to look out for. Confirmation bias occurs when executives look for supportive evidence to back up their decision making, attempting to justify a decision. When a leader has an idea, he looks only for things to support his idea. If he comes across something ambiguous, it will be diverted to support the idea or strategy. Anything that points to the idea/strategy not to work is ignored. Confirmation bias is very dangerous.

In their current situation, it is difficult for risk managers to intervene and prevent confirmation bias and overconfidence. It depends on management having an open mind, or due consideration for risk management efforts. At this stage, most risk managers are in no position to try direct confrontation. It is about being comfortable pointing out where confirmation bias might be operating. How receptive are the CEO and Chair to ideas like this? Still too often risk managers are not involved in strategy development. If the leadership has found necessary to appoint Chief Risk Officer for the company, with the mission to develop and implement an ERM programme, clearly, he or she should be involved in all the strategic decisions the company is making.

## Culture and Talent Management

Risk management is at a rupture point, pivoting from an operational to a strategic role. Corporate culture – the way risk is treated and the way we treat those involved in loss events – is critical to that change. The right culture is vital to truly embed risk in decision-making at the top level, and to deal with more uncertain risks, especially those involving human performance.

Risk managers must have exposure to the very top of their organisation and across the company to the chains of management to inform the highest level of leadership. Therefore, risk professionals are now more likely to be kept awake with concerns over business model threats from start-ups, the changing demographics of customers and employees, and emerging risks that could damage a new portfolio of intangible assets.

The risk landscape is volatile, uncertain, complex, and wrapped up in strategic disruption. And with this new context comes a critical period for risk management as a practice and a profession. New opportunities are being created for risk managers to take a more strategic role, helping management and the board make decisions on strategy as well as risk managing the threats to these plans. Risk managers need to elevate their positions from operational risk management to strategic risk management.

However, this requires that risk managers acquire the competencies and talents required to justify their seat at the top table to make a positive impact on strategy. This challenge can be viewed in two parts: culture and talent management.

## Being Heard by Leadership

The first challenge is board and C-suite engagement. Few risk managers are actively involved in management conversations about creating strategy and defining corporate objectives. Too often the situation is such that executive management creates the strategy, defines the objective, and then asks risk managers to identify and manage the risks. Instead, strategy and risk management should go in tandem and should be a process embedded at the point of creating strategy and defining corporate objectives.

This means that a corporate cultural shift is needed to ensure that risk management is recognised as a strategic-making tool across the company. But to achieve this, risk managers must have a seat at the top table. Without this, risks cannot successfully be embedded and discussions about strategic risk management will not take place. However, it may prove difficult to make ERM work because colleagues tend to still view the risk manager as middle management, and not as the facilitator of the process. A direct reporting to the CEO may prove necessary to obtain a greater buy-in from executive management and from all departments across the company.

## Talk the Language of All Departments

Engaging colleagues from other departments is equally as important as getting buy-in from the very top. But this challenge is more about changing the perception of risk management from a function that 'prevents business opportunities' to one that 'enables business development'.

To make this happen, risk managers need to articulate their value by adopting their company's 'corporate language' and fit into the organisation's culture. For department heads and operational managers, RM language may not be readily understandable; terms like 'risk tolerance' and 'risk appetite' may be lost on them. When considering their mission, they are more attuned to performance and how it is related to the achievement of corporate and strategic objectives.

Risk managers must develop indexes to measure and monitor performance, and think about risk management in terms of how the chances of successfully achieving each of the objectives can be increased. Corporate language and communication, that is understanding corporate culture, is the key to successful grafting of ERM.

At the same time, it is essential to apply different approaches to different internal stakeholders. It may prove necessary to take a velvet glove approach with the executives, and a more forceful approach with business unit heads and project managers. After the top-down approach, the bottom-up consists of filtering the risks to expose only strategic-impact risk to the executives.

Thus, the ownership of risk at the appropriate level leads to ERM maturity and reduces the reaction against change in the middle management ranks. Risk managers can play a key role in promoting the cultural change needed in some organisations.

The evolving risk context suggests that the demand for risk management is generally growing. Change is propelling shifts in risk management and risk professionals must step confidently into this strategic role. This is particularly true when it comes to the fourth industrial revolution.

**Activity | The case of analytics culture**

Organisational culture can accelerate the application of analytics, amplify its power and steer companies away from risky outcomes.

Read the seven principles that underpin a healthy data culture at www.mckinsey.com/business-functions/mckinsey-analytics/our-insights/why-data-culture-matters

## Empower Staff to Speak Up

In many high-pressured and results-driven companies, there is a propensity to remain quiet about personal and emotional issues that could affect performance and lead to large-scale losses.

The issue is then to ensure that all members of staff are fit to work, especially as personal problems can interfere with the staff fitness. This is a corporate culture issue. Companies need to foster a culture that enables employees to raise such issues and feel comfortable with asking to be redeployed. For example, an employee might not have slept much because their child was ill, so they should be able to ask if someone could cover for them so that they can be deployed in a position that isn't safety-critical.

The culture must be such that employees, particularly those in critical safety roles, have a responsibility to do this. However, it is the manager's responsibility to ensure the right culture exists for staff to speak openly.

For many businesses, production is often prioritised over safety. This is an inadvertent trade-off: profits and volume capture the board's attention – much more so than human performance integrity risks. And so, the primary focus across the company will be on profits above all else, said a risk manager from a metals and mining industry. To this date, staff are human not robots. So, the human element in risk will always be a factor that businesses need to manage.

From an enterprise risk management perspective, the human factor should be something that everyone talks about. This ensures that people-related risks can be prevented and mitigated. It is a corporate culture issue and, in many organisations, priority changes are needed.

**Activity | Talent management**

Read about how to manage and capitalise on the talent in your organisation in 'An agenda for the talent-first CEO' from McKinsey Quarterly.

www.mckinsey.com/business-functions/organisation/our-insights/an-agenda-for-the-talent-first-ceo

## ERM and Communication on Risk

Information and consultation are clearly mentioned in the two leading Standards for managing risks, ISO 31000 and COSO ERM 2017, and they see information on risk a key to successfully implementing an ERM programme. Some might take the stance that the issue of 'communication on risk' is not new or emerging.

However, in addition to the new COSO ERM framework, the ISO recently released ISO 31000:2018, *Risk Management – Guidelines*, another widely used standard for ERM, which provides a more simplified framework focused on the principles and processes for managing risk.

Used by organisations regardless of their size, activity or sector, it also stresses the importance of leadership by top management and the integration of risk management to include the streamlining of information/consultation content with greater focus on sustaining an open systems model to fit the multiple needs and contexts of different organisations.

Furthermore, there are aspects of communication that are becoming essential to risk managers and two have been selected here that are at the heart of the credibility of risk management professionals as they move up the food chain in their organisation: the riskiness of interpersonal communication and communication with the executive already touched in previous topics.

> **Activity | The riskiness of interpersonal communication**
>
> 'The riskiness of interpersonal communication' makes it clear how important the consultation aspect of an efficient two-way communication with stakeholders is.
>
> https://erm.ncsu.edu/library/article/the-riskiness-of-interpersonal-communication

### *Communication with the C-suite and the Board: Visualising Enterprise Risk Management Information*

This report investigates enterprise risk management and offers strategies on how to decide what to report to an organisation's decision-makers.

> Without robust information about risk, directors cannot offer effective oversight. Therefore, management should carefully evaluate the format and purpose of board risk communication with consideration to risk governance responsibilities, risk appetite, and the intersection between risk and strategy. This process also ensures that the risk information is of value to the management team as well and not simply 'paperwork'.

Indeed, with increasing global uncertainty and accelerating pace of change impacting business on many levels, expectations for improved risk management and information reporting have significantly increased since that paper was published. Stakeholder pressures, regulatory requirements, credit rating agency calculations, massive increases in cyber risk and disclosure requirements, and the threat of reputation damage have moved enterprise-wide risk management (ERM) to the front of the conversation regarding risk and its impact on organisational performance.

Accordingly, board reporting needs to focus on the key risk portfolio – the aggregate view of all the key enterprise risks. The key risk portfolio allows the board to consider the overall view of risk the company is facing relative to its strategy, operational goals, and objectives. That is where ERM comes into play.

Based on the volume of suggested reportable ERM information to the C-suite and board of directors as compared to an organisation's current information reporting practices, an evolutionary path has emerged with respect to the state of ERM within an organisation. This evolution can often serve as a guide to how ERM information can best be communicated throughout the organisation. The path can be broken down into three categories:

- *Emerging:* Emerging organisations may only be armed with a risk register and a desire to implement an ERM programme with adequate executive reporting. While it can be difficult for them to demonstrate the return on investment (ROI) of implementing a working program, they recognise that there are many downsides to not acting on this initiative, from financial to operational.
- *Evolving*: In these organisations, an ERM programme has been implemented and is in the process of continuous improvement.
- *Exploiting:* An organisation with a fully implemented and monitored ERM programme is delivering significant value to the organisation and allowing it to exploit risk to the benefit of all stakeholders. Executive leadership is keenly aware of both upside and downside risks facing the organisation and adjusts strategy to mitigate key risks and avoid the negative ramifications.

Key risk information must be communicated to the highest levels to help the organisation reach its objectives. Where once ERM was a supporting function for the board, executives are now charged with the oversight of these programmes and are increasingly aware of the consequences of not integrating the ERM process into their organisations' missions.

ERM will continue to evolve, both as a discipline and within organisations to help better manage the volatility of existing and emerging risks. As a result, ensuring that the most effective methods are used to inform senior management of critical ERM information is the surest path to organisational success, stability, and resiliency.

### *Lost in Translation: Why Are Risk Managers and Decision Makers Still Not Speaking the Same Language?*

According to Jonathan Blackhurst, author of the winning dissertation from the 2018 Cass Risk Leadership Programme (available at www.airmic.com/sites/default/files/Dissertation-Lost-in-Translation-Jonathan-Blackhurst.pdf), many of the traditional professional disciplines are either over-used in a strategic setting or perhaps should be discarded altogether in order to create a more useful and meaningful dialogue with top management. As he writes in the introduction, 'If something is getting lost in translation then the onus is on risk management – not business – to learn a new language'.

*Cutting Out the Noise.* The report is particularly critical of people who rely too much on the bottom-up approach to risk management such as risk registers and heat-maps to engage with top management. As far as board members are concerned this can simply add to the noise that makes well informed strategic decision-making more difficult. The challenge is to 'distil all this noise, these messages and best practices into something that could add value'. Or, as it says towards the end, 'Keep it simple'.

Somewhat radically, it argues that company overviews of consolidated information should not include a section on risk. Instead, risk should permeate all aspects of the discussion. The current practice, by contrast, can foster a superficial risk oversight, as often illustrated by the compliance mentalities of the risk and audit committees.

### *Focus on Strategic Risks*

The shortcomings of this bottom-up approach are well illustrated, the paper says, by the obligatory risk sections in annual reports. Too often these are best practice adherence exercises that quite simply miss the big picture – the important, real-time, strategic risks facing the company. These big-ticket items are where risk management could make itself truly relevant and do more to inform the board in a way that it finds genuinely helpful.

The critical risks represent the exposures that can threaten the strategy, business model and the viability of the business and should consequently warrant the most attention from decision makers. Senior management also needs to be mindful of emerging trends triggered by unanticipated events of varying significance, ranging from catastrophic new events to existing risks accelerating in their impact.

### *ISO 31000 – Getting It Right in Practice*

The author puts meat on these broad ideas with a more detailed critique of the internationally accepted risk management standard ISO 31000. Rather than challenging the standard, it questions the way its proposed process is applied.

Starting with Step one of the standard (Establishing the scope, context, criteria), it argues:

> Risk management, and the context in which it is delivered, must therefore serve as a guidepost for when a new opportunity or significant risk emerges. Dialogue around this often turns to the phrase 'risk appetite', but this falls back into the trap of a risk language not necessarily aligned to a strategic conversation. The better focus should be on executive management and the board agreeing on the strategic, operational and financial parameters and drivers around their opportunity-seeking behaviour - all in 'business' not risk language. … The context of risk management is therefore realigned in order to call attention to the level of risk the organisation is facing, directly corresponding to the decisions it is making in pursuit of value creation.

On Steps two, three, and four (risk assessment), it urges risk managers not to just focus on

> short-term business-as-usual conditions affected by such things as market changes, but also the effect these have on the overarching

> strategic drivers in the company. ... The point is that the focus on these day-to-day risks is not the right one when it comes to decision-making.

On Step five (risk treatment), it warns that in practice this too often amounts to 'rubber-stamping what is already known'.

> A far more useful exercise for supporting decision makers is for risk treatment to play out the full scenario of the big strategic assumptions that the company depends upon. ... Instead of reducing risk treatment to a single most likely outcome, these big assumption scenarios attempt to identify the major forces driving external change and the key uncertainties that lead to a wide range of possible outcomes.
>
> By way of example, it cites a military aircraft manufacturer selling to the Middle East. Conventional risk management considerations like supply chains, materials and logistics are still needed, but so are the big-picture considerations such as political stability and how fluctuations in the price of oil might affect the underlying economic strength of the customer, potentially impacting longer term military spend.

### *Is the Risk Reporting Model Out of Date?*

The author concludes by arguing for a radical overhaul of the risk reporting model, which needs to provide insightful, honest, and well-synthesised information. Risk reporting, it says, needs to answer the question: 'What are the responses needed from management in considering these risks?'

In short, decision makers need to know whether the risk profile of their company performance has changed, why and how might this affect the decisions in front of them. In such a highly competitive corporate landscape, with a constantly evolving economic environment, knowing how and why the level of risks is fluctuating – or spotting the trends that hint how it is about to change – is a significant advantage.

The author confronts risk practitioners with a challenge: to change their mindset if they are to be genuinely useful to the board in making strategic decisions.

Some people may question or dispute some of the arguments, but it is certain to stimulate new thought and discussion and it is timely in view of the rapid changes taking place in the business world.

## ***Further Food for Thought from Two ERM Professionals***

> *The only other thing is to truly keep it simple and streamlined. This is really critical. So many companies make it too complicated and bureaucratic and it falls apart under its own weight. And it really*

*needs to be pragmatic. If you try to get fancy, it really doesn't bring the value. You need to produce insights and information that people can grab and run with, and that's been my goal here.*

*Rob Gould, Harley-Davidson*

*We're all individuals, you know? We're all different and have different personalities. Some of our executive team members are very formal. And when I'm dealing with them, I will be polite and ask questions. I might not be as provocative. I won't be as aggressive as with another executive team member who I know can take it.*

*Jette Birkeholm Møller, LEGO*

## Top Management and Value Creation

Although the risk environment is growing more perilous and costly, it is still difficult for risk management professionals to demonstrate how ERM is creating value. Many researchers have tried different approaches and did not come up with very conclusive results. The key issues are the timeline and performance measure; risk management is a long-term effort that may prove costly in the short term and requires considering value to stakeholders to be fully appreciated.

However, the rapid development of the fourth industrial revolution is changing the game with artificial intelligence and business analytics forcing innovation and for many executives a dive into the unknown.

Starting an ERM programme in any organisation is never easy. Many have embarked on this initiative, with some organisations having long started and have reached a certain level of maturity level. There are nonetheless even more organisations who have finally realised the importance and essence of such a programme and are in the preparation and planning stage on how to start one.

Nevertheless, many leading companies set an example in embarking on a path to resilience and value by embedding strategic risk capabilities throughout the organisation. Below are two articles on how executives view risk management.

**Activity | Value and resilience through better risk management**

Read 'Value and resilience through better risk management' from McKinsey & Company to learn how vital the role of the board is in risk management.

Focus particularly on the introduction, the sections titled 'Toward proactive risk management', 'Debiasing and stress testing' and 'The three dimensions of effective risk management', and the conclusion.

www.mckinsey.com/business-functions/risk/our-insights/value-and-resilience-through-better-risk-management

**Activity | The value proposition for ERM: From intangible to tangible**

Read through the report, 'The value proposition for ERM: From intangible to tangible', for more on the executive role.

Pay particular attention to the introduction, the sections titled 'Focusing on what matters', 'Improving resource allocation', 'Enabling proactive responses' and 'Spotlighting hidden risks', the conclusion and Appendix F: 'How ERM adds value' and 'Future goals and changes for ERM'.

https://erm.ncsu.edu/az/erm/i/chan/library/The_Value_Proposition_for_ERM_-_From_Intangible_to_Tangible.pdf

## The Future of Enterprise Risk Management

In the turbulent times we are going through, uncertainty is ever higher and rupture may appear always requiring a complete strategy overhaul. This creates an unprecedented opportunity for risk management professionals to rise in the 'food chain' provided they have a clear vision of where the context in which their organisation operates is going. With the enhanced position of risk management, there will be competition and the current bread of risk managers must fast develop their talents and acquire new competencies.

Predicting the future is more fluid than ever and we have gathered here four visions of the ERM future that will help the reader develop their own vision and rise to the level expected of them to justify their seat at the table.

**Activity | Vision: Roads to revolution**

Read an executive summary of the 'Roads to revolution' report, written by Airmic with Cass Business School. https://www.airmic.com/technical/library/roads-revolution

**Activity | Vision: The chief risk officer's role in the era of disruption**

Read the article, 'The chief risk officer's role in the era of disruption' for a suggestion of how chief risk officers should adapt to meet the changing demands of the current era.

www.strategic-risk-europe.com/the-chief-risk-officers-role-in-the-era-of-disruption/1428797.article?adredir=1

**Activity | Vision: Forward-looking risk management – Navigating an ever-changing business landscape**

Read the article 'Forward-looking risk management' for an explanation of forward-looking risk management and how it can be effective.

https://assets.metricstream.com/pdf/insights/Forward-Looking-Risk-Management-Navigating-an-Ever-Changing-Business-Landscape.pdf

**Activity | Vision: Next-generation enterprise risk management**

Read about next-generation enterprise risk management in Ernst and Young's article about the new COSO publication, 'Enterprise risk management – Integrating with strategy and performance'.

www.ey.com/Publication/vwLUAssets/ey-next-generation-enterprise-risk-management/$FILE/ey-next-generation-enterprise-risk-management.pdf

**Activity | 8 key considerations for CROs after strategic planning**

Read about what a chief risk officer can do after the strategic decisions have been made in '8 key considerations for CROs now that strategic planning is over' from Strategic Risk Europe.

www.strategic-risk-europe.com/8-key-considerations-for-cros-now-that-strategic-planning-is-over/1429036.article

## Summary

Please keep the following points from this chapter in mind:

- Complexity is increasingly unavoidable in organisations, but the answer is not to simplify but instead, to focus on building processes, skills, and culture to embrace complexity on a multitude of levels to gain a competitive advantage.
- Today, organisations are constantly transforming, with new markets, labour pools, and technologies disrupting the world of work as we knew it.
- Organisations are finding that change management needs to be conducted throughout an entire project to ensure the best results.
- Risk management is at a rupture point, pivoting from an operational to a strategic role.
- New opportunities are being created for risk managers to take a more strategic role – helping management and the board makes decisions on strategy as well as risk managing the threats to these plans. Risk managers need to elevate their positions from operational risk management to strategic risk management.
- The rapid development of the fourth industrial revolution is changing the game with artificial intelligence and business analytics forcing innovation and for many executives a dive into the unknown.

# Appendices

# Appendix 1 – Risk Reporting Examples

## Bubble Chart

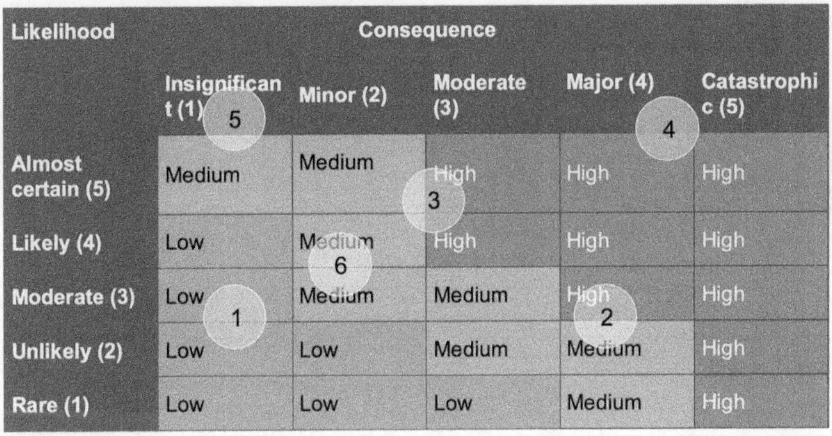


The bubble chart is one common form of risk report. In practice, the bubble chart is more complex than this example as it shows the distribution of risks across an organisation.

A bubble chart analysis is normally accompanied by a tabular analysis of the:

- material risks
- controls
- action plans.

## High-Level Summary of Data

Another form of common risk reporting is a high-level summary of data extracted from the risk register.

| Risk category | Current rating | Trend | Action status | Prior rating |
|---|---|---|---|---|
| **Corporate and strategy** | | | | |
| | | ↔ | **Yes** | |
| | | ↓ | **No** | |
| | | ↑ | **Monitor** | |
| **Human resources** | | | | |
| | | | | |
| | | | | |
| **Legal** | | | | |
| | | | | |
| | | | | |
| **Operations** | | | | |
| | | | | |
| | | | | |
| **Bid process** | | | | |
| | | | | |
| | | | | |
| **Finance and administration** | | | | |
| | | | | |
| | | | | |

Again, this form of summary would be accompanied by more detailed risk data as a director needs to understand what the risk is and how it is being managed.

## Notes

## Notes

## Notes

# Appendix 2 – Supply Chain Risk – A Taxonomy

Below is an example of a detailed taxonomy.

| Risk Source | Risk | Risk Description |
|---|---|---|
| **Product characteristics** | Raw materials | Nature and availability of raw materials |
| | Product composition | Changes in product composition during transit through the supply chain |
| | Suitability for end use | Changes in the suitability of a product for its intended end use which could be due to contamination or damage during transit through the supply chain |
| | Packaging | Product damage due to inadequate packaging during transportation or for sale |
| | Labelling | Risk to end users of a product due to its mislabelling |
| | Diversion | Product loss due to diversion during transit through the supply chain |
| | Intellectual property | Product-related IP lost due to lack of data security in the supply chain |
| | Design changes | Frequent product design changes |
| | Development delay | Inordinate delays in product development, innovation risk |
| | Product quality | Unacceptable product quality |
| | Product obsolescence | Product obsolescence and perishability |
| | Substitution alternatives | Product substitution with its alternatives |

| Risk Source | Risk | Risk Description |
|---|---|---|
| **Information systems** | IT infrastructure failure | Failure of IT and /or telecommunication networks |
| | System integration | Incompatibility of IT systems between organisations in the supply chain |
| | Cyber attack | Vulnerability of IT system to cyber-attack due to for e.g. viruses/ bugs/hackers |
| | E-commerce | Risks associated with e-commerce implementation |
| | Information delays | Delay in transmission of information across the supply chain |
| | Information distortion | Delay in transmission of information across the supply chain |
| | Data breach | Data breach in information network |
| **Transportation** | Transport network | Disruption of transport network |
| | Network complexity | Network complexity |
| | Multimodal transport | Product damage during product handling in multimodal transport |
| | Transhipment | Product damage during handling in transhipment |
| | Transport delay | Risk to on-time/on-budget delivery due to delays in the transport network |
| **Financial factors** | Funding liquidity | Inability to obtain funding to meet obligations |
| | Currency | Currency exchange rate fluctuations |
| | Interest rate | Interest rate fluctuations/market risk |
| | Insolvency | Insolvency of supply chain partners |
| | Market | Due to unexpected movement in market prices |
| | Contracts | Implications of contract terms, short-term vs long-term contract |
| | Fiscal risk | Due to changes in taxation |
| | Asset impairment risk | • Due to for example physical damage to an asset, other reasons causing permanent<br>• Reduction in the market value of the asset or reduction in asset utilisation |

| Risk Source | Risk | Risk Description |
|---|---|---|
| | Market liquidity | Inability to sell assets when needed |
| **Manufacturing facilities** | Facility breakdown | Breakdown of machinery, equipment, or production facilities |
| | Worker strikes | Lost production due to worker strikes/ labour disputes |
| | Inventory | Inventory holding costs |
| | Capacity | Manufacturing capacity constraints |
| | Cost | Increases in labour and production costs |
| | Flexibility | Inability to service market demand due to lack of production flexibility |
| | Process stability | Production breakdown due to manufacturing process instability |
| | Yield | Production shortfall due to insufficient process yields |
| | HSE incident | Production disruption due to health, safety, or environmental incidents |
| | Working conditions | Reduction in worker productivity due to poor working conditions |
| | Maintenance | Plant breakdowns due to poor or insufficient maintenance |
| | Plant obsolescence | Production inefficiencies or shortfalls due to obsolete production technology or equipment |
| **Source process** | Single sourcing | Supply disruption from a sole supplier |
| | Sourcing flexibility | Cost of switching between suppliers, capacity, and responsiveness of alternate suppliers |
| | Outsourcing | Additional risks due to outsourcing/ offshoring of supplies, supplier reliability, transport risk, country risk, exchange rate risk, etc. |
| | Delivery | Supplier delivery failures |
| | Relational | Associated with a lack of cooperation from a supply chain partner or with his opportunistic behaviour |
| | Quality | Supplier quality issues |

| Risk Source | Risk | Risk Description |
|---|---|---|
| | Yield | Low process yields at supplier facility |
| | Material cost | Increase in material costs |
| | Capacity | Supplier capacity constraints |
| | Market shortages | Limited qualified sources of supply |
| | Intellectual property | Supplier monopoly due to patents |
| | Technology | Technological obsolescence |
| **Make process** | Operational disruptions | Disruptions due to natural disasters, breakdown of manufacturing facilities, human resources, policies, and processes |
| | Capacity | Production shortfall due to capacity constraints |
| | Design changes | Inability to reconfigure manufacturing processes due to changes in product/ process design |
| **Deliver process** | Product delivery | Deficient product delivery according to criteria such as quantity, quality, and delivery time |
| | Customer | Affects the likelihood of customer placing orders |
| | Demand volatility | Changes in demand due to seasonality and volatility due to factors such as bullwhip effect or changes in customer preferences |
| **Return process** | Legal | Legal implications of environmental impact due to disposal of returned products |
| | Recycling / reprocessing | Loss incurred in recycling the product or in selling the product in the secondary market |
| | Inventory | Inventory holding costs due to the inability to recycle, dispose or reprocess returned products |

| Risk Source | Risk | Risk Description |
|---|---|---|
| **Plan process** | Strategic | Lack of strategic planning and failure to sense and respond to market changes |
| | Forecasting | Excessive inventories or product shortages due to errors in forecasting |
| | Integration | Lack of integration, shared risk management, accountability or team work across the supply chain |
| | Capacity | Over capacity or underutilisation of capacity due to poor capacity planning |
| **Human resources** | Lack of skills | Impact due to lack/loss of skilled employees |
| | Business ethics incident | Impact due to violation of ethics codes of conduct such as due to violation of human rights, corruption |
| | Employee dissatisfaction | Operational risks such as low quality, schedule delays |
| | Employee accident/ injury | Financial, legal, and reputational implications |
| | Workplace rights | Legal implications of violating employee workplace rights |
| | Employee illness | Impact on supply chain due to illness in a single employee or a group of employees |
| **Organisation** | Organisation | Policies and processes, managerial risk taking, risks to reputation |
| | Employee turnover | Turnover costs and possible impact on wages |
| **External environment** | Natural disasters | Supply chain disruptions due to natural disasters |
| | Security | Supply chain disruptions due to acts of war, pirate attacks, highway thefts |
| | Terrorism | Supply chain disruptions due to terrorism |
| | Political instability | Implications due to political instability |

| Risk Source | Risk | Risk Description |
|---|---|---|
| | Legal | Cost impact of legal compliance or litigation |
| | Government regulations | Cost impact of compliance with government regulations |
| | Economic | Economic instability in the country of operation, changes in CPI/GDP |
| | Social instability | Implications due to social unrest in a region where supply chain operates |
| | Cultural | Implications due to risks caused by cultural differences |
| | Sovereign default | Financial implications of sovereign default in countries where supply chain operates |
| | Fire | Supply chain disruptions due to fire |
| | Diseases / epidemics/ pandemics | Food supply chain disruptions due to animal disease |
| | Market characteristics | Implications of market size, market growth rate in relation to supplier capabilities |
| | Competitive | Inability to differentiate products from competitor |
| | Energy | Energy shortage, unreliable energy sources, cost of energy |

*Source*: Deshpande, S, Jakhar, S, Rathod, U and Hudnurkar, M 2017 'Supply chain risk classification schemes: A literature review', *Operations and Supply Chain Management: An International Journal*, 10, pp. 182–199. 10.31387/oscm0290190.

www.researchgate.net/publication/319136432_Supply_Chain_Risk_Classification_Schemes_A_Literature_Review

## Notes

## Notes

# References and Recommended Reading


## Standards and Handbooks

Equator Principles III, www.equator-principles.com (site accessed 4 October 2019).

Extractive Industries Transparency Initiative (EITI) Standard, https://eiti.org (site accessed 4 October 2019).

Global reporting initiative (GRI), www.globalreporting.org (site accessed 4 October 2019).

Guiding Principles for business and human rights (UN), www.unglobalcompact.org/library/2 (site accessed 4 October 2019).

IFC Sustainability Framework, www.ifc.org/sustainabilityframework (site accessed 14 September 2017).

International Organisation for Standardization, ISO 26000:2010 *Guidance on social responsibility*, International Organisation for Standardization (ISO), Geneva, www.iso.org/standard/42546.html (site accessed 4 October 2019).

International Organisation for Standardization, *IWA 26:2017 Using ISO 26000 guidance on social responsibility in management systems*, International Organisation for Standardization (ISO), Geneva, www.iso.org/standard/72669.html (site accessed 4 October 2019).

OECD 2011, 'OECD guidelines for multinational enterprises', http://mneguidelines.oecd.org/guidelines (site accessed 4 October 2019).

SAI Global 2003, AS 8000-2003 *Corporate governance — Good governance principles*, Standards Australia, Sydney. www.saiglobal.com/PDFTemp/Previews/OSH/as/as8000/8000/8000-2003(+A1).pdf (site accessed 4 October 2019).

UN Global Compact, www.unglobalcompact.org (site accessed 4 October 2019).

UN Principles for Responsible Investment (PRI), www.unpri.org (site accessed 4 October 2019).

Voluntary Principles on Security and Human Rights, www.voluntaryprinciples.org (site accessed 4 October 2019).

## Print Material

Bartol, K et al. 2005, *Management: A Pacific Rim focus*, 4th edn, McGraw-Hill, Sydney.

Becht, M, Bolton, P and Röell, AA 2002, Corporate Governance and Control, ECGI - Finance Working Paper No. 02/2002.

Cadbury Sir, A 2002, 'Role of the Independent Chairman', Global Corporate Governance Forum, International Finance Corporation, Washington, DC.

Davidson, P and Griffin, RW 2003, *Management: An Australian perspective*, 2nd edn, John Wiley & Sons, Milton, Qld.

Felton, R et al. 1996, 'Putting a Value on Board Governance', *The McKinsey Quarterly*, 170, 1996.

Gaultier-Gaillard, S and Louisot, J 2006, 'Risks to Reputation: A Global Approach', *Geneva Papers on Risk & Insurance*, 31, pp. 425–445. http://dx.doi.org/10.1057/palgrave.gpp.2510090

Hanson, D et al. 2002, *Strategic management: Competitiveness and globalisation*, Nelson Thomson Learning, Australia.
Maxeiner, JR 2003, 'Standard terms contracting in the global Electronic Age: European alternatives (January 1, 2003)', *Yale Journal of International Law*, 28(1), SSRN: https://ssrn.com/abstract=1150508
McLaughlin, Y 1994, *Australian management: A practical guide for managers, supervisors and administrators*, 3rd edn, TAFE Publications, Collingwood, Victoria.
Mukhi, SK, Hampton, DR and Barnwell, N 1988, *Australian management*, McGraw-Hill, Sydney.

## Online Material

'Climate change reporting: New guidelines by European Commission', FERMA, 5 July 2019, www.ferma.eu/european-commission-publishes-guidelines-on-the-disclosureof-climate-change-related-information (site accessed 15 October 2019).
'Commission guidelines on non-financial reporting', European Commission, 26 June 2017, https://ec.europa.eu/info/publications/non-financial-reporting-guidelines_en (site accessed 15 October 2019).
Committee on the Financial Aspects of Corporate Governance and Gee and Co. Ltd 1992, 'The financial aspects of corporate governance', Gee, London, www.ecgi.org/codes/documents/cadbury.pdf (site accessed 4 October 2019).
COSO WBCSD, Enterprise Risk Management | Applying enterprise risk management to environmental, social and governance-related risks, COSO WBCSD, October 2018, https://www.ferma.eu/app/uploads/2019/04/COSO_WBCSD_ESGERM_Guidance.pdf
COSO, 'Demystifying sustainability risks', COSO and Ernst and Young, May 2013, www.coso.org/documents/COSO-ERM%20Demystifying%20Sustainability%20Risk_Full%20WEB.pdf (site accessed 2 October 2019).
COSO WBCSD, Executive Summary – Enterprise Risk Management | Applying enterprise risk management to environmental, social and governance-related risks, COSO WBCSD, October 2018, https://www.ferma.eu/app/uploads/2019/04/COSOWBCSD-ESGERM_Executive_Summary.pdf
'Enterprise risk management: Applying enterprise risk management to environmental, social and governance-related risks', FERMA, October 2018, www.ferma.eu/app/uploads/2019/04/COSO-WBCSD-ESGERM_Executive_Summary.pdf (site accessed 15 October 2019).
'Enterprise risk management: Applying enterprise risk management to environmental, social and governance-related risks', FERMA, October
European Commission 2014, 'The corporate social responsibility strategy of the European Commission: Results of the public consultation', European Commission, November 2014, https://ec.europa.eu/growth/content/european-commission%E2%80%99sstrategy-csr-2011-2014-achievements-shortcomings-and-future-challenges_en_ (site accessed 4 October 2019).
European Commission 2017, Non-Financial Reporting Guidelines, European Commission, June 2017, https://ec.europa.eu/info/publications/non-financial-reporting-guidelines_en (site accessed 10 October 2019).
European Commission 2019, Guidelines on reporting climate-related, European Commission, June 2019, https://ec.europa.eu/info/publications/non-financialreporting-guidelines_en#climate
European Parliament 2012, 'Code of conduct for members of the European Parliament with respect to financial interests and conflicts of interest', www.europarl.europa.eu/pdf/meps/201305_Code_of_conduct_EN.pdf (site accessed 4 October 2019).

FERMA 2016, 'Position paper: Response to the European Commission consultation on non-financial reporting guidelines', 15 April 2016, www.ferma.eu/app/uploads/2016/04/FINAL-response-to-the-2016-consultation-on-non-financialreporting-guidelines.pdf (site accessed 4 October 2019).

FERMA article available on the Non-Financial Reporting Guidelines, https://www.ferma.eu/non-financial-reporting-guidelines-a-supportive-tool-with-risk-managementconcepts/ (site accessed 10 October 2019).

FERMA article on climate-related information reporting, https://ec.europa.eu/info/publications/non-financial-reporting-guidelines_en#climate (site accessed 10 October 2019).

FERMA webinar replay "How risk management can contribute to sustainable growth?" about the COSO WBCSD guidance, https://www.ferma.eu/webinar-replay-howrisk-management-can-contribute-to-sustainable-growth/

FERMA's statement on the Non-Financial Reporting Guidelines, https://www.ferma.eu/european-commission-publishes-guidelines-on-the-disclosure-of-climate-changerelated-information/ (site accessed 10 October 2019).

OECD 2009, 'Corporate governance and the financial crisis: key findings and main messages', Corporate Governance, OECD Publishing, www.oecd.org/daf/ca/corporategovernanceprinciples/43056196.pdf (site accessed 4 October 2019). Also available at: www.oecd.org/daf/ca/corporategovernanceprinciplescorporategovernanceandthefinancialcrisis.htm (site accessed 4 October 2019).

OECD 2009, 'Corporate governance lessons from the financial crisis', Financial market trends, OECD Publishing, www.oecd.org/daf/ca/corporategovernanceprinciples/42229620.pdf (site accessed 4 October 2019). Also available at: www.oecd.org/daf/ca/corporategovernanceprinciples/corporategovernanceandthefinancialcrisis.htm (site accessed 4 October 2019).

OECD 2014, 'Risk Management and Corporate Governance', Corporate Governance, OECD Publishing. http://dx.doi.org/10.1787/9789264208636-en (site accessed 4 October 2019). Also available at: www.oecd-ilibrary.org/governance/risk-management-and-corporategovernance_9789264208636-en (site accessed 4 October 2019).

OECD 2014, 'Risk management and corporate governance', Corporate Governance, OECD Publishing, http://dx.doi.org/10.1787/9789264208636-en (site accessed 4 October 2019).

## Print Resources

Harvey-Jones, J 1988, *Making it happen: Reflections on leadership*, Fontana Press.

Larkin, J 2003, *Strategic reputation risk management*, Palgrave Macmillan.

Nordhaus, WD 1994, *Managing the global commons: The economics of climate change*, MIT Press, Cambridge, MA.

Obersteiner, M, 'Managing climate risk', Interim Report IR-01-051, *International Institute for Applied Systems Analysis.*

Revi, A 2008 (April), 'Climate change risk: an adaptation and mitigation agenda for Indian cities', *Environment & Urbanization*, 20(1), pp. 207–229.

Righi, B 2018 (March), 'Five tips for better communication with executives', *Risk Management*, 65(2).

## Online Resources

### Supply Chain Risk Management

'Adidas reaps reputational rewards for best-in-class modern slavery strategy' from *Commercial Risk Europe*, http://edition.pagesuite-professional.co.uk/html5/reader/

production/default.aspx?pubname=&edid=fd34b341-ae79-42aa-ad45-236970ddeba9 (site accessed 18 September 2019).

'Modern slavery index reveals depth of supply chain risk' from Commercial Risk, www.commercialriskonline.com/modern-slavery-index-reveals-depth-of-supply-chain-risk (site accessed 18 September 2019).

'Top 10 third party management mistakes — Addressing supplier disruption with intelligence', *KPMG*, June 2018, www.kpmgspectrum.com/content/dam/spectrum/pdf/GM-TL-01007%20-%20Spectrum%20-%20Forbes%20ebook_V8_web.pdf (site accessed 18 September 2019).

Deshpande, S, Jakhar, S, Rathod, U and Hudnurkar, M 2017 (August), 'Supply chain risk classification schemes: A literature review', *Operations and Supply Chain Management: An International Journal*, 10, 182–199. 10.31387/oscm0290190. www.researchgate.net/publication/319136432_Supply_Chain_Risk_Classification_Schemes_A_Literature_Review

Investopedia, www.investopedia.com/terms/s/supplychain.asp (site accessed 18 September 2019).

The BCI Supply Chain Resilience Report 2018, www.thebci.org/uploads/assets/uploaded/c50072bf-df5c-4c98-a5e1876aafb15bd0.pdf (site accessed 18 September 2019).

## Project Management

'Critical Path Analysis and PERT Charts', *MindTools*, www.mindtools.com/pages/article/critical-path-analysis.htm (site accessed 18 September 2019).

'Multiplex losses head skywards with soaring Wembley woes', *The Telegraph*, 20 December 2005, www.telegraph.co.uk/finance/2928727/Multiplex-losses-head-skywards-with-soaring-Wembley-woes.html (site accessed 15 October 2019).

Chapman, JR, 'Project Risk Management', ©1997. www.hyperthot.com/pm_risk.htm (site accessed 3 September 2019).

Project Management Institute's *Guide to the Project Management Body of Knowledge (PMBOK®)*.

Williams, S 2017, 'Advantages of PERT charts vs GANTT charts', *Lucidchart*, 16 May 2017, www.lucidchart.com/blog/advantages-of-pert-charts-vs-gantt-charts (site accessed 18 September 2019).

## Mergers and Acquisitions

'How to mitigate risk with an effective exit strategy', *Rodriques Law*, 12 April 2017. https://rodriqueslaw.com/blog/how-mitigate-risk-effective-exit-strategy (site accessed 10 September 2019).

'Mergers and acquisitions', *Investopedia*, www.investopedia.com/terms/m/mergersandacquisitions.asp (site accessed 10 September 2019).

'Practical aspects of risk management in M&A transactions', *Korpus Prava Analytics*, www.korpusprava.com/en/publications/analytics/practical-aspects-of-risk-management-in-m&a-transactions.html (site accessed 10 September 2019).

Derenthal, JB 2018, 'Mitigating risk in M&A transactions', *Crain's Cleveland Business*, 16 January 2018. www.crainscleveland.com/article/20180116/custom1718/148816/mitigating-risk-ma-transactions (site accessed 10 September 2019).

Dhawan, E 2016, 'Mergers and acquisitions today: Higher risks require new methods', *Forbes*, 5 October 2016. www.forbes.com/sites/ericadhawan/2016/10/05/

mergers-acquisitions-today-higher-risks-require-new-methods/#74a750e27e9d (site accessed 10 September 2019).

Duff, V 2017, 'Mergers and acquisition risks', *Bizfluent,* 26 September 2017. https://bizfluent.com/info-7869097-mergers-acquisition-risks.html (site accessed 20 September 2019).

Elwin, T, 'Mergers and acquisitions failures are project management failures', https://tobyelwin.com/mergers-acquisitions-project-failure (site accessed 10 September 2019).

LexCounsel 2018, 'M&A: Three easily mitigated but commonly overlooked pitfalls', *Alliot Group*, 17 December 2018. www.alliottgroup.net/practice-management-resources-for-owner-managed-firms/ma-pitfalls-lexcounsel (site accessed 10 September 2019).

McCaw, I 2019, 'Top Five Cyber Risks in Mergers & Acquisitions', *Aon*, 9 July 2019, www.aon.com/unitedkingdom/insights/top-5-cyber-risks-in-mergers-and-acquisitions.jsp (site accessed 10 September 2019).

Schmidt, JA 2001, 'The Correct Spelling of M&A Begins with *HR*', *SHRM*, June 1, 2001, www.shrm.org/hr-today/news/hr-magazine/Pages/0601schmidt.aspx (site accessed 10 September 2019).

## Cyber Security and Managing Cyber Risks

'At the junction of corporate governance and cyber security', ECIIA and FERMA, October 2018, www.eciia.eu/wp-content/uploads/2019/02/FERMA-Perspectives-Cyber-risk-governance-09.10.2018_0.pdf (site accessed 4 September 2019).

'Cyber and data loss overtake regulatory concerns as top priority facing senior managers', *Strategic Risk Europe*, 29 November 2018. www.strategic-risk-europe.com/cyber-and-data-loss-overtake-regulatory-concerns-as-top-priority-facing-senior-managers/1428922.article (site accessed 4 September 2019).

'Forcepoint sur la cybersécurité', 2019, www.forcepoint.com

'Gartner Says By 2020, 60 Percent of Digital Businesses Will Suffer Major Service Failures Due to the Inability of IT Security Teams to Manage Digital Risk', press release, Gartner, 6 June 2016, www.gartner.com/en/newsroom/press-releases/2016-06-06-gartner-says-by-2020-60-percent-of-digital-businesses-will-suffer-major-service-failures-due-to-the-inability-of-it-security-teams-to-manage-digital-risk (site accessed 3 September 2019).

'Hacking humans: The social engineering threat', Sword & Shield Enterprise Security, 12 November 2018. www.swordshield.com/blog/hacking-humans-social-engineering (site accessed 4 September 2019).

'How can technology enable risk management and mitigation? What steps should I be taking to use technology as a risk manager?', *Strategic Risk: Knowledge*, 17 July 2018, www.strategicrisk-asiapacific.com/the-knowledge/how-can-technology-enable-risk-management-and-mitigation-what-steps-should-i-be-taking-to-use-technology-as-a-risk-manager/1427431.article (site accessed 11 September 2019).

'Preparing for cyber insurance', FERMA, October 2018, www.ferma.eu/app/uploads/2019/02/preparing-for-cyber-insurance-web-04-10-2018.pdf (site accessed 4 September 2019).

'Small business insurance and cyber-attacks: Are you covered?', Liberty Mutual Insurance, https://protectmybusiness.libertymutual.com/article/small-business-insurance-cyber-attacks-covered/ (site accessed 4 September 2019).

'Thetoptenmostfamoussocialengineeringattacks',Infosec,26July2018.https://resources.infosecinstitute.com/the-top-ten-most-famous-social-engineering-attacks/#gref (site accessed 4 September 2019).

Allen & Overy LLP and Willis Towers Watson, 'Directors' liability. D&O: Personal exposure to global risk', November 2018. www.allenovery.com/SiteCollectionDocuments/Directors%E2%80%99%20liability_DO%20Personal%20Exposure%20to%20Global%20Risk.pdf (site accessed 4 September 2019).

Bailey, T, Kolo, B, Rajagopalan, K and Ware, D 2018, 'Insider threat: The human element of cyber risk', *McKinsey & Company*, September 2018. www.mckinsey.com/business-functions/risk/our-insights/insider-threat-the-human-element-of-cyberrisk (site accessed 3 September 2019).

Bevan, O, Boehm, J, Manocaran, M and Riemenschnitter, R 2018, 'Cyber security and the risk function', *McKinsey & Company*, November 2018, www.mckinsey.com/business-functions/risk/our-insights/cybersecurity-and-the-risk-function (site accessed 3 September 2019).

Catlin, T, LaBerge, L and Varney, S 2018, 'Digital strategy: The four fights you have to win', *McKinsey Digital*, October 2018, www.mckinsey.com/business-functions/digital-mckinsey/our-insights/digital-strategy-the-four-fights-you-have-to-win (site accessed 10 September 2019).

Datesh, J, Dietz, M and Radnai, M 2018, 'Learning from digital threats', *McKinsey Digital*, December 2018, www.mckinsey.com/business-functions/digital-mckinsey/our-insights/learning-from-digital-threats (site accessed 10 September 2019).

Diagram of 6 steps in ISO 27001 risk management, *27001Academy,* https://advisera.com/27001academy (site accessed 10 September 2019).

Díaz, A, Rowshankish, K and Saleh, T 2018, 'Why data culture matters', *McKinsey and Company*, September 2018, www.mckinsey.com/business-functions/mckinsey-analytics/our-insights/why-data-culture-matters (site accessed 10 September 2019).

Dyson, B 2017, 'UK firms "severely unprepared" for cyber attacks', *Strategic Risk*, 14 August 2017. www.insurancetimes.co.uk/uk-firms-severely-unprepared-for-cyber-attacks/1422258.article (site accessed 4 September 2019).

Goldman, A and Vogt, PJ 2018, Episode #130 'The Snapchat thief', *Reply All*, 8 November 2018. https://gimletmedia.com/shows/reply-all/v4he6k (site accessed 20 September 2019).

How do you help the board get to grips with cyber risk and exposure? Airmic. www.airmic.com/news/guest-stories/how-do-you-help-board-get-grips-cyber-risk-and-exposure (site accessed 4 September 2019).

Lynn, J 2017, 'Ransomware attacks rising but human error a cause for concern', Insurance Business Australia, 9 August 2017. www.insurancebusinessmag.com/au/news/breaking-news/ransomware-attacks-rising-but-human-error-a-cause-for-concern-75415.aspx (site accessed 3 September 2019).

Stacy Moran and Steve Piper, 'Cyber exposures for dummies', Wiley, www.dummies.com

Tucker, B 2017, 'The 3 pillars of enterprise cyber risk management', Carnegie Mellon University, 9 November 2017, https://insights.sei.cmu.edu/insider-threat/2017/11/the-3-pillars-of-enterprise-cyber-risk-management.html (site accessed 4 September 2019).

## Terrorism

'The changing face of terrorism risk', *Strategic Risk*, 3 July 2018, www.strategicrisk-asiapacific.com/latest-updates/the-changing-face-of-terrorism-risk/1427565.article (site accessed 13 September 2019).

'The terrorism risk landscape is changing', *Strategic Risk Europe*, 27 June, 2018. www.strategic-risk-europe.com/the-terrorism-risk-landscape-is-changing/1427514.article (site accessed 16 October 2019).

'Types of terrorism', Encyclopaedia Britannica, www.britannica.com/topic/terrorism/Types-of-terrorism (site accessed 13 September 2019).

Baubion, C 2013, 'Strategic crisis management', OECD Working Papers on Public Governance, *OECDiLibrary*, 29 August 2013. https://doi.org/10.1787/5k41rbd1lzr7-en (site accessed 16 October 2019).

DeAngelis, T 2009, 'Understanding terrorism', American Psychological Association, November 2009, www.apa.org/monitor/2009/11/terrorism (site accessed 13 September 2019).

Goodman, SE 2007, 'Chapter 5: Cyberterrorism and security measures', *Science and Technology to Counter Terrorism: Proceedings of an Indo-U.S. Workshop*, 2007. www.nap.edu/read/11848/chapter/6 (site accessed 13 September 2019).

Gould, NC 2004, 'Managing terrorism', *IRMI*, July 2004. www.irmi.com/articles/expert-commentary/managing-terrorism-risk (site accessed 13 September 2019).

Gragera, JP and Sansó, D 2014, 'A phenomenological analysis of terrorism and organized crime from a comparative criminological perspective', *Journal of Law and Criminal Justice*, December 2014. www.researchgate.net/publication/273350927_A_Phenomenological_Analysis_of_Terrorism_and_Organized_Crime_from_a_Comparative_Criminological_Perspective (site accessed 16 October 2019).

Hoffman, B 2006, 'Defining terrorism' *Inside terrorism*, Columbia University Press, June 2006, http://movies2.nytimes.com/books/first/h/hoffman-terrorism.html (site accessed 13 September 2019).

Leetaru, K 2018, 'The problem with using AI to fight terrorism on social media', *Forbes*, 15 May 2018. www.forbes.com/sites/kalevleetaru/2018/05/15/the-problem-with-using-ai-to-fight-terrorism-on-social-media/#1d7c65056fed (site accessed 16 October 2019).

Summary of a conference given on October 27, 2009 at the Sorbonne for graduate students in Risk Management by General Jean Louis Esquivié, c.r. from the French Special Forces and advisor to the President of the French Republic updated under his supervision

Tutun, S, Akça, M, Bıyıklı, Ö and Khasawneh, MT 2017, 'An outlier-based intention detection for discovering terrorist strategies', *Procedia Computer Science*, on ScienceDirect, 2017. https://doi.org/10.1016/j.procs.2017.09.006 (site accessed 16 October 2019).

Zieba, S, Vanderhaegen, F and Polet, P 2010, 'Towards learning processes in a resilient human-machine system', *IFAC Proceedings Volumes*, on ScienceDirect, 2010, https://doi.org/10.3182/20100831-4-FR-2021.00068 (site accessed 16 October 2019).

## Reputation

Drinkwater, Doug, 'Does a data breach really affect your firm's reputation?', CSO Online, 7 January 2016. www.csoonline.com/article/3019283/does-a-data-breach-really-affect-your-firm-s-reputation.html (site accessed 20 September 2019).

Gaultier-Gaillard, S, Louisot, J-P and Rayner, J, 'Managing reputational risk – From theory to practice', in Joachim Lewes and Robert Wreschniok, 'Reputation capital: Building and maintaining trust in the 21st century', www.researchgate.net/

publication/227012643_Managing_reputational_risk_-_From_theory_to_practice (site accessed 11 September 2019).
OECD 2013, The OECD privacy framework www.oecd.org/internet/ieconomy/privacy-guidelines.htm (site accessed 11 September 2019).

## Emerging Risks

'The global risks report 2019', *World Economic Forum*, 14th edition, 2019. www3.weforum.org/docs/WEF_Global_Risks_Report_2019.pdf (site accessed 18 September 2019).
'The top evolving risk concerns and challenges', *AIG*, 12 June 2018. www.aig.co.uk/insights/top-evolving-risk-concerns-and-challenges (site accessed 18 September 2019).

### *Geopolitical Risk*

'Bold steps to manage geopolitical threats', PWC, 2017, www.pwc.com/gsiss (site accessed 11 September 2019).
'Managing geopolitical risk amid global instability', *Marsh*, www.marsh.com/us/insights/research/managing-geopolitical-risk-amid-global-instability.html (site accessed 11 September 2019).
'Managing geopolitical risk', Willis Towers Watson, 8 May 2018, www.reuters.com/article/us-sponsored-sovereignty/the-end-of-sovereignty-idUSKBN1I928T (site accessed 11 September 2019).
'Political risk', *InvestingAnswers*, https://investinganswers.com/dictionary/p/political-risk (site accessed 18 September 2019).
'The end of sovereignty?', PGIM/Reuters, 9 May 2018, www.reuters.com/article/us-sponsored-sovereignty/the-end-of-sovereignty-idUSKBN1I928T (site accessed 11 September 2019).
Aon, 'Global risk management survey report', *Aon*, 2017 and 2019, www.aon.com/2017-global-risk-management-survey/index.html www.aon.com/2019-top-global-risks-management-economics-geopolitics-brand-damage-insights/index.html (sites accessed 11 September 2019).

### *Climate Change Risk*

'Climate change and green finance', *Financial Conduct Authority*, October 2018, www.fca.org.uk/publication/discussion/dp18-08.pdf (site accessed 11 September 2019).
'Reducing risk from a changing ocean', *Strategic risk*, 14 June 2018, www.strategic-risk-europe.com/reducing-risk-from-a-changing-ocean/1427414.article?adredir=1 (site accessed 11 September 2019).
Agrawala, S, Carraro, M, Kingsmill, N, Lanzi, E, Mullan, M and Prudent-Richard, G 2011, 'Private sector engagement in adaptation to climate change', OECD Environment Working Papers No. 39, 30 November 2011, https://read.oecd-ilibrary.org/environment/private-sector-engagement-in-adaptation-to-climate-change-approaches-to-managing-climate-risks_5kg221jkf1g7-en#page4 (site accessed 18 September 2019).

*Climate change impacts & risk management: A guide for business and government*, Australian Greenhouse Office, Department of the Environment and Heritage, 2006, www.environment.gov.au/system/files/resources/21c04298-db93-47a6-a6b0-eaaaae9ef8e4/files/risk-management.pdf (site accessed 18 September 2019).

O'Brien, G, O'Keefe, P, Rose, J, Wisner, B 2006, 'Climate change and disaster management', Wiley, 1 March 2006, https://onlinelibrary.wiley.com/doi/abs/10.1111/j.1467-9523.2006.00307.x (site accessed 11 September 2019).

OECD 2018, the UN and the World Bank Group, 'Financing climate futures: Rethinking infrastructure', *OECD*, 28 November 2018, www.oecd.org/environment/financing-climate-futures-9789264308114-en.htm (site accessed 18 September 2019).

Tchakert, P and Ann Dietrich, K 2010, 'Anticipatory learning for climate change adaptation and resilience', Resilience Alliance Inc., www.ecologyandsociety.org/vol15/iss2/art11/ (site accessed 18 September 2019).

Wired, 'What is climate change? The definition, causes and effects', *Wired*, 15 May 2018, www.wired.co.uk/article/what-is-climate-change-definition-causes-effects (site accessed 11 September 2019).

Wise, RM, Fazey, I, Stafford Smith, M, Park, SE, Eakin, HC, Archer Van Garderen, ERM and Campbell, B 2014 (September), 'Reconceptualising adaptation to climate change as part of pathways of change and response', *Global Environmental Change*, www.sciencedirect.com/science/article/pii/S095937801300232X (site accessed 18 September 2019).

### *Regulatory Risk*

'FERMA European risk manager report', FERMA, 2018, www.ferma.eu/app/uploads/2019/02/ferma-european-risk-manager-report-2018_final_19-12.pdf (site accessed 11 September 2019).

'GDPR survival basics: 5 ways to help prepare', whitepaper, RSA, www.rsa.com/content/dam/en/white-paper/gdpr-survival-basics.pdf (site accessed 11 September 2019).

'Individual rights guide', *TrustArc*. https://info.trustarc.com/guide-to-individual-rights-management.html (site accessed 18 September 2019).

'Managing third parties under GDPR', *MetricStream*. https://assets.metricstream.com/pdf/insights/Insight_Managing_third_parties_under_GDPR.pdf (site accessed 18 September 2019).

'Measuring privacy operations', *IAPP and TrustArc*, 3 January 2019, www.trustarc.com/blog/2019/01/03/benchmarking-gdpr-privacy-operations-new-iapp-trustarc-research-report-reveals-how-companies-are-managing-compliance-dpias (site accessed 18 September 2019).

'Qu'est-ce que le RGPD?', *AXA Corporate Solutions*, April 2018, https://corporatesolutions.cdn.axa-contento-118412.eu/corporatesolutions%2F7faa20a1-e0b0-4ed3-a4f8-6c29d860161a_axa+erw+avril+2018+-+gdpr+france.pdf (site accessed 18 September 2019).

Elliot, J 2017, 'GDPR without the hype', *RSA conference*, 30 June 2017, www.youtube.com/watch?v=HgYl7OQsiLY (site accessed 18 September 2019).

Elliot, J 2018, *Dark reading*, 4 September 2018, www.darkreading.com/endpoint/privacy/gdpr-without-the-hype/d/d-id/1331471 (site accessed 18 September 2019).

Mancini, J and Pery, A 2019, 'Information privacy and security — GDPR is just the tip of the iceberg', AIIM e-book, 2019, https://info.aiim.org/eu-gdpr-aiim (site accessed 18 September 2019).

Regulation (EU) 2016/679 of the European Parliament and of the Council, *Official Journal of the European Union*, 27 April 2016, https://eur-lex.europa.eu/legal-content/EN/TXT/PDF/?uri=CELEX:32016R0679 (site accessed 18 September 2019).

Schuman, E 2016, 'GDPR', SC Media and RSA, www.rsa.com/content/dam/en/e-book/how-gdpr-could-impact-your-business-organization.pdf (site accessed 11 September 2019).

Shomura, P, 'GDPR: How to establish a strong defensible position', Source Media and ACL. https://img1.wsimg.com/blobby/go/e086db95-5227-456c-a743-9254a88a6fed/downloads/1c86v3slh_744954.pdf (site accessed 11 September 2019).

Williams, O and Henbest, G 2018, 'The implications of GDPR for captives', XL Catlin, 3 May 2018. www.commercialriskonline.com/implications-gdpr-captives/ (site accessed 11 September 2019).

### *Algorithms and Artificial Intelligence*

'AI and risk management — Innovating with confidence', *Deloitte*, 2018, www2.deloitte.com/content/dam/Deloitte/global/Documents/Financial-Services/deloitte-gx-ai-and-risk-management.pdf (site accessed 2 October 2019).

'Artificial intelligence in the United Kingdom: Prospects and challenges', *McKinsey Global Institute*, June 2019, www.mckinsey.com/featured-insights/artificial-intelligence/artificial-intelligence-in-the-united-kingdom-prospects-and-challenges (site accessed 18 September 2019).

'Managing algorithmic risks: Safeguarding the use of complex algorithms and machine learning', Deloitte Development LLC, 2017. www2.deloitte.com/content/dam/Deloitte/us/Documents/risk/us-risk-algorithmic-machine-learning-risk-management.pdf (site accessed 11 September 2019).

'Managing risks raised by algorithmic applications', *Wall Street Journal: Risk & Compliance Journal*, 1 February 2018. https://deloitte.wsj.com/riskandcompliance/2018/02/01/managing-risks-raised-by-algorithmic-applications-2 (site accessed 18 September 2019).

'The future of risk management in the digital era', *McKinsey & Company*, December 2017. www.mckinsey.com/business-functions/risk/our-insights/the-future-of-risk-management-in-the-digital-era (site accessed 11 September 2019).

'What's now and next in analytics, AI, and automation', *McKinsey Global Institute*, May 2017. www.mckinsey.com/featured-insights/digital-disruption/whats-now-and-next-in-analytics-ai-and-automation (site accessed 11 September 2019).

'Why AI is both a risk and a way to manage risk', *EY*, 2018, www.ey.com/en_gl/assurance/why-ai-is-both-a-risk-and-a-way-to-manage-risk (site accessed 2 October 2019).

Batra, G, Queirolo, A and Santhanam, N 2018, 'Artificial intelligence: The time to act is now', *McKinsey & Company*, January 2018. www.mckinsey.com/industries/advanced-electronics/our-insights/artificial-intelligence-the-time-to-act-is-now (site accessed 18 September 2019).

Bughin, J, Hazan, E, Ramaswamy, S, Chui, M, Allas, T, Dahlström, P, Henke, N and Trench, M 2017, 'How artificial intelligence can deliver real value to companies',

*McKinsey Global Institute*, June 2017, www.mckinsey.com/business-functions/mckinsey-analytics/our-insights/how-artificial-intelligence-can-deliver-real-value-to-companies (site accessed 11 September 2019).

Gehani, A, Zaniewski, L and Subramani, K 2011, 'Algorithmic aspects of risk management', *Formal modelling*, Springer-Verlag Berlin, 2011, https://link.springer.com/chapter/10.1007%2F978-3-642-24933-4_13 (site accessed 18 September 2019).

Sikich, G 2017, 'Mathematical Models, Algorithms, and Risk Management Methodologies', CERM® Risk Insights, 29 April 2017. https://insights.cermacademy.com/172/#more-10035 (site accessed 11 September 2019).

## *Intellectual Property and Intangible Assets*

'Expert view: Managing business interruption in the intangible economy', *Strategic Risk*, 8 December 2018, www.strategic-risk-europe.com/expert-view-managing-business-interruption-in-the-intangible-economy/1428921.article (site accessed 13 September 2019).

'From asset heavy to asset light: risk-managing AirAsia's new digital business', *Strategic Risk Europe*, 8 December 2018, www.strategic-risk-europe.com/from-asset-heavy-to-asset-light-risk-managing-airasias-new-digital-business-/1428931.article?adredir=1 (site accessed 13 September 2019).

'How risks to intangible assets could harm profits and revenue', *Strategic Risk*, 1 December 2018, www.strategic-risk-europe.com/how-risks-to-intangible-assets-could-harm-profits-and-revenue/1428953.article (site accessed 13 September 2019).

'Intangible risk a tangible threat', *Strategic Risk*, 18 December 2018, www.strategic-risk-europe.com/intangible-risk-a-tangible-threat/1428912.article?adredir=1 (site accessed 11 September 2019).

'The rise of the intangible economy and how its risks have grown', *Strategic Risk Europe*, 8 December 2018, www.strategic-risk-europe.com/the-rise-of-the-intangible-economy-and-how-its-risks-have-grown/1428918.article (site accessed 13 September 2019).

'Intellectual property: Risk landscape', *Aon*, November 2018, www.aon.com/getmedia/3bc3c273-9b6a-4ac1-99fe-ccc4a6fa0a39/Aon-Intellectual-Property-Risk-Landscape-2019.aspx (site accessed 13 September 2019).

## *Bribery Risks*

'Anti-bribery and corruption risk assessment checklist', *NAVEX Global*. www.navexglobal.com/en-us/file-download-canonical?file=/anti-bribery-corruption-risk-assessment-checklist-white-paper.pdf&file-name=anti-bribery-corruption-risk-assessment-checklist-white-paper.pdf (site accessed 13 September 2019).

'Bribery risk guide', Transparency International UK & IRM, 2016, www.theirm.org/media/2218767/IRM-TI-UK-Bribery-Guide-A5-V6-Low-Res-proof.pdf (site accessed 13 September 2019).

'ISO 37001 Standard for anti-bribery management systems: What you need to know', *MetricStream*. www.metricstream.com/insights/ISO-37001-Standard-for-Anti-Bribery-Mgmt.htm (site accessed 13 September 2019).

Rubenfeld, S 2017, 'SFO chages Unaoil executives with corruption', *The Wall Street Journal*, 16 November 2017, https://blogs.wsj.com/riskandcompliance/2017/11/16/sfo-charges-unaoil-executives-with-corruption (site accessed 13 September 2019).

### Organisational and Contextual Complexity

'Navigating a world of disruptions', *McKinsey Global Institute*, Briefing note prepared for the World Economic Forum, January 2019, www.mckinsey.com/~/media/mckinsey/featured%20insights/innovation/navigating%20a%20world%20of%20disruption/mgi-briefing-note-navigating-a-world-of-disruption-jan-2019.ashx (site accessed 18 September 2019).

Birkinshaw, J and Heywood, S 2010, 'Putting organisational complexity in its place', *McKinsey Quarterly*, May 2010, www.mckinsey.com/business-functions/organisation/our-insights/putting-organisational-complexity-in-its-place (site accessed 17 September 2019).

Pederzin, GDA, 'Managerial learning challenges in a complex world', *Journal of Work-Applied Management,* 11(1), pp. 17–29. 10.1108/JWAM-04-2018-0009 (site accessed 17 September 2019).

Reeves, M, Levin, S and Ueda, D 2017, 'Think biologically: Messy management for a complex world', BCG Henderson Institute, 19 July 2017, https://bcghendersoninstitute.com/think-biologically-messy-management-for-a-complex-world-7be3f5b08b44 (site accessed 17 September 2019).

### Change Management

'An introduction to change management', *Prosci*, http://businessenmotion.com/files/7414/9988/5822/An-Introduction-Guide-to-Change-Management.pdf (site accessed 17 September 2019).

'Cost-benefit analysis of change management', *Prosci*, www.prosci.com/resources/articles/cost-benefit-analysis-change-management (site accessed 18 September 2019).

'Reducing risk from a changing ocean', *Strategic Risk*, 14 June 2018, www.strategic-risk-europe.com/reducing-risk-from-a-changing-ocean/1427414.article?adredir=1 (site accessed 17 September 2019).

'Risk? What risk?', Strategic Risk, 11 July 2018. www.strategicrisk-asiapacific.com/the-knowledge/risk-what-risk-how-do-you-get-buy-in-from-risk-owners-who-want-to-tell-you-they-have-no-problems/1427368.article (site accessed 18 September 2019).

Andonian, A, Horii, M, Iwatani, N, Raviscioni, M and Sato, K 2018, 'A more effective model for managing change in Japan could accelerate economic growth', *McKinsey & Company*, June 2018, www.mckinsey.com/business-functions/organisation/our-insights/a-more-effective-model-for-managing-change-in-japan-could-accelerate-economic-growth (site accessed 18 September 2019).

Benkert, C and van Dam, N 2015, 'Experiential learning: What's missing in most change programs', *McKinsey & Company*, August 2015. www.mckinsey.com/business-functions/operations/our-insights/experiential-learning-whats-missing-in-most-change-programs (site accessed 18 September 2019).

Bossert, O, Kretzberg, A, and Laartz, J 2018, 'Unleashing the power of small, independent teams', *McKinsey Quarterly*, July 2018, www.mckinsey.com/business-functions/organisation/our-insights/unleashing-the-power-of-small-independent-teams (site accessed 18 September 2019).

Fine, D, Hansen, MA and Roggenhofer, S 2008, 'From lean to lasting: Making operational improvements stick', *McKinsey Quarterly*, November 2008, www.

mckinsey.com/business-functions/operations/our-insights/from-lean-to-lasting-making-operational-improvements-stick (site accessed 18 September 2019).

Pollack, JM 2018, 'The riskiness of interpersonal communication', NC State University: Poole College of Management, 2 January 2018. https://erm.ncsu.edu/library/article/the-riskiness-of-interpersonal-communication (site accessed 18 September 2019).

Jones, J, Aguirre, DA and Calderone, M 2004, 'Ten Principles of Change Management Tools and techniques to help companies transform quickly', *Strategy and Business*, 15 April 2004, www.strategy-business.com/article/rr00006?gko=dab72 (site accessed 17 September 2019).

## *Decision Making Under Uncertainty*

'Decision making under uncertain and risky situations', *ResearchGate*, www.researchgate.net/publication/228876125_Decision_Making_Under_Uncertain_and_Risky_Situations (site accessed 17 September 2019).

'Decision making under uncertainty and reinforcement learning'., www.cse.chalmers.se/~chrdimi/downloads/book.pdf (site accessed 17 September 2019).

'Decision making under uncertainty with fuzzy targets'. www.researchgate.net/publication/29682360_Decision_making_under_uncertainty_with_fuzzy_targets (site accessed 17 September 2019).

Courtney, H, Kirkland, J and Viguerie, P 1997, 'Strategy under uncertainty', *Harvard Business Review*, November–December 1997, https://hbr.org/1997/11/strategy-under-uncertainty (site accessed September 2019).

Dimitrakakis, C and Ortner, R, 'Decision making under uncertainty and reinforcement learning', www.cse.chalmers.se/~chrdimi/downloads/book.pdf (site accessed 17 September 2019).

Hosni, H, 'Mathematical fuzzy logic in reasoning and decision making under uncertainty', www2.cs.cas.cz/~cintula/slides/fmfl_hosni.pdf (site accessed 17 September 2019).

Meissner, P, Sibony, O, and Wulf, T 2015, 'Are you ready to decide', April 2015, www.mckinsey.com/business-functions/strategy-and-corporate-finance/our-insights/are-you-ready-to-decide (site accessed 17 September 2019).

## *Culture and Talent Management*

Barton, D, Carey, D and Charan, R 2018, 'An agenda for the talent-first CEO', *McKinsey Quarterly*, March 2018, www.mckinsey.com/business-functions/organisation/our-insights/an-agenda-for-the-talent-first-ceo (site accessed 17 September 2019).

Díaz, A, Rowshankish, K and Saleh, T 2018, 'Why data culture matters', *McKinsey and Company,* September 2018, www.mckinsey.com/business-functions/mckinsey-analytics/our-insights/why-data-culture-matters (site accessed 17 September 2019).

## *ERM and Communication on Risk*

'Communication with the C-suite and the board: Visualizing enterprise risk management information', RIMS report, August 2018, www.riskmanagementmonitor.com/new-rims-report-establishing-and-communicating-erm-info (available free to RIMS members).

Blackhurst, J, 'Lost in translation: Why are risk managers and decision makers still not speaking the same language?', winning dissertation from the Cass Risk Leadership Programme 2018, www.airmic.com/sites/default/files/Dissertation-Lost-in-Translation-Jonathan-Blackhurst.pdf (site accessed 17 September 2019).

Díaz, A, Rowshankish, K and Saleh, T 2018, 'Why data culture matters', *McKinsey and Company*, September 2018, www.mckinsey.com/business-functions/mckinsey-analytics/our-insights/why-data-culture-matters (site accessed 10 September 2019).

Pollack, JM 2018, 'The riskiness of interpersonal communication', NC State University: Poole College of Management, 2 January 2018, https://erm.ncsu.edu/library/article/the-riskiness-of-interpersonal-communication (site accessed 18 September 2019).

### *Top Management and Value Creation*

'The value proposition for ERM: From intangible to tangible', NC State ERM Practicum Team and published by North Carolina Poole College of Management, ERM Initiative 2018, https://erm.ncsu.edu/az/erm/i/chan/library/The_Value_Proposition_for_ERM_-_From_Intangible_to_Tangible.pdf (site accessed 18 September 2019).

Gius, D, Mieszala, JC, Panayiotou, E and Poppensieker, T 2018, 'Value and resilience through better risk management', *McKinsey & Company*, October 2018, www.mckinsey.com/business-functions/risk/our-insights/value-and-resilience-through-better-risk-management (site accessed 18 September 2019).

### *The Future of Enterprise Risk Management*

'8 key considerations for CROs now that strategic planning is over', *Strategic Risk Europe*, 14 December 2018, www.strategic-risk-europe.com/8-key-considerations-for-cros-now-that-strategic-planning-is-over/1429036.article (site accessed 18 September 2019).

'Enterprise risk management—Integrating with strategy and performance', *Ernst and Young*, November 2017, www.ey.com/Publication/vwLUAssets/ey-next-generation-enterprise-risk-management/$FILE/ey-next-generation-enterprise-risk-management.pdf (site accessed 18 September 2019).

'Forward-looking risk management', *MetricStream,* https://assets.metricstream.com/pdf/insights/Forward-Looking-Risk-Management-Navigating-an-Ever-Changing-Business-Landscape.pdf (site accessed 18 September 2019).

'Roads to revolution', *Airmic*, 12 June 2018, www.airmic.com/technical/library/roads-revolution (site accessed 18 September 2019).

'The chief risk officer's role in the era of disruption', *Strategic Risk Europe*, 15 November 2018, www.strategic-risk-europe.com/the-chief-risk-officers-role-in-the-era-of-disruption/1428797.article?adredir=1 (site accessed 18 September 2019).

www.ingramcontent.com/pod-product-compliance
Lightning Source LLC
LaVergne TN
LVHW052001080425
807968LV00004B/20